PRECIOUS AND FEW

Don Breithaupt and
Jeff Breithaupt

PRECIOUS AND FEW

Pop Music in the
Early Seventies

St. Martin's Griffin 🐾 New York

For Rikki and the boys, who held the fort

—D.B.

For Shelley, my playmate and my inspiration

—J.B.

PRECIOUS AND FEW. Copyright © 1996 by Don Breithaupt and Jeff Breithaupt. All rights reserved. Printed in the United States of America. No part of this book may be used or reproduced in any manner whatsoever without written permission except in the case of brief quotations embodied in critical articles or reviews. For information, address St. Martin's Press, 175 Fifth Avenue, New York, N.Y. 10010.

Design by Pei Koay.

Library of Congress Cataloging-in-Publication Data

Breithaupt, Don.
    Precious and few : pop music of the early '70's / by Don Breithaupt and Jeff Breithaupt.
        p.   cm.
    ISBN 0-312-14704-X
    1. Popular music—History and criticism. I. Breithaupt, Jeff. II. Title.
    ML3470.B74   1996
    781.64'09'04—dc20   96-24779
                                              CIP
                                              MN

First Edition: November 1996

10   9   8   7   6   5   4   3   2   1

CONTENTS

ACKNOWLEDGMENTS

Thanks to Mom, Dad, and Ross for the love and support; Shelley for suggesting we write this book; Rikki for suggesting we finish it; Marian Lizzi for her undying enthusiasm and insightful edits; Walter Becker and Donald Fagen; Scott Barkham; Donald Lehr; 1050 CHUM; Jane LaMantia; Laura Krakowec; Carol Bonnett; Jane L. Thompson; David Taylor; the staff at the Brittany; David Brown; Dave Donald; NARAS; BPI Communications, Inc.; Walt Grealis and Stan Klees at *RPM;* Gary Fern at K-Tel International; and all the record labels for their gracious cooperation. Quotation from Pauline Kael's *For Keeps* used with permission. Copyright © 1994 by Pauline Kael. New York: Dutton, 1994. Quotation from Philip Roth's *Portnoy's Complaint* used with permission. Copyright © 1967, 1968, 1969 by Philip Roth. New York: Random House, 1969.

INTRODUCTION

Strange how potent cheap music is.

—NOËL COWARD, *PRIVATE LIVES*

Early May 1985. The last either of us had seen of our extensive collection of Watergate-era 45s had been at a house party where the Mountain Dew flowed like water and the beanbag chair lured the horny. We asked ourselves: What had become of those singles in the intervening years? Were they haggled away at some ill-conceived garage sale? Were they deep in a landfill?

And then it came to us.

Mom's voice crackled over the phone with all the reassurance of a public health official at a nuclear disaster. "The crawl space—I think they're in the crawl space," she said. "Don't worry." *Worry?* Those singles had cost us 79 cents apiece at a time when our combined annual income was in the low two figures. But it wasn't the money; our lost youth was at stake.

When we found our mock-denim record storage box in the crawl space, cramped quarters prevented the full expression of our glee. So, for a few moments, we crawled in tight circles like wet dogs. Then, with great ceremony, we loosened the box's rusty buckle. A faint mustiness issued forth.

Who knows why we chose to play our less-than-mint-condition

copy of Hamilton, Joe Frank & Reynolds's "Don't Pull Your Love" first. Maybe we picked it because it harked back to the beginning of our love affair with Top 40 radio. Probably we picked it because it was the only record in the box equipped with one of those little plastic 45 rpm adaptors.

As the song's heavily orchestrated intro filled the basement, instantly transporting us back to the long, hot summer of 1971, we had an idea. First, we had to find every record that made Toronto's CHUM Chart (the local Top 30) between June and September 1971. Then we'd use them as the soundtrack for a retro picnic at the family cottage on Georgian Bay, where, fourteen years earlier, we had discovered the power of popular music at what is normally considered an inauspicious moment in its history. Having asserted for years that the early seventies were not a musical wasteland, we were going to prove it to ourselves, once and for all.

The ritual, dubbed the Stoned Soul Picnic (after the 1968 hit by the 5th Dimension), has become an annual event. In the meantime, the world has caught up with us. Beginning in the late eighties, Contemporary Hit Radio grew crowded with freeze-dried covers of early-seventies classics. Long-dormant names like Eugene Record (whose band, the Chi-Lites, helped define seventies soul) resurfaced as songs like "Oh Girl" and "Have You Seen Her" were revived by artists as disparate and desperate as Paul Young and (The Artist Formerly Known as M.C.) Hammer. A whole generation experienced Gamble and Huff's "If You Don't Know Me by Now" as a Simply Red song, Stevie Wonder's "Higher Ground" as a Red Hot Chili Peppers song, and, unlikeliest of all, Paul McCartney's "Live and Let Die" as a Guns N' Roses song.

Through the black magic of digital sampling, snippets of seventies R & B records have become the basis for groove construction in the nineties. Imagine Salt-n-Pepa's "Let's Talk About Sex" without the Staple Singers' "I'll Take You There" cadence, or Coolio's "Gangsta's Paradise" without the loop from Stevie Wonder's "Pastime Paradise." These soul-searching hip-hop records directly link the mid-seventies to the present. Isn't it about time someone put the post-Beatles/pre-disco era into perspective?

The story of pop music from 1971 to 1975 is a story of hacks competing with heroes. July 1972 was a month in which the radio audience could choose from among recent releases by Eric Clapton, Wayne Newton, Aretha Franklin, Donny Osmond, Alice Cooper, Sammy Davis, Jr., the Eagles, Elton John, Procol Harum, Bobby Vinton, Stevie Wonder, the cast of *Godspell,* Cher, the Rolling Stones, and—ahem—the Pipes and Drums and the Military Band of the Royal Scots Dragoon Guards. These were the last days of radio's unformatted innocence; MOR, country, bubblegum, hard rock, folk, soul, and sundry oddities could coexist on an urban playlist with no fear of listener backlash.

The dearth of critical writings on the subject can be chalked up to two things: First, it's hard to write seriously about an era that was so willfully goofy; and second, the era is distinguished mostly by its lack of a single distinguishing characteristic. Without a prime mover like the Beatles or a dramatic development like punk, the early seventies have been anathema to critics. The rock press has a good ear for innovation, but has shown little patience with the slower process of consolidation—and consolidation was the stock-in-trade of the early seventies.

By 1971, it was time to plug the full-tilt musical tumult of the late sixties into older models. Cross the sixties' darker lyrical avenues with Duke Ellington and you get Steely Dan. Cross Arlo Guthrie with Tin Pan Alley and you get James Taylor. Cross the cosmic headspeak of the drug culture with chamber music and you get, yes, Yes. And so on.

This book takes as its subject five years' worth of singles. The records under discussion were active on the *Billboard* Hot 100 chart between December 31, 1970, when Paul McCartney took the first legal step to disband the Beatles, and December 31, 1975, by which time Donna Summer's "Love to Love You Baby" had disco panting its way into the rumpus rooms of middle America. Years listed refer to the date the song first appeared in the *Billboard* Top 100. Completionists will note that the 45s-only criterion excludes some acknowledged classics like Led Zeppelin's "Stairway to Heaven," which was never released as a single, but it also makes more room for discussion of beloved one-hit wonders like Jean Knight ("Mr. Big Stuff"), King Harvest ("Dancing In The Moonlight"), David Essex ("Rock

On") and the Undisputed Truth ("Smiling Faces Sometimes").

We begin with the careers of the solo Beatles and end with disco's emergence into the mainstream, but by and large, we've ignored chronology in favor of stylistic categorizations. Some of these are familiar (hard rock, MOR, Philly soul); others were suggested by the records themselves (feminist pop, buzzwords, self-pity). The thirty-one chapters that result amount to a complete overview of the five years between Van Morrison's "Domino" and Fleetwood Mac's "Over My Head." All chart positions are from *Billboard*.

Writing the book has been a labor of love, and a great excuse to sit around listening to the aforementioned record collection. In every pock-marked groove we have glimpsed forgotten corners of the old neighborhood, in every fading chorus heard the tinny voices of old-school deejays babbling their way through million-dollar weekends. The only downside has been having to walk into respected old libraries and ask respected old librarians for information on Barry Manilow. In those awkward moments we have held on to our conviction that the under-appreciated O'Jays are at least as important as the revered Velvet Underground, and that it is somehow up to us to prove it.

We do not intend to apologize for the seventies. We know the decade was an orgy of ridiculous trends, facile sloganeering, and blow-dried, self-involved, edible-underwear-munching talk show guests. (Hey, at least they weren't all talk show *hosts*.) But come on, have a little fun—just for a moment, re-embrace the ethos of the Me Decade. Put on your clogs. Dress yourself in colors not found in nature. Or, better yet, take it all off and streak across the smoggy landscape with your closest friends in a mellow, fleshy convoy. Don't pretend you don't understand. You remember it all. The first step to recovery is admitting you were there.

The thing is, those strange days produced a bumper crop of great popular music. The half-decade between 1971 and 1975 saw the emergence of Steely Dan, Randy Newman, Al Green, Elton John, Chaka Khan, Bruce Springsteen, Isaac Hayes, Todd Rundgren, Earth, Wind & Fire, David Bowie, the Eagles, Bob Marley, James Taylor, Hall & Oates, the Staple Singers, Little Feat, and the Philly soul explosion. Paul Simon, Neil Young, Smokey Robinson, Diana Ross, Michael

Jackson, Carole King, Eric Clapton, Curtis Mayfield, and the individual Beatles came into their own as solo artists. Joni Mitchell, Stevie Wonder, the Rolling Stones, Led Zeppelin, the Isley Brothers, Van Morrison, the Temptations, and Gladys Knight & the Pips made the best music of their careers. And then there are all those memorable one-offs, like Ashton, Gardner & Dyke's "Resurrection Shuffle," Rick Derringer's "Rock and Roll, Hoochie Koo," the Stampeders' "Sweet City Woman," Minnie Riperton's "Lovin' You," and Johnny Bristol's "Hang On in There Baby."

By way of goals, let's just say that if after reading this book, just one person searches out a long-forgotten favorite song and finds himself or herself willing to admit the early seventies weren't all bad, then all of this—even the swimsuit competition—will have been worth it.

THE LONG, UNWINDING ROAD
Solo Beatles

"Another Day" • Paul McCartney (Apple, 1971)
"Imagine" • John Lennon/Plastic Ono Band (Apple, 1971)
"Uncle Albert/Admiral Halsey" • Paul & Linda McCartney (Apple, 1971)
"Day After Day" • Badfinger (Apple, 1971)
"Mind Games" • John Lennon (Apple, 1973)
"Photograph" • Ringo Starr (Apple, 1973)
"Give Me Love (Give Me Peace on Earth)" • George Harrison (Apple, 1973)
"Whatever Gets You Through the Night" • John Lennon/Plastic Ono Nuclear Band
(Apple, 1974)
"Band on the Run" • Paul McCartney & Wings (Apple, 1974)
"Lucy in the Sky with Diamonds" • Elton John (MCA, 1974)

On New Year's Eve 1970, Paul McCartney filed for divorce. The marriage he was suing to dissolve was not his recent one to photographer Linda Eastman, but a decade-long musical collaboration with three friends from his hometown. The next morning, the world found itself officially without the Beatles.

It's difficult now to understand how cataclysmic the split seemed at the time. Pop culture, especially pop music, has been so fragmented for so long that the concept of a single galvanizing force like the Beatles seems far-fetched. But during the roughly seven (could it have been only seven?) years they were going full steam, the Beatles tallied twenty Number 1 singles and thirteen Number 1 albums. They played before the largest concert audiences of their day. With producer George Martin, they expanded the creative scope of the recording studio, bringing to rock and roll artistic heft it had never had before. Their fans were legion, their influence pervasive. They became musical-political-spiritual gurus during a period of furious social upheaval. What John Lennon meant when he opined in 1966 that the group was "more popular than Jesus" was simply that, at the time, they were the four best-known blokes on the face of the earth.

Apologies to Michael Jackson, Madonna, and U2, but there will never be another Beatles.

In the aftermath of the unthinkable breakup, abandoned fans, journalists, and fellow artists searched for someone to blame. They found McCartney. All Paul had really done, though, was the paperwork: each of the Beatles had already issued solo albums by the end of 1970 (including McCartney's *McCartney,* Lennon's *Live Peace in Toronto,* Harrison's *All Things Must Pass,* and Ringo Starr's *Sentimental Journey*); Harrison and Starr had each quit temporarily at least once; and Lennon, now collaborating mainly with his new bride, conceptual artist Yoko Ono, had long since announced his intention to leave permanently. In point of fact, the breakup took seven years. It began with *The Beatles* (1968), essentially a bunch of solo albums in one (white) package, and wasn't really over until Apple Corps., Ltd., was dissolved in 1975. Still, McCartney frequently found himself called upon to explain his actions.

He answered with music. "Another Day," his tuneful slice-of-life debut single, would have been at home on any late-model Beatles album. It may not have ranked with grand statements like "Let It Be," but it was long on melody and lyrical detail, strengths that continued to inform McCartney's work for several more years. From astounding, multisectioned singles like "Uncle Albert / Admiral Halsey," "Live and Let Die," "Band on the Run," and "Venus and Mars/Rock Show" to straight-ahead rockers like "Hi, Hi, Hi," "Jet," "Junior's Farm," and "Helen Wheels" (named for Paul's Land Rover), McCartney was the consummate pop melodist.

Oddly enough, friends and foes alike described him this way. In rock criticism, "melodic" is a pejorative term, implying a kind of weak-kneed, sing-along commerciality, and McCartney probably exacerbated the situation with 1976's defensive "Silly Love Songs." The single, his biggest of the seventies, marked the end of a fertile five-year period and was a mission statement for much of his later career.

Meanwhile, John Lennon was following his muse wherever it led him, sometimes down blind alleys. "How Do You Sleep?," his vindictive attack on McCartney, indicated an unwillingness to give peace a chance, at least where band relations were concerned. Besides, after experiments with populism, minimalism, and rock revivalism, the eldest Beatle had a solo catalog that compared rather unfavorably to his old mate's. Exceptions included the Spectorian "Mind Games," a chamber-rock classic whose hypnotic flow made its big ideas digestible; "Whatever Gets You Through The Night," a loping R&B duet with Elton John; and a few acknowledged classics like "Imagine" and "Jealous Guy."

George Harrison was the Buzz Aldrin of the Beatles—always second to Lennon and McCartney—but after two acclaimed triple albums *(All Things Must Pass* and *The Concert for Bangla Desh)*, a blockbuster hit single ("My Sweet Lord" / "Isn't It a Pity") and several Grammy nominations, Harrison seemed ready to put an end to all that second-fiddle stuff. His early-seventies oeuvre presented a new set of questions, chief among them being: Why are love songs about God so often boring? When Harrison's singles succeeded, it was in spite of their spiritual intentions: "Give Me Love (Give Me Peace on Earth)" had a quirky, rhythmically restless melody that made the utopian lyrics a red herring. But go deeper into the albums at your peril.

One of Harrison's best cracks at a pure pop song was a minor masterpiece he co-wrote for *Ringo*, the 1973 Richard Perry–produced blockbuster that made Ringo Starr a commercial force (if only briefly). "Photograph" went to Number 1 in eight weeks, and gold shortly thereafter. The song's opening lines reflected the mood of many fans as they watched the solo Beatles lumber forward under the weight of recent history: "Every time I see your face / It reminds me of the places we used to go." Starr's other hits, mostly retreads and novelties, were more or less what people expected from the world's drollest drummer.

In addition to a spate of Beatles covers by names big (Elton John's "Lucy in the Sky with Diamonds" with Lennon on guitar, Stevie Wonder's "We Can Work It Out," Joan Baez's "Let It Be," Blood, Sweat & Tears' "Got to Get You into My Life," Richie Havens's "Here Comes the Sun") and small (Johnny Rodriguez's "Something," the Gary Toms Empire's "Drive My Car," Katfish's "Dear Prudence"), the early seventies not surprisingly produced a number of Fab Four imitators. Of these, Badfinger was the only authorized one. The Liverpool quartet was signed to Apple in 1968, and songs like the McCartney-penned "Come and Get It" and the Harrison-produced "Day After Day" probably stayed truer to the Beatles' legacy than the lads themselves did. To this day, many people mistakenly remember Badfinger's hits as Beatles songs.

Beatles-style pop ran the gamut from the sublime (the Raspberries' "Go All the Way") to the ridiculous (the Hudson Brothers' "So You Are a Star"), and was ultimately unnecessary; as of 1971, the solo Beatles had plenty of creative ammunition left. Compare the band's twenty-one Top 10 hits from 1965 to 1970 to the individual members' twenty-two during the following five years.

To the generation that had come of age with them, though, the Beatles would never be good enough again. Collectively they had raised expectations they could never live up to individually, and it fell to their original fans' younger brothers and sisters to sort through four erratic solo careers. Too young to remember firsthand Beatlemania, these proto-X'ers listened to the Beatles as exactly what Lennon had insisted they were all along: four individuals. Or, as the joke goes, did you know Paul McCartney was in another band before Wings?

REVOLUNCHEON
Late Sixties Continued

"Riders on the Storm" • The Doors (Elektra, 1971)
"Family Affair" • Sly & the Family Stone (Epic, 1971)
"Won't Get Fooled Again" • The Who (Decca, 1971)
"Me and Bobby McGee" • Janis Joplin (Columbia, 1971)
"Don't Let the Green Grass Fool You" • Wilson Pickett (Atlantic, 1971)
"High Time We Went" • Joe Cocker (A&M, 1971)
"Have You Ever Seen the Rain" • Creedence Clearwater Revival (Fantasy, 1971)
"Life Is a Carnival" • The Band (Capitol, 1971)
"Draggin' the Line" • Tommy James (Roulette, 1971)
"Knockin' on Heaven's Door" • Bob Dylan (Columbia, 1973)

I n mid-August 1969, a "music and art fair" in Bethel, New York, attracted a pretty good crowd—roughly a hundred visitors for each of the three thousand local residents. Despite quicksandlike conditions, water shortages, and horrendous sanitation problems, the event was declared a resounding success, and Woodstock (as it became known) went down in history as not only the mother of all rock festivals, but the climactic moment of a generation that thought flowers had power.

Later that year, the Woodstock dream came to a gory end at a racetrack outside San Francisco. Altamont (or, if you will, "Hoodstock"), infamous for the stabbing death of audience member Meredith Hunter at the hands of a makeshift Hell's Angels "security" force, was supposed to have been a grand gesture to complete the Rolling Stones' 1969 tour. Instead, the group, still reeling from the recent drowning of guitarist Brian Jones, wound up presiding over the de facto death of the sixties. *Gimme Shelter*, the feel-bad movie of 1970, provided a visual account of the event. Its chilling footage of Mick Jagger watching the Altamont murder sequence on an editing machine was the love decade literally coming face to face with its dark side.

In fairness to Jagger and company, the sixties died more than once. To many, the 1970 Kent State massacre, in which the Ohio National Guard killed four student protesters, was the end. Others point to the Manson murders. Or the deaths of Jimi Hendrix, Janis Joplin, and Jim Morrison. Or the breakup of the Beatles. But whatever the final act, one thing is certain: No one told the musicians the show was over.

Joplin and Morrison enjoyed posthumous success in 1971 with "Me and Bobby McGee" and "Riders on the Storm." Sly Stone, who many believed was losing his ability to produce meaningful work, released the landmark *There's a Riot Goin' On* album, featuring the hits "Runnin' Away" and "Family Affair," the latter propelled by Sly's languid baritone. John Fogerty continued his swamp rock crusade with late Creedence Clearwater Revival hits like "Have You Ever Seen the Rain" and "Sweet Hitch-Hiker." And a slew of other sixties artists released either career-defining singles (Joan Baez's "The Night They Drove Old Dixie Down," Ike and Tina Turner's "Proud Mary," the Grateful Dead's "Truckin' ") or minor classics (The Band's "Life Is a Carnival," Joe Cocker's "High Time We Went," Wilson Pickett's "Don't Let the Green Grass Fool You").

Some veterans were hard to spot. The "Derek" in Derek & the Dominos was none other than Eric Clapton, in a short-lived configuration that might be forgotten by now had it not spawned the FM rock staple "Layla." Former Jefferson Airplane copilots Grace Slick and Paul Kantner launched Jefferson Starship and scored with the sprawling, sultry single "Miracles." Keyboardist Rod Argent, late of the Zombies, switched to the other end of the record bin by dubbing his new group Argent, but disappeared after one fist-pumping anthem ("Hold Your Head Up"). Tommy James, the sixties' quintessential popster, shed his Shondells and cracked the Top 10 one last time with the atypical "Draggin' the Line," a lazy psychedelic shuffle whose hypnotic feel perfectly expressed its title.

Not all the rock and roll personnel changes were this superficial, however. Simon and Garfunkel split for real, freeing Paul Simon's muse and making Art Garfunkel the Andrew Ridgely of the sixties folk scene. Simon wasted no time in crafting a remarkable string of hits, blending his literate folk approach with, at various times, Latin music, reggae, gospel, jazz, and country. Meanwhile, Garfunkel pursued a film career (with roles in Mike Nichols's *Catch-22* and *Carnal Knowledge*), finding pop success only occasionally. His lone Top 10 hit, 1973's "All I Know," pales before even one-off Simon and Garfunkel reunions like "My Little Town."

Crosby, Stills, Nash & Young, another folk-rock powerhouse of the late sixties, disbanded after 1970's *Déjà Vu*, but the breakup only increased the quartet's pop radio presence. Consider: Neil Young's "Heart of Gold" and "Old Man," Stephen Stills's "Love the One You're With" and "Marianne," Graham Nash's "Chicago," and Nash and David Crosby's "Immigration Man" represent about eighteen months' worth of singles. Factor in knockoffs like America's "A Horse with No Name" and Redeye's "Games," and you have an early-seventies bull market in peace and (close) harmony.

While other artists inspired tributes of clonelike precision—compare the Hollies' "Long Cool Woman (In a Black Dress)" (1972) to CCR's "Green River" (1969) or Shirley Brown's "Woman to Woman" (1974) to Aretha Franklin's "Angel" (1973)—none had the pervasive

influence of Bob Dylan. For years after Dylan became the poet laureate of the baby boom, it seemed every halfway literate dude with an acoustic guitar was dubbed "the new Dylan." From John Prine to Harry Chapin, though, the label proved to be more albatross than accolade. Then, in late 1973, the new Dylan turned out to be none other than Dylan himself. "Knockin' on Heaven's Door" was more affecting and less affected than most of Sir Bob's mid-sixties classics, and its moody fatalism was all the more remarkable for sharing the Top 20 with, among others, the DeFranco Family and Cheech & Chong. Use of the "new Dylan" label went into remission until Bruce Springsteen had it permanently grafted onto his career in 1975.

Then as now, the late sixties loomed large over the pop cultural world. The credibility acquired by having been on the bill at Woodstock, for example, far outweighed equivalent early-seventies success. (An exact formula for this can be derived by dividing Country Joe & the Fish by Dr. Hook & the Medicine Show.) But the milder days that followed the revolution were anything but a total loss, musically speaking. Sure, the Who's landmark album *Tommy* (1969) morphed into Ken Russell's over-the-top film *Tommy* (1975), featuring *über*babe Ann-Margret squirming orgasmically in a roomful of baked beans, but many sixties veterans actually peaked creatively in the early seventies: Paul Simon, Marvin Gaye, the Rolling Stones, Neil Young, Stevie Wonder, and the Who, to name a few.

Who's Next (1971), widely regarded as the Who's best album, contained "Won't Get Fooled Again," Pete Townshend's definitive comment on his g-g-generation. The revolution was bloody and pointless, Townshend suggests, so let's get on with rocking and rolling, shall we? It was, no doubt, a personal statement, but it was perfectly in tune with the new decade's zeitgeist. "Viet Nam made it clear that the ordinary citizen had no way to approach his government, not even by civil disobedience or by mass demonstration," said Kurt Vonnegut, Jr., in a 1973 *Playboy* interview. He was right. Idealism, student radicalism, communal living, and collectivist thinking in general were on the wane, giving way to an era of social apathy and self-fulfillment.

How did the shift from "we" to "me" affect popular music? In allowing for multiple points of view, it splintered the scene—irrevocably, as it turns out. In the five-year period from 1966 to 1970, only thirteen artists accounted for all American Number 1 hits. In the next five-year period, that figure more than doubled, to twenty-eight. The relatively unified front of the Beatles, Stones, and Motown shattered into a million Hamiltons, Joe Franks, & Reynoldses. It was more than just a change of flavors (from Moby Grape and Strawberry Alarm Clock to Wild Cherry and the Raspberries); it was a wholesale reshaping of the world's musical diet, with old ingredients reconstituted in fresh, unexpected combinations. These odd new recipes are the subject of this book. *Bon appétit.*

WHERE WERE YOU IN '62?
Early Sixties Revisited

"Spanish Harlem" • Aretha Franklin (Atlantic, 1971)
"Puppy Love" • Donny Osmond (MGM, 1972)
"Monster Mash" • Bobby "Boris" Pickett & the Crypt-Kickers (Parrot, 1973)
"You're Sixteen" • Ringo Starr (Apple, 1973)
"The Loco-Motion" • Grand Funk (Capitol, 1974)
"Surfin' U.S.A." • The Beach Boys (Capitol, 1974)
"Another Saturday Night" • Cat Stevens (A&M, 1974)
"Please Mr. Postman" • The Carpenters (A&M, 1975)
"Heat Wave" • Linda Ronstadt (Asylum, 1975)
"Breaking Up Is Hard to Do" • Neil Sedaka (Rocket, 1975)

In George Lucas's landmark coming-of-age film, *American Graffiti,* rock and roll was part of the environment. It emanated from secret transmitters, hummed through the thick southern California air, echoed out the back doors of high-school sock hops, blared from hamburger joints, jukeboxes, and a million souped-up cars. It was, in a near-perfect ensemble film, the main character. So many movies have used the retro soundtrack technique since that it now seems impossible to imagine any late-twentieth-century story being told cinematically without the help of vintage rock and roll, but the trend started somewhere—in the fall of 1973.

In 1972, there had been several Eisenhower-era tributes—the musical *Grease,* WCBS–FM's shift to "all oldies," a Buddy Holly eulogy ("American Pie")—but after *American Graffiti,* the early sixties were everywhere. In 1974 alone, at least twenty hits dating from 1960 to 1965 reappeared on the *Billboard* Hot 100, in new versions or, in the case of the Beach Boys' "Surfin' U.S.A.," with a re-release of the original. (The two-disc Beach Boys compilation *Endless Summer* went to Number 1 that year.) And that's not counting new retrograde songs like "Crocodile Rock," "Beach Baby," and "Dancin'

(On a Saturday Night)." The pop audience, confused and embittered after the tumultuous late sixties, was craving the comfort of a simpler era; before long, *Happy Days* (starring *American Graffiti* cast member Ronny Howard) were here again.

Trend-spotters might have noticed early warning signs of pre-Beatles nostalgia as early as 1971, when Aretha Franklin revived Ben E. King's "Spanish Harlem" (1960), Andy Kim de-Spectored the Ronettes' "Be My Baby" (1963) and Roberta Flack and Donny Hathaway tackled the Righteous Brothers' ultimate duo vehicle "You've Lost That Lovin' Feeling" (1964). These were songs from the Brill Building, home to the early sixties' most productive songwriting teams; "Spanish Harlem" was written by Jerry Leiber and Phil Spector; "Be My Baby" by Jeff Barry and Ellie Greenwich; and "You've Lost That Lovin' Feeling" by Barry Mann and Cynthia Weil.

Here was fresh proof that the singer-songwriter approach was not the only route to success. The Brill Building writers (who also included Gerry Goffin and Carole King, Burt Bacharach and Hal David, Doc Pomus and Mort Shuman, and Howard Greenfield and Neil Sedaka) seldom recorded their own material. They were descendants of the craft-oriented teams of the thirties and forties—their subject was romance, not revolution. If that made their work seem quaint by early-seventies standards, it wasn't stopping the hottest acts of the day from jumping on the bandwagon.

Case in point: Grand Funk. In 1974, right around the time they dropped the "Railroad" from their name, Mark Farner and company decided it would be a hoot for a hard rock group to record "The Loco-Motion" and "Some Kind of Wonderful," both lightweight Goffin-King classics. They were right.

The ultimate Brill Building remake, of course, was Neil Sedaka's 1975 cover of his self-penned 1962 hit, "Breaking Up Is Hard to Do." The new version, featuring the artist's mousy tenor and strings galore, completed a banner year for Sedaka—the Number 1 success of "Laughter in the Rain" (his comeback hit), "Bad Blood" (with Elton John, whose Rocket Records roster included Sedaka) and "Love Will Keep Us Together" (for Captain & Tennille) must have had some accountant scrambling for tax shelters.

Don Kirshner, godfather of the Brill scene, had spent the late sixties developing TV-ready projects like the Monkees and the Archies, and his latest venture was the unforgettable series *Don Kirshner's Rock Concert*. Kirshner (whose languorous introductions were often more amusing than the bands' performances) was competing directly with *The Midnight Special* and its soft-rocking host Helen Reddy. (The *Special*, which featured deejay emeritus Wolfman Jack, aka Bob Smith, was part of a Wolfman mini-revival that had begun with Todd Rundgren's "Wolfman Jack" (1972) and included the Wolfman's role in *American Graffiti* and guest shots on two tribute records: the Stampeders' "Hit the Road Jack" and the Guess Who's "Clap for the Wolfman").

Motown, lest we forget, had enjoyed its first blush of success in the early sixties; accordingly, its catalog was strip-mined by a host of seventies artists. Linda Ronstadt dug up the Miracles' "Tracks of My Tears" and Martha and the Vandellas' "Heat Wave," two songs in no particular need of reinterpretation, and reinterpreted them. The Doobie Brothers boogied enthusiastically through Kim Weston's "Take Me in Your Arms (Rock Me a Little While)." James Taylor filed the rough edges off Marvin Gaye's "How Sweet It Is (To Be Loved by You)" while keeping its essence intact, beginning a series of J.T. early-sixties covers that would eventually include "Handy Man" (1977) and "(What a) Wonderful World" (1978). The California approach to Motown represents the high end of the scale; for the other extreme, try Petula Clark's version of "My Guy."

The seventies' prolonged nostalgia-fest contains many strains, including the bubblegum connection (*eight* Osmonds covers!), the startling return of the "Monster Mash," and the reemergence of early-sixties stalwarts like Rick Nelson, Little Anthony & the Imperials, Frankie Valli, and Bobby Vinton. Space limitations and good taste prevent a full discussion—if we dig too deep, we'll be talking about Tony Orlando—but the chart below should give some idea of the pervasiveness of the trend.

Conventional wisdom has it that the early sixties were the crass repackaging of the first rock revolution ("Blue Suede Shoes" devolves into "Blue Velvet") and the early seventies were the crass repackaging of the second rock revolution ("Sunshine of Your Love" devolves into "Sunshine on My Shoulders")—as though there were ever a time when rock and roll was undiluted by commercialism. Yes, the emphasis shifted from innovation to consolidation in the early seventies, but thanks in part to the return of the Brill Building song-lab approach, studio artists as dissimilar as Steely Dan, Earth, Wind & Fire, Carole King, Todd Rundgren, and Curtis Mayfield found mass acceptance.

"Where where you in '62?" read the tag line for *American Graffiti,* and it turned out to be one of those rare slogans that becomes an instant catch phrase. Maybe it was pure nostalgia; we're talking about a decade in which a reprint of the 1897 Sears, Roebuck catalog could sell 200,000 copies. Or maybe it was a desire to find new lessons in old places, to reject the politics of change that had fueled the recent youth movement. Either way, it's good the question wasn't "Where where you in '69?," because no one would have remembered.

SONG	EARLY SIXTIES		EARLY SEVENTIES	
Brill Building				
"Hey Girl" (Goffin/King)	Freddie Scott	1963	Donny Osmond	1972
"It Might As Well Rain Until September" (Goffin/King)	Carole King	1962	Gary & Dave	1974
"The Loco-Motion" (Goffin/King)	Little Eva	1962	Grand Funk	1974
"Some Kind of Wonderful" (Goffin/King)	The Drifters	1961	Grand Funk	1974
"Will You Love Me Tomorrow" (Goffin/King)	The Shirelles	1960	Melanie	1974
"Be My Baby" (Barry/Greenwich)	The Ronettes	1963	Andy Kim	1971
"Chapel of Love" (Barry/Greenwich)	The Dixie Cups	1964	Bette Midler	1973
"Da Doo Ron Ron" (Barry/Greenwich)	The Crystals	1963	Ian Matthews	1972
"Walk on By" (Bacharach/David)	Dionne Warwick	1964	Gloria Gaynor	1975
"What the World Needs Now Is Love" (Bacharach/David)	Jackie DeShannon	1965	Tom Clay	1971
"You'll Never Get to Heaven" (Bacharach/David)	Dionne Warwick	1964	The Stylistics	1973
"Ruby Baby" (Leiber/Stoller)	Dion	1963	Billy "Crash" Craddock	1974
"Stand by Me" (Leiber/Stoller)	Ben E. King	1961	John Lennon	1975
"Spanish Harlem" (Leiber/Spector)	Ben E. King	1960	Aretha Franklin	1971
"Breaking Up Is Hard to Do" (Greenfield/Sedaka)	Neil Sedaka	1962	The Partridge Family	1972

SONG	EARLY SIXTIES		EARLY SEVENTIES	
Brill Building *(con't.)*				
"Breaking Up Is Hard to Do" (Greenfield/Sedaka)	Neil Sedaka	1962	Neil Sedaka	1975
"You've Lost That Lovin' Feelin' " (Mann/Weil)	The Righteous Brothers	1964	Flack & Hathaway	1971
"Save the Last Dance for Me (Pomus/Shuman)	The Drifters	1960	The DeFranco Family	1974
Motown				
"Ain't That Peculiar"	Marvin Gaye	1965	Fanny	1972
"Can I Get a Witness"	Marvin Gaye	1963	Lee Michaels	1971
"How Sweet It Is (To Be Loved by You)"	Marvin Gaye	1965	James Taylor	1975
"Stop! In the Name of Love"	The Supremes	1965	Margie Joseph	1971
"Where Did Our Love Go"	The Supremes	1964	Donnie Elbert	1971
"The Tracks of My Tears"	The Miracles	1965	Linda Ronstadt	1975
"You've Really Got a Hold on Me"	The Miracles	1963	Gayle McCormick	1972
"My Guy"	Mary Wells	1964	Petula Clark	1972
"You Beat Me to the Punch"	Mary Wells	1962	Charity Brown	1975
"Take Me in Your Arms (Rock Me a Little While)"	Kim Weston	1965	Charity Brown	1975
"Take Me in Your Arms (Rock Me a Little While)"	Kim Weston	1965	The Doobie Brothers	1975
"Heat Wave"	Martha & the Vandellas	1963	Linda Ronstadt	1975
"Please Mr. Postman"	The Marvelettes	1961	Carpenters	1975
"I Can't Help Myself (Sugar Pie, Honey Bunch)"	The Four Tops	1965	Donnie Elbert	1972
Bubblegum				
"A Million to One"	Jimmy Charles	1960	Donny Osmond	1973
"Are You Lonesome Tonight?"	Elvis Presley	1960	Donny Osmond	1974
"Go Away Little Girl"	Steve Lawrence	1963	Donny Osmond	1971
"Hey Girl"	Freddie Scott	1963	Donny Osmond	1972
"Puppy Love"	Paul Anka	1960	Donny Osmond	1972
"Deep Purple"	N. Tempo/A.	1963	Donny & Marie Osmond	1975

SONG	EARLY SIXTIES		EARLY SEVENTIES	
Bubblegum *(con't.)*				
"I'm Leaving It Up to You"	Dale & Grace	1963	Donny & Marie Osmond	1974
"Paper Roses"	Anita Bryant	1960	Marie Osmond	1973
"Breaking Up Is Hard to Do"	Neil Sedaka	1962	The Partridge Family	1972
"Save the Last Dance for Me"	The Drifters	1960	The DeFranco Family	1974
"Little Bitty Pretty One"	Frankie Lymon	1960	The Jackson 5	1972
"Daddy's Home"	Shep & The Limelites	1961	Jermaine Jackson	1973
Miscellaneous				
"Tell Laura I Love Her"	Ray Peterson	1960	Johnny T. Angel	1974
"Surfin' U.S.A."	The Beach Boys	1963	The Beach Boys	1974
"Jambalaya (On the Bayou)"	Fats Domino	1962	The Blue Ridge Rangers	1973
"Hot Rod Lincoln"	Johnny Bond	1960	Commander Cody	1972
"Hang On Sloopy"	The McCoys	1965	Rick Derringer	1975
"Iko Iko"	The Dixie Cups	1965	Dr. John	1972
"I'm Gonna Love You Too"	The Hullaballoos	1965	Terry Jacks	1973
"The Lion Sleeps Tonight"	The Tokens	1961	Robert John	1972
"Just One Look"	Doris Troy	1963	Anne Murray	1974
"You Can Have Her"	Roy Hamilton	1961	Sam Neely	1974
"He Don't Love You (Like I Love You)"	Jerry Butler	1960	Tony Orlando & Dawn	1975
"Runaway"	Del Shannon	1961	Tony Orlando & Dawn	1972
"Monster Mash"	Bobby "Boris" Pickett	1962	Bobby "Boris" Pickett	1973
"I Really Don't Want to Know"	Tommy Edwards	1960	Elvis Presley	1971
"Help Me, Rhonda"	The Beach Boys	1965	Johnny Rivers	1975
"When Will I Be Loved"	The Everly Brothers	1960	Linda Ronstadt	1975
"Tossin' and Turnin'"	Bobby Lewis	1961	Bunny Sigler	1973
"Mockingbird"	Inez Foxx	1963	C. Simon/J. Taylor	1974
"Hit the Road Jack"	Ray Charles	1961	Stampeders	1975
"New Orleans"	Gary "U.S." Bonds	1960	Stampeders	1975

SONG	EARLY SIXTIES		EARLY SEVENTIES	
Miscellaneous (con't.)				
"You're Sixteen"	Johnny Burnette	1960	Ringo Starr	1974
"Another Saturday Night"	Sam Cooke	1963	Cat Stevens	1974
"Twistin' the Night Away"	Sam Cooke	1962	Rod Stewart	1973
"Our Day Will Come"	Ruby & the Romantics	1963	Frankie Valli	1975
"Sealed with a Kiss"	Bryan Hyland	1962	Bobby Vinton	1972
"Last Kiss"	J. F. Wilson & the Cavaliers	1964	Wednesday	1973
"Teen Angel"	Mark Dinning	1960	Wednesday	1974

POST-NUCLEAR FAMILIES
Bubblegum

"One Bad Apple" • The Osmonds (MGM, 1971)
"Doesn't Somebody Want to Be Wanted" • The Partridge Family (Bell, 1971)
"Sweet and Innocent" • Donny Osmond (MGM, 1971)
"Cried Like a Baby" • Bobby Sherman (Metromedia, 1971)
"Sugar Daddy" • The Jackson 5 (Motown 1971)
"Rockin' Robin" • Michael Jackson (Motown, 1972)
"Heartbeat—It's a Lovebeat" • The DeFranco Family (20th Century, 1973)
"So You Are a Star" • The Hudson Brothers (Casablanca, 1974)
"I'm Leaving It (All) Up to You" • Donny & Marie Osmond (MGM, 1974)
"Saturday Night" • The Bay City Rollers (Arista, 1975)

Bubblegum music is as old as Frank Sinatra and as contemporary as Boyz II Men. The mostly pejorative term was not used widely until the late sixties, however, when Buddah Records producers Jerry Kasenetz and Jeff Katz gave rock and roll an extended sugar high with records like the 1910 Fruitgum Co.'s "Goody Goody Gumdrops" and Ohio Express's "Chewy Chewy" and "Yummy Yummy Yummy." The designation was new, but bubblegum's guiding principle, "calculated innocence" (a term coined by Lester Bangs in what may be the only serious treatise on the subject), had been in place since Sinatra had 'em fainting in the aisles.

By 1971, novelty acts like the ones in the Buddah confectionery were growing scarce; like the flavor in a wad of Dubble Bubble, bubblegum's hooks lacked staying power. But even as the Surgeon General would link saccharine to cancer in rats, a new sugar substitute was emerging. Perhaps in response to the decline of traditional North American family life, real and fictitious musical families, sporting a reassuring average of 5.1 kids per brood, burst onto the scene with an implicit message: Big, happy families are everywhere.

This flew in the face of the facts. In the United States, the divorce

rate was approaching half the marriage rate, the birthrate had dipped to its lowest point since 1917, and, according to a 1971 Yankelovich Survey, 34 percent of college students believed marriage was "becoming obsolete." Still, inspired by the success of sixties pilgrims the Cowsills (five brothers, little sister, Mom, four Top 40 hits) and the Five Stairsteps (four brothers, big sister, one Top 10 hit), "family acts" would, over the next five years, come to dominate the early-teen pop market.

Though Michael Jackson (b. 1958) was the acknowledged star of the Jackson 5, he and his brothers were marketed as a group. Likewise, the Osmonds were sold as a quintet of singing siblings even though Donny (b. 1957) attracted the lion's share of the hysteria. Record executives were deliberately shifting the emphasis away from heartsick solo stars in the Paul Anka–Frankie Avalon mold and placing it on the cozier all-in-the-family formula. Maybe parents doling out cash for albums, singles, and dreamy posters found it easier to accept their little girls' mania for young male stars in the context of a family (even if the family was fictitious). After all, you didn't see that awful Alice Cooper with any nice brothers and sisters, now, did you?

The Osmond-Jackson similarities were eerie: five brothers, the youngest being the star (an unwitting public was not yet aware of the existence of youngsters Jimmy Osmond and Randy Jackson); two "middle" children, Merrill and Jermaine, who shared lead vocal duties; established showbiz mentors (Andy Williams and Diana Ross); music sympathetic to the concerns of their audience ("Yo-Yo" and "ABC"); and all the trappings of teen stardom—fanzine dream date features, Saturday morning cartoon spinoffs, and official merchandise. The only difference, and it wasn't one that weighed heavily on the minds of *Tiger Beat* readers, was racial.

Of the two groups, Papa Joe's Jacksons from Gary, Indiana, were first on the scene and, in the long run, the more satisfying musically. They had already had four Number 1 hits ("I Want You Back," "ABC," "The Love You Save," and "I'll Be There"), classics all, in the year preceding the Osmonds' 1971 chart debut. The now forgotten "Sugar Daddy," a Top 10 sweet fix of the highest order, advances the hilarious conceit that the thirteen-year-old Michael is attempting to buy a girl's love away from his rival, "Henry." The rival might have remained nameless, if not for Michael's brothers' unison exclamation "Oh, Henry!" Just in case the allusion to the eponymous candy bar escapes us, Michael drives it home with a pun on its key ingredient: "He's driving me *nuts!*"

The Osmonds hailed from Ogden, Utah. MGM president Mike Curb repackaged the group as a white Jackson 5, even sending them to Rick Hall's legendary Muscle Shoals studio in Alabama. "One Bad Apple," the result of this improbable field trip, stayed at Number 1 for five weeks in early 1971. Though the Osmonds never quite matched the success of that first release, the follow-up single "Double Lovin'," whose lyrics read like a Doublemint gum ad ("You get two for the price of one!"), at least extended "Apple" 's cheerful legacy. Subsequent hits, like "Yo-Yo" (yeah, we liked it at the time; so what?), "Down by the Lazy River" (with its persistent use of the word "mosey"), and "Love Me for a Reason" (listen to Merrill's inimitable pronunciation—"keeses"), were not as appealing.

What matters twenty years later is not each band member's favorite color, hobbies, or astrological sign; what matters is that Michael Jackson and Donny Osmond were great pop singers at an absurdly young age. They had crystal clarity, uncanny phrasing, and, not incidentally, a knowing touch with grown-up lyrics like "Got to be there in the morning" ("Got to Be There") and "You're too young to know the score" ("Sweet and Innocent"). Ironically, Jackson seemed more at ease with sexually charged lyrics in these early teen performances than he does now as the self-proclaimed King of Pop. His almost supernatural poise lent credibility to "Got to Be There" (a new and improved "I'll Be There") and "Ben" (a beautiful ballad wasted on a rat). Meanwhile, Osmond made the most of the late fifties–early sixties covers he was asked to record ("Puppy Love," "Go Away Little Girl," "Twelfth of Never," and "Lonely Boy").

For a time, Michael and Donny were omnipresent. Taking into account their solo and group efforts, they amassed an astonishing total of forty-three Top 40 hits by the end of 1975, including seven Number 1s. One day in 1972, KHJ Radio in Los Angeles played "Puppy Love" *for a full hour.* And although history has been kinder to Jackson's early music—at least in part because it represents the last days of Motown's golden age—for one brief, shining moment the two were equally lunch box–friendly. In both cases, more than two decades after bubblegum's family affair, the original packaging still lingers; for those who remember Shelley Winters best as the only buoyant object in *The Poseidon Adventure,* Donny and Michael will always be one fifth of the Osmonds and the Jackson 5.

Though David Cassidy, Jeremy Gelbwaks, and Danny Bonaduce shared a surname on TV, most fans conceded they weren't really brothers. The closest thing to a blood relationship on the set of *The Partridge Family* was this: Shirley Jones was David Cassidy's real-life stepmother. But as the writer Sara Davidson observed in 1973, "David Cassidy is visualized less as Cassidy the actor—the only child of separated parents—than as Keith Partridge, who lives in a family with lots of other children." It was testament to Bell Records' faith in the family that every Partridge had to participate musically, or at least learn how to fake it: If you bought a 'Tridge disc having seen the group's TV "jam sessions," you might have thought bored young Suzanne Crough (Tracy) was an actual percussionist. Tolerance for this kind of musical duplicity has all but vanished in the nineties; witness the outrage when lip-synchers Rob and Fab of Milli

Vanilli turned out to be no more musical than tambourine-totin' Tracy Partridge. (Incidentally, there was another television precedent for the Milli Vanilli debacle: Fred Flintstone was onstage lip-synching Rock Roll's "The Twitch" when his bird-powered turntable fell asleep.)

Having adults like mother Shirley and band manager Reuben Kincaid (former *Laugh-In* regular Dave Madden) as chaperones made *The Partridge Family*'s rock-and-roll premise palatable to parents; at least when the band hit the road, there would be a "Nervous Mother Driving." Kids, however, could still thrill to the idea of skipping school, hopping on the magic bus (a Piet Mondrian painting on wheels), and playing groovy music for throngs of hysterical fans. An attractive scenario, but the group's "sets" never seemed to last longer than one song and, although they occasionally performed in alternative venues like a maximum-security prison (magically taming a mob of cold-blooded inmates with "Only a Moment Ago"), their on-screen venue was more often than not a dimly lit lounge containing a crowd of middle-aged men and women.

A much younger audience catapulted the Partridges into the real-life world of Top 40 radio. "I Think I Love You," now everyone's favorite make-fun-of-the-seventies song, broke on the show's eighth episode, the one where the skunk sneaks onto the bus and sends everyone running for the deodorizing tomato juice bath. The song's harpsichord-driven track gave "keyboard player" Susan Dey a lot to do onscreen, but the pseudo-classical trilling wore thin pretty quickly. Cassidy's arch vocal, full of Merrill Osmond–esque mannerisms (*"Wa* think I love you") pushed the limits of tolerance, finally arriving at the too-easy capitulation "If you say, 'Hey, go away,' I will." He wouldn't, though; "I Think I Love You" stayed on the charts for twenty-two weeks. (David/Keith was no Teddy Pendergrass, but he *could* sing, though as late as the pilot episode, he was lip-synching, no one on the production team apparently having bothered to ask if he could carry a tune.)

Other singles hatched by the Partridge Family included "Doesn't Somebody Want to Be Wanted" (Cassidy hated the song's sensitive-guy soliloquy because it threatened his "cool"); "I'll Meet You Halfway" (used in a mid-seventies U.S. Army recruitment ad); and

"I Woke Up in Love This Morning" (no nocturnal emission jokes, please).

There was no end to the TV show's onslaught of gimmicky off-shoots: "concept" albums that took the form of a photo album, a family birthday log, a shopping bag, and a Christmas card; a small library of books (including not only novelizations of *Partridge Family* episodes but also every girl's bedside bible, *Boys, Beauty and Popularity and How to Have Your Share of Each,* "written" by Susan Dey); and collectibles that included lunch boxes, trading cards, coloring books, paper dolls, clocks, posters, pens, gumballs, comic books, toy guitars, toy tour buses, bulletin boards, Viewmaster reels, David Cassidy "Luv" Stickers, David Cassidy Choker "Luv" Beads ("Make and Wear Choker Beads Like David Does"), a striped Nehru jacket with David's face on the breast pocket, and, finally, a Patti Partridge doll ("Tracy's Own Performing Doll, which even plays patticake"—yeah, sure, just like Tracy plays tambourine).

The Partridge Family, loosely based on the real-life Cowsills, aired from 1970 to 1974. By 1975, Cassidy had signed with RCA, whose execs felt "confident that his future as a performer, composer, and lyricist, will far surpass his previous accomplishments." Not true, as it turns out, although David's half-brother Shaun would enter the fray two years later with "Da Doo Ron Ron." The elder Cassidy told *Rolling Stone* in 1972, "I said to [Partridge Family producer Wes Farrell], 'I don't want to cut bubblegum records.' And he said, 'No, man, we're not going to cut bubblegum records.' " But they did, and they should thank their lucky stars.

The Partridge Family's only direct musical competition came from their Friday night lead-in, *The Brady Bunch,* featuring TV's symmetrical suburbanite clan. Here was the ultimate healing force for the splintered nuclear family: a sort of wonderland in which two former single parents, each with three kids, lived the good life, notwithstanding minor crises (Peter's volcanic science project, Mrs. Brady's broken vase, Jan's orthodonture). The usually nonmusical Brady kids attempted some prime-time pop of their own, concluding the Peter's-in-puberty episode with "It's Time to Change." This was a stroke of genius by producer Sherwood Schwartz; without an actual vocalist like David Cassidy in the clan, why not include a song that dodged the question of musicality altogether (Peter's voice is changing, so he can't sing)? The adolescent anthem has not worn nearly as well as Peter's oft-quoted Bogart imitation—"pork chops and apple sauce."

Whereas television responded to North America's runaway divorce rate and the emergence of alternative lifestyles with nontraditional but wholesome TV family units like the ones in *The Partridge Family, The Brady Bunch, The Courtship of Eddie's Father,* and *Family Affair,* pop music marketers stuck to actual families. In addition to the Osmonds and Jacksons, the mid-seventies would see the DeFranco Family going to Number 1 with "Heartbeat—It's a Lovebeat," the Hudson Brothers going to Number 21 with "So You Are a Star," the Sylvers going to Number 1 with "Boogie Fever," and the Bay City Rollers (two of whom were brothers—bet you can't guess which ones) riding a wave of tartan mania to the top of the charts with "Saturday Night." Naturally, there were traditional solo teen idols around in the first half of the seventies—Bobby Sherman, who guest-starred on *The Partridge Family*'s Lionel Poindexter episode, had his last Top 20 hit, "Cried Like a Baby"—but the era's contribution to bubblegum history is first and foremost the Mom-and-Pop pop of the families mentioned here.

Disco, the music of single people having a good time, would come to dominate the pop charts in the latter half of the seventies. As the dance floors of North America heated up, David Cassidy would become an England-only phenomenon; the Osmonds would devolve into Donny and Marie's little-bit-country-little-bit-rock-and-roll variety show; and Michael Jackson would endure a four-year hitless streak before embarking on a legendary (though scandal-plagued) adult career. But while Evel Knievel was still selling tickets to his own funeral and Richard Nixon's office was still ovoid, the pop family unit remained intact, held in place with nothing more than a little bubblegum.

BORN TO BE MILD
Soft Rock

"Sooner or Later" • The Grass Roots (Dunhill, 1971)
"Baby I'm-a Want You" • Bread (Elektra, 1971)
"Don't Pull Your Love" • Hamilton, Joe Frank & Reynolds (Dunhill, 1971)
"Here Comes That Rainy Day Feeling Again" • The Fortunes (Capitol, 1971)
"Nice to Be with You" • Gallery (Sussex, 1972)
"Beautiful Sunday" • Daniel Boone (Mercury, 1972)
"Precious and Few" • Climax (Rocky Road, 1972)
"Thank God I'm a Country Boy" • John Denver (RCA, 1975)
"I Write the Songs" • Barry Manilow (Arista, 1975)
"Magic" • Pilot (EMI, 1975)

Just as Parker Brothers had to reformulate the Nerf Ball in 1971 because it was flammable, the early seventies' soft-rocking, bell-bottomed male Caucasians defused rock and roll's incendiary character, rounding its edges and making it safe for children. The musical equivalent of a leisure suit, Cauc Rock was a benign but dominant chart force during the first half of the decade. The songs were performed by musical sales reps skilled in the soft sell, who quietly affirmed and stoically lamented love from both sides, while moving counter to their rebellious rock and roll predecessors. Moms and dads could sing along, and this antagonized rock critics (even as many of these scribes were becoming parents themselves), who were anxious to keep rock out of the "older" generation's hands.

The new breed was typified by Bread, whose pretty melodies and mawkish cornpone had millions of "Bread-heads" (as one critic dubbed the band's fans) standing in line for concert tickets and singles, and sensitive couples everywhere adopting Bread songs as their songs. David Gates, who wrote, produced, and sang all the group's hits, was responsible for ten Top 40 singles during the first half of the seventies. As digestible as their namesake, songs like "Baby I'ma Want You," "If," and "Everything I Own" featured Gates's quiet desperation and a minimum of electric guitars.

In 1973, bickering between Gates and "Guitar Man" James Griffin finally broke Bread. The band, whose fans-a wanted them one more time, reunited briefly in 1976 for the weepy "Lost Without Your Love." Gates returned in 1978 with a couple of hits, including "Goodbye Girl," a Top 20 ballad from the Neil Simon film. His band, however, was toast.

The genre that bred Bread also gave rise to artists that were able to transcend soft rock's inner wimp and create stand-alone classics that left their mark on the era. Chief among these artists was Hamilton, Joe Frank & Reynolds, whose "Don't Pull Your Love" (1971) was an uplifting, arranged-to-the-hilt pure pop record and as close as any song can come to laying claim as the inspiration for this book. From its triumphant overture and the crafty decision to start the record in full flight, chorus-first, to its tension-building bridge and last blissful release, it was a mainstream monument to the joys of summer radio. Chief among its pleasures was the tug-of-war between the exhilarating arrangement and desperate lyric (including the threat to "cry for a hundred years").

HJF&R would land only one more Top 20 hit, 1975's chart-topping "Fallin' in Love." Few people noticed that by that time, Alan Dennison had replaced Tommy Reynolds, one of the band's founding members, who left the group in 1972. The confusion was no doubt exacerbated by the fact that the band continued to record under its original law-firm-style name. In retrospect, slipping Dennison into the band recalls television's tendency to replace cast members with totally different actors playing the same role. (Remember the double-Darrin hubbub on *Bewitched* when Dick York was replaced by Dick Sargent, or *The Partridge Family*'s Chris-cross when, after one season, swarthy Jeremy Gelbwaks was replaced by blue-eyed blond Brian Forster?)

Cleveland-born singer Sonny Geraci, on the other hand, had the good sense to institute a name change when his band the Outsiders (who had four Top 40 hits, all in 1966) split, leaving Geraci and guitarist Walter Nims to form the portentously named Climax, whose chart life indeed climaxed with 1972's "Precious and Few," the band's first and only hit. The track, another of those memorable one-offs that seem to evoke the era in people's memories, recalled the melody of "Cherish" (a trance-inducing ballad recorded by the Association in 1966 and David Cassidy in 1971), but worked better than that song on almost every level. Despite its wistful lyric, the track succeeded brilliantly, with the help of a seamless pop arrangement, a last-verse key change, and a carefully placed Geraci voice-crack that miraculously sounded sincere.

Sincerity was not lacking in the Fortunes' chart swan song. Despite soft rock's abundance of creative pitfalls, where one wrong step can mean the difference between "Cherish" and "Precious and Few," "Here Comes That Rainy Day Feeling Again" (another great summer '71 hit) made every listening seem like you were watching the clouds part. Soft rock's lonely hearts club bands were not always so satisfying. The Grass Roots, melodic chart stalwarts since 1967, had the biggest year of their career in 1971, with "Temptation Eyes," "Sooner or Later," and "Two Divided by Love" going Top 20. These Nerf-rock tracks, especially the latter, made sexual relations seem about as exciting as long division. They were catchy but unremarkable songs, and after a couple of minor hits the following year, this Bay-area band made like Bedouins (the group's original name) and left quietly. The Glass Bottle scored its only hit in the fall of 1971. "I Ain't Got Time Anymore," a cloying requiem for a lost love, realized the worst fears of soft rock's detractors, and the Bottle's lead singer Gary Criss, who by his own musical admission didn't even have time to wipe away his tears, somehow found two minutes and twenty-seven seconds to tell us about it.

Occasionally, the male Caucasians did enjoy life, but only in carefully calibrated doses. Gallery, a Detroit band featuring singer-guitarist Jim Gold, epitomized this restrained euphoria with "Nice to Be with You" (1972), a musical greeting card that sounded like a Neil Diamond castoff. Prior to being rechristened Daniel Boone by Troggs producer Larry Page, Peter Lee Stirling played session guitar, most notably on Tom Jones's "It's Not Unusual," and made the first recording of the eventual Wayne Newton hit "Daddy Don't You Walk So Fast." He's best known, however, for the unflinching cheeriness of "Beautiful Sunday," a mellow wonder that was a hit three different times: two years after its initial Number 15 chart peak, the track was rereleased to additional sales; two years after *that,* it was used as the theme of a successful Japanese television program and catapulted to four months at Number 1 in that country.

John Henry Deutscherdorf, alias John Denver, the seventies performer who most resembles a Happy Face button, was behind such hits as "Take Me Home, Country Roads," "Rocky Mountain High," and "Sunshine on My Shoulders" (written just before ozone depletion became a burning issue). With a catalog of mild-mannered pop that fell somewhere between folk and country, Denver visited the Top 10 eight times between 1971 and 1975. In 1975, he thanked God that he had thanked God he was a country boy; his hillbilly prayer, which had wannabe hayseeds in the suburbs earnestly singing along, do-si-do'd its way to the top of the charts.

Denver's only rival for the title of Soft-Rock Solo Artist of the Millennium is Barry Alan Pincus, or Barry Manilow. Playing piano in a Manhattan bar-cum-bathhouse in 1972, Manilow met Bette Midler, also unknown at the time. He began working with her as an accompanist and arranger, producing her first two albums before charting for the first time himself with "Mandy," a pleasant ballad that went to Number 1 in 1974. As Manilow's hugely successful career began to unfold, many of the people who confessed to liking his first hit jumped ship with a parting concession, and "I hate Barry Manilow, but I love the song 'Mandy' " became the cry of a generation.

His second single, the perky "It's a Miracle" (1975), sounded less like a milquetoast Manilow hit and more like one of his jingles, perhaps for a fast-acting cleaning fluid or headache medication ("I took one tablet and in five minutes, my headache was gone! It's a miracle!"). Manilow, who recognized the importance of being earnest, followed with the somber "Could It Be Magic," inspired by Chopin's "Prelude in C Minor." "I Write the Songs," Manilow's other chart-topper from the first half of the seventies, was next. (Ironically, it was one of the few hits he *didn't* write himself; "I Write [*Most* of] the Songs" would have been more accurate.)

If John Denver was soft rock's answer to the Happy Face button, it was Paul Williams, the world's unlikeliest rock star, who most resembled a Jim Henson creation. Williams was first and foremost a songwriter for acts like the Carpenters, but he made his name as a singer in his own right with a tight-lipped vocal style that was a staple on television specials, where he usually performed self-penned songs that other artists had made famous. He had his own minor hit in 1972 with "Waking Up Alone," and ventured into film acting as the Mephistophelean record producer in Brian DePalma's 1974 musical *The Phantom of the Paradise*. (Williams also scored the film.)

England's own Leo Sayer debuted in 1975 with "Long Tall Glasses (I Can Dance)." The song came across like a soft-rock epiphany; Sayer's exuberant hero discovered rhythm—*he can dance!*—a big moment for soft rockers everywhere. Sayer tripped the chart fantastic with hits like "You Make Me Feel Like Dancing" during the late seventies, but gradually ran out of steam. (Is it a coincidence that right around the time Leo Sayer disappeared from the charts in 1980, cherubic aerobics guru Richard Simmons came to prominence? *Is it?!*)

Until the first half of the seventies, "soft rock" would have been dismissed as an oxymoron, and there are many who would have preferred it to stay that way. In June 1975, even as the Alan Parsons–produced "Magic" by Pilot was leaving its cheerful mark on the charts, Cher divorced longtime hubby Sonny Bono and four days later married Southern rocker Gregg Allman—a sign that perhaps soft rock's cushy Top 40 ride might soon be over. Not so. In the last half of the seventies, the genre gathered steam as the likes of England Dan & John Ford Coley, Rex Smith ("sexy Rexy"), Kenny Nolan, and Alan O'Day abandoned the gently engaging pop of Hamilton, Joe Frank & Dennison (just testing) for the suffocating smarm that had always lurked there. These latter-day saints served up some of the dullest pop of the decade—Denver without the sincerity, Manilow without the grand gestures, Bread without the crusts.

DANCING IN THE MOONLIGHT
Seventies Pop

"Maggie May" • Rod Stewart (Mercury, 1971)
"It's Too Late" • Carole King (Ode, 1971)
"American Pie" • Don McLean (United Artists, 1971)
"Doctor My Eyes" • Jackson Browne (Asylum, 1972)
"Summer Breeze" • Seals & Crofts (Warner, 1972)
"Dancing in the Moonlight" • King Harvest (Perception, 1972)
"Goodbye Yellow Brick Road" • Elton John (MCA, 1973)
"Shambala" • Three Dog Night (Dunhill, 1973)
"Long Train Runnin' " • The Doobie Brothers (Warner, 1973)
"Rock On" • David Essex (Columbia, 1973)

When George Martin and the Beatles proved that an album could be more than a depository of unconnected songs, they sounded the death knell of the single. Until *Sgt. Pepper's Lonely Hearts Club Band* (1967) and its introduction of the concept album concept, 45s had been pop's basic currency, but by the early seventies, the hit single was slipping as a commercial force while LP sales surged.

Like the largely unheralded hitmakers of the early sixties who were the custodians of rock and roll during the JFK years, early seventies "singles acts" like the Doobie Brothers, Chicago, and Three Dog Night made sense of their predecessors' excesses. Gone was the compulsion to reinvent the wheel with each new release; the best records from this taking-stock period used the tools at hand instead of searching for new ones. Pop had arrived at an evolutionary resting point that allowed for a bonanza of great songs neither heavy enough to be considered rock, nor light enough to be considered MOR.

Several of pop's most distinguished careers peaked in the early seventies. Veteran songwriter Carole King found her solo touch in

1971 with the blockbuster album *Tapestry.* "It's Too Late," a breakup song in which the narrator endeavors to make a clean break from a relationship that's beyond saving, supported King's typically first-rate lyric (co-written with Toni Stern) with a sparse, moody arrangement. More hits followed, including "Sweet Seasons" (1972), "Jazzman" (1974), and "Nightingale" (1975).

Elton John, who, like King, was a master of melodies that sounded as if they'd always been with us, also peaked during the early seventies. Behind the smokescreen of his ultra-flamboyant wardrobe (the monumental prescription specs, the towering platform shoes) lurked one of the most prolific pop songwriters of any era. With lyricist Bernie Taupin, John went on a spree, churning out eight gold albums and sixteen Top 40 hits between 1971 and 1975. It's testament to the duo's embarrassment of riches that radio-ready tracks like "Mona Lisas and Mad Hatters" (1972), "Teacher I Need You" (1973), and "Pinky" (1974) weren't even released as singles.

Among John's stunning Watergate-era output (he's the closest thing the first half of the seventies has to a defining force), "Goodbye Yellow Brick Road" stands out. Like another of the era's greatest hits, "Midnight Train to Georgia," it chronicled the displacement

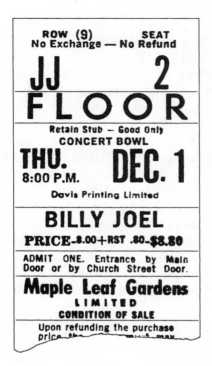

ROW (9)   SEAT
No Exchange — No Refund

JJ   2
FLOOR
Retain Stub — Good Only
CONCERT BOWL

THU.   DEC. 1
8:00 P.M.

Davis Printing Limited

BILLY JOEL
PRICE-8.00+RST .80-$8.80

ADMIT ONE. Entrance by Main
Door or by Church Street Door.

Maple Leaf Gardens
LIMITED
CONDITION OF SALE
Upon refunding the purchase
price

of a rural man stuck in the big city. John's light-as-air pop singing negotiated the melody with ease, bringing in the chorus with a swooping and soaring falsetto: "Beyond the yellow brick *roh-oh-oooh-aaaaaah-eeee-aaaaa-yaaa-yaaaahh*"—Bernie's gone for coffee—"*aaaaah-ooohhhh-ooooohhhh,*" etc. The song launched the eponymous album, one of the biggest-selling and best of its time.

Elton John's importance to MCA was such that by 1975 the label saw fit to take out a $25 million life insurance policy on its franchise player. That same year, anticipation of John's *Captain Fantastic and the Brown Dirt Cowboy* LP rivaled the buildup that had preceded Comet Kohoutek's fly-by two years earlier. Whereas Kohoutek fizzled, *Captain Fantastic* shot to the top, becoming the first release ever to debut in the Number 1 position (June 7, 1975) on *Billboard*'s album chart. Since then, except for flashes of brilliance on *Blue Moves* in 1976, John hasn't come close to the level of mastery that he and Taupin exhibited throughout the early seventies.

It was vocal chops, not songwriting, that kept Three Dog Night successful from 1969 to 1975; the band was frequently knocked for not having written more of its own material. This was a double standard, as many of the era's soul acts, for example, weren't expected to write their own stuff. Here was a tight, versatile rock group fronted by three capable lead singers (Cory Wells, Chuck Negron, and Danny Hutton), each bringing a distinct vocal color to the proceedings, yet they couldn't get arrested by rock critics. They were prone to parroting well-known vocalists (Negron's vocal on "You" was ridiculously close to the Marvin Gaye original, and Cory Wells's idea of a tribute to Otis Redding on "Try a Little Tenderness" was an all-out raid on Redding's phrasing), but their commercial instincts advanced the careers of many an underappreciated songwriting talent (Nilsson, Laura Nyro, and Randy Newman, to name a few).

Among Three Dog Night's myriad hits, "Shambala" (1973) shines as a triumph of pure pop. Scooped from B. W. Stevenson, whose own version went into a Kohoutek-like tailspin as the Dogs' soared to Number 3, "Shambala" was a utopian celebration of a place where "everyone is helpful, everyone is so kind." It's notable for the classic guitar interplay of the intro and for Wells's playful, "Mama Told Me"–like vocal. The extro, in which the band dug into the groove like kids dismissed from school, was a typical Three Dog Night fade; their "heavy" reputation probably demanded that a light pop song like "Shambala" be counterbalanced with some rock-and-roll muscle (if only for their original fans).

Patrick Simmons, Tom Johnston, and the pre–Michael McDonald Doobie Brothers grooved just on the pop side of rock and roll with early hits like "Long Train Runnin' " (1973) and "China Grove" (1973). By the time of their first Number 1 record ("Black Water," 1975), the band had welcomed Steely Dan alumnus Jeff "Skunk" Baxter into the fold and had come to a fork in the road (they followed the "Mellow" sign).

Like the Doobies, Chicago was rarely well reviewed—critics preferred Little Feat and Blood, Sweat & Tears—but the brass-driven popsters could take solace in the success of hits like the piano-slamming "Saturday in the Park" (not to mention their sales figures: 20 million "units" in 1975 alone).

In the old-standby department, prominent Pauls McCartney and Simon weighed in whenever they felt like it with carefully crafted pop confections like Simon's "Kodachrome" (that "all-the-crap-I-learned-in-high-school" line was a can't-miss with the AM audience) and McCartney's majestic "Listen to What the Man Said" (propelled by Tom Scott's euphoric soprano sax and McCartney's cold-glass-of-milk vocal, the song is a true celebration of love and his last great single).

It wasn't just artists with longevity who crafted classic pop during the early seventies. In some ways, it's the one-hit wonders who truly did justice to the concept of a "single." King Harvest achieved pop perfection with one hit only, and the buoyant rush of "Dancing in the Moonlight" (1973) still serves as a concise reminder of what pop music's all about. Like the folks populating the song's moonlit dance party, it "keeps things loose," and if drummer David Montgomery found it difficult to contain himself (you can hear him trying very hard, but he really does want to speed up), it's forgivable; he just wanted to join the party.

David Essex, another one-hit pure popster, left his mark on the charts in 1973 with one of the seventies' most original recordings. "Rock On" was a pastiche of ethereal singing, syncopated percussion, and a repeated baritone vocal reference to "Ja-ay-mes Dean." It has never dated, because nothing has ever sounded like it before or since. Heading into the fade with the tom-toms way up in the mix and a string section that sounded as if it had leaked in from a neighboring studio, Essex repeated insistently that we should "rock on." Maybe he realized that this would be his one opportunity to say it. If so, he made the most of it.

The best hit singles offer the unforgettable listening experience that comes only with unique records like "Rock On." Back in the early seventies, when you heard "Brandy (You're a Fine Girl)" by Looking Glass, "Don't Pull Your Love" by Hamilton, Joe Frank & Reynolds, "Stuck in the Middle with You" by Stealers Wheel, "Come and Get Your Love" by Redbone, "How Long" by Ace, "Summer Breeze" by Seals & Crofts, "Jackie Blue" by the Ozark Mountain Daredevils, or

"The Joker" by the Steve Miller Band, you were hearing songs that transcended their status as disposable "product".

Which brings us to Don McLean's "American Pie," unusual in its length (radio stations had the option to play an edited version, but most of them had the good sense to play the whole thing) and for its maze of pop-music allusions. Lester Bangs described the song's reference-heavy lyrics as "just a bunch of words that could have as much meaning as you wanted." Which was a good thing. People hungering for literal meaning from every lyric likely imploded with sheer interpretive angst every time they heard the song. You were much better off enjoying the words' cumulative effect and bringing your own "meaning" to it. If we now know that "the day the music died" was meant to be the day Buddy Holly's plane went down, that the "sergeants" were the Beatles and that the "jester" was Dylan, so what? It's more fun *not* knowing. Just sing along with any one of the ten or so rounds of "Bye, bye, Miss American Pie" (who is *she,* anyway?), and don't sweat it!

The wonderful, lightweight singles that flourished in the early seventies existed not in spite of but *because of* a spate of depress-

ing headlines (take your pick from the Watergate cover-up, Nixon's Christmas bombing of Hanoi and Haiphong, the PLO slaughter of Israeli athletes at the 1972 Munich Olympics, the Manson murders). Pop radio was a tonic; it provided an endless long weekend, what with "Saturday in the Park," "Saturday Night," "Another Saturday Night," "Saturday Night's Alright for Fighting," "Saturday Morning Confusion," and "Beautiful Sunday" cramming the airwaves.

Things really were different then. It's only when a song like "Dancing in the Moonlight" sneaks up from behind and wrenches you back to a time when true variety was valued that you realize what's been missing all these years. Don McLean may have been mourning Buddy Holly, but "the day the music died" is better translated as the day the *hit single* died.

COLOR BLIND
Blue-eyed Soul

"Do You Know What I Mean" • Lee Michaels (A&M, 1971)
"Wild Night" • Van Morrison (Warner, 1971)
"I Just Want to Celebrate" • Rare Earth (Rare Earth, 1971)
"Thunder and Lightning" • Chi Coltrane (Columbia, 1972)
"Tight Rope" • Leon Russell (Shelter, 1972)
"Right Place Wrong Time" • Dr. John (Atco, 1973)
"Brother Louie" • Stories (Kama Sutra, 1973)
"Hello It's Me" • Todd Rundgren (Bearsville, 1973)
"I've Got the Music in Me" • The Kiki Dee Band (Rocket, 1974)
"Jive Talkin'" • Bee Gees (RSO, 1975)

The history of white singers trying to sing like black ones didn't begin with Elvis Presley (remember Al Jolson?); it's just that he was the first to combine a genius for derivation with the chops to channel R&B and gospel traditions for a waiting white world. As hard as it is to believe for those who grew up in his fat-postage-stamp period, Presley is *a* king of rock and roll, sharing that cushy throne with Chuck Berry ("My Ding-A-Ling" aside) and anyone else for whom sound claim can be made. He wasn't the first white man to appropriate or ransack (your call) African-American musical traditions, but it's in Presley's blistering pre-1958 recordings that modern "blue-eyed soul" is rooted.

In pinpointing its arrival as a genre, however, we'll have to take a quick trip across the Atlantic and acknowledge the faux–R&B intentions of the British invasion; the Beatles, as they frequently pointed out, were steeped in early black rockers like Berry, Little Richard, and Fats Domino, and the Rolling Stones were—and still are—fueled by the blues. (Mick Jagger's first band was called Blues Inc., after a Muddy Waters song.) Back in New York, the Young Rascals were concocting a smooth popsoul extraction, and it was in

1966 that they shot to Number 1 with their first hit, blue-eyed soul's opening salvo, "Good Lovin'." More than any other single, "Good Lovin' " opened the door for an early-seventies mini-wave of white singers schooled in soul.

Van Morrison seems to have spent most of his Belfast youth glued to a radio listening to and learning from his R&B heroes. His seventies catalog is riddled with lyrical references to them; in "Jackie Wilson Said (I'm in Heaven When You Smile)" (1972), Morrison quotes gleefully from Wilson's first hit, "Reet Petite." But it was on "Domino" (1970) and "Wild Night" (1971) that Morrison really hit his stride. The latter record featured the kind of loose, street-smart recitative that would figure so prominently in Bruce Springsteen's early albums a few years later. It also typified the ease with which Morrison could tap into R&B's emotional charge. When he sang that "the wild night is calling," you almost believed he might tear himself away from his radio right then in search of some action.

On "Domino," with its elastic rhythm guitar, its honking baritone sax, and Morrison's growling vocal copping soul licks left, right, and center ("Lord have mercy!"), he invokes the Domino who inspired the title (Antoine "Fats") and evokes the inevitable forward motion of falling dominoes. By the time the record fades, with Morrison testifying that he just wants to hear some R&B on the radio, it's clear he's gone one better: He's *sung* some R&B on the radio. And, in his case, it's as good as the real thing.

Another Fats Domino descendant, this time with a geographical claim, was boogie-woogie piano specialist Dr. John, who sprang from the same swampy New Orleans R&B tradition. If his sound wasn't as directly indebted to Domino's as Morrison's was, the good doctor nonetheless proved to be a great musical ambassador for his hometown. His 1973 hit "Right Place Wrong Time" was produced by Allen Toussaint and featured backing by the Neville Brothers.

Dr. John's super-cool rasp (cross Wolfman Jack with Tom Waits) was one of several quirky voices in the blue-eyed-soul genre. Lee Michaels ("Do You Know What I Mean"), J. J. Cale ("Crazy Mama") and Leon Russell ("Tight Rope," "Lady Blue") were vocally unmistakable. Michaels made his name as a rock organist, Cale as a rock songwriter and blues guitarist; Russell, a veteran session man and husband of Sly Stone "Family" member Mary McCreary, penned some of the era's most enduring melodies, including George Benson's "This Masquerade" and Donny Hathaway's "A Song for You." In all three cases, early-seventies pop success proved unrepeatable.

Todd Rundgren and Daryl Hall represented the slick side of blue-eyed soul. Their vocals had more in common with the contemporary R&B of their native Philadelphia than with past masters like Otis Redding. Rundgren, who produced Badfinger, Grand Funk, Patti Smith, the New York Dolls, and the Tubes, went to Number 5 in 1973 with "Hello It's Me," a brilliantly constructed pop monologue (basically one side of a late-night phone conversation) from his landmark *Something/Anything?* album. Hall and partner John Oates found Top 10 success in 1976 when "She's Gone" (which originally charted in 1974) hit Number 7. Half a dozen gold singles later, it's still the duo's best record.

The Stories scored big in 1973 with a wah-wah-enhanced saga of interracial love called "Brother Louie." The "Louie-Louie-Louie-Lou-ee / Louie, Louie, Louie, Lou-ahh" of the story was a white man dating a black woman; when he took her home to meet his parents, the shit hit the fan and the ominous Norman Whitfield–inspired string arrangement began to make sense. The song's blue-eyed-soul pedigree, reinforced by the *Guess Who's Coming to Dinner* plot, was not consistent with the band's vision of themselves, however, and there would be no future Stories in the Top 40.

Another interracial romance of sorts took place at Motown, when Detroit's black-music monolith signed Rare Earth, a white rock band, in 1969. Easing them out of the gate in 1970 with a couple of Smokey Robinson tunes that had already been hits for the Temptations ("Get Ready", "[I Know] I'm Losing You"), the powers that be decided that the band deserved a shot at "originating" a hit. Three followed: "Born to Wander," a strutting defense of aimlessness; "I Just Want to Celebrate," a seize-the-day power anthem; and "Hey Big Brother," a Whitfield/Strong–style ode to paranoia.

Another of Motown's "white" signings, British soul shouter Kiki Dee, didn't work out quite as well. It wasn't until Elton John signed her to his Rocket Records that Dee scored on the charts, tearing into "I've Got the Music in Me" (1974) with her high-octane delivery, perhaps fueled by a desire to show Motown what they were missing. John had soul aspirations of his own: "Bennie and the Jets" was the first song by a white artist to make Number 1 on the R&B chart; "Honky Cat" featured the "boppin'" reminiscences of an urban sophisticate on his redneck past; and "Philadelphia Freedom" was as much a tribute to Philly soul as it was to Billie Jean King's tennis team.

Dee was not the only female singer to crack the male-dominated world of blue-eyed soul; Chi (pronounced "Shy") Coltrane burst out of Columbia's new talent stable in 1972 with a "Knock on Wood" knockoff called "Thunder and Lightning." Anything but shy, Coltrane's sexually charged singing in the verse ("Oooohhh, what a good thing I got") seemed to be champing at the bit, waiting for that "thunder and lightning" chorus to come along. When it did, the track broke open into a Stax-y pastiche of gutsy vocal, muscular horn section, and gospel piano. As a first single, it was a remarkable achievement—Coltrane also wrote, coproduced, and played piano on the record—and an unsung (except by Chi) classic.

Paul Simon, the Zelig of stylistic assimilation, recruited Phoebe Snow ("Poetry Man") for the gospel-charged workout "Gone at Last" (1975). The pair seemed perfectly at home in the no-holds-barred atmosphere of calling and responding and fronting for the Jessy Dixon Singers. Simon had scored with another shuffling call-and-response gospel hit, "Loves Me Like a Rock," two years earlier.

In the shuffle category, the champions were the British studio trio Ashton, Gardner & Dyke, whose propulsive "Resurrection Shuffle" (1971) competed with the concurrent Tom Jones version. The two records split the vote, going to Number 40 and Number 38, respectively. AGD's version was a minor classic, an adults-only romp masquerading as a traditional soul dance step. Its only appeal for young children was the lead vocal, which sounded uncannily like the Cookie Monster, but its galloping drum track and rough energy provided long-lasting charms. Put it in the "must find" category.

Steely Dan occasionally crossed into blue-eyed-soul territory, using the blues as a building block for singles like "Pretzel Logic" (1974) and "Black Friday" (1975). "Dan" alumnus Michael McDonald would come to define blue-eyed (literally) soul in the latter half of the decade as the smooth-crooning leader of the Doobie Brothers.

For the Bee Gees, whose soulful "Jive Talkin' " quietly hinted at their *Fever*-ish disco takeover, 1975 marked the beginning of a very good thing. Producer Arif Mardin had brought the group to Miami ("KC" country) to funkify their sound, and the late seventies would reward the field trip with more chart-toppers and more money.

In the meantime, the early seventies saw a change in the musical weather. The white-artist tradition of recording black artists' hits (Ricky Nelson covering Fats Domino's "I'm Walkin'," Pat Boone covering Little Richard's "Tutti Frutti") continued apace with "blue-eyed" covers like James Taylor's version of Marvin Gaye's "How Sweet It Is (To Be Loved by You)" and the Rolling Stones' version of the Temptations' "Ain't Too Proud to Beg." However, the reverse was also true: Wilson Pickett covered the Archies' "Sugar, Sugar"; Aretha Franklin covered Elton John's "Border Song (Holy Moses)" and Simon & Garfunkel's "Bridge over Troubled Water"; Stevie Wonder covered the Beatles' "We Can Work It Out"; Al Green covered the Bee Gees' "How Can You Mend a Broken Heart"; Gladys Knight & the Pips covered Sammi Smith's "Help Me Make It Through the Night"; and Tavares covered Hall & Oates' "She's Gone." The work of rock and country songwriters was appealing increasingly to R&B artists. If Jughead jamming with Wilson Pickett was a stretch, it was easy to see what the Tavares brothers saw in "She's Gone," the best Philly soul this side of Gamble and Huff (and the blueprint for later missing-you tracts like Player's "Baby Come Back").

Those seeking a pop-cultural visual to represent blue-eyed soul's early-seventies peak should look no further than syndicated reruns of *The Brady Bunch*. There you will rediscover a powerful metaphor for the white world's coopting of black culture: *Mr. Brady's Afro.* Mike Brady—architect, father, provider—was a blue-eyed soul man.

HOW SWEET IT WAS
The Twilight of Motown

"Just My Imagination (Running Away with Me)"
• The Temptations (Gordy, 1971)
"Got to Be There" • Michael Jackson (Motown, 1971)
"Want Ads" • The Honey Cone (Hot Wax, 1971)
"Nathan Jones" • The Supremes (Motown, 1971)
"Never Can Say Goodbye" • The Jackson 5 (Motown, 1971)
"If You Really Love Me" • Stevie Wonder (Tamla, 1971)
"Reach Out I'll Be There" • Diana Ross (Motown, 1971)
"Ain't No Woman (Like the One I've Got)" • The Four Tops (Dunhill, 1973)
"Neither One of Us (Wants to Be the First to Say Goodbye)" • Gladys Knight &
the Pips (Soul, 1973)
"My Mistake (Was to Love You)" • Diana Ross & Marvin Gaye (Motown, 1974)

By the end of the sixties, the fall of Hollywood's studio system was a fait accompli. MGM, Universal, and Paramount had long since ceased functioning as they had in the thirties and forties, movie moguls having surrendered creative (if not financial) control to their actors, writers, and directors. But in 1971 Motown Records founder and president Berry Gordy was still presiding over his empire, a musical analog of the old Hollywood system, as though nothing had changed.

Since its inception in 1960, Motown had produced an astonishing total of twenty Number 1 singles, giving the British Invasion a run for its money and transmogrifying American R&B. Stars like the Supremes, Stevie Wonder, the Four Tops, the Miracles, Martha & the Vandellas, Gladys Knight & the Pips, Marvin Gaye, and the Temptations had been supported by white radio to a degree that would have been impossible only a decade earlier. And like a musical David O. Selznick, Gordy had controlled the careers of his charges right down to matters of grooming and speech.

Then, on May 13, 1971, Steve Wonder turned twenty-one. The former "boy genius" negotiated a new contract with Motown, one that

VOCAL

G 7121F
(61517)
© 1972
Stone Diamond
Music Corp.
(BMI)
Time: 6:58

Produced by
Norman Whitfield
Arr. & Cond. By:
Paul Riser
In Album
"All Directions"
G 962L

PAPA WAS A ROLLIN' STONE
(N. Whitfield, B. Strong)
THE TEMPTATIONS

DISTRIBUTED BY AMPEX MUSIC OF CANADA 108 Skyway Ave., Rexdale, Ont. Canada

R 5038F
© 1971
Jobete, BMI
Q-G1/01-T2-
934M02
Time: 3:04

Produced by
Rare Earth

"HEY BIG BROTHER"
(D. Fekaris, N. Zesses)
RARE EARTH

granted him total artistic freedom. *Music of My Mind, Talking Book, Innervisions, Fulfillingness' First Finale*, and *Songs in the Key of Life* followed, making Wonder a bargain at any price. The same year, Marvin Gaye completed *What's Going On?*, the first Motown album to fully address the political, social, and environmental (at the time the word was "ecological") ills of the day. Free agency had arrived, and Berry Gordy's benevolent dictatorship would never be the same.

By 1973, Diana Ross had left the Supremes, Smokey Robinson had left the Miracles, David Ruffin and Eddie Kendricks had left the Temptations, and Martha Reeves had left the Vandellas. Gladys Knight & the Pips moved to Buddah Records, striking gold and topping the pop chart for the first time with "Midnight Train to Georgia," and the Four Tops had their biggest hit of the seventies, "Ain't No Woman (Like the One I've Got)" on their new label, Dunhill.

The only indication that corporate Motown was still alive was the ongoing success of Gordy's latest triumph, the Jackson 5. Up to and including their last big hit, "Dancing Machine," the Jackson brothers were model Motown citizens, recording catchy, up-tempo material written by Gordy's "Corporation," dancing up a synchronized storm, and smiling their way into the hearts of preteen America. Though less well known than their 1969–70 breakout hits, 1971's "Mama's Pearl," "Never Can Say Goodbye," "Maybe Tomorrow," and "Sugar Daddy" make a strong argument for production-line pop.

Still, the writing was on the wall, and the final masterworks of the high Motown era—records like the post-Diana Supremes' "Nathan Jones," Michael Jackson's "Got to Be There," the Temptations' "Just My Imagination (Running Away with Me)," and Gladys Knight & the Pips' "Neither One of Us (Wants to Be the First to Say Goodbye)"— soon gave way to fierce competition from without and within. As Motown struggled to maintain its identity after moving from Detroit to Los Angeles, Philadelphia International Records cofounders Kenny Gamble and Leon Huff were trying on Gordy's crown, writing and producing for a stable of artists that included the O'Jays, Harold Melvin & the Bluenotes, and Billy Paul. Memphis-based Stax/Volt Records, though past its creative prime, still had major clout and top-drawer talent like Isaac Hayes, the Dramatics, and the Staple Singers.

The burgeoning, beat-driven Miami disco scene (home of K.C. & the Sunshine Band) was using soul idioms for its own sinister purposes. Worse, pop artists at large had begun aping Motown's style, with mixed results; hands up if you'd rather listen to Diana Ross than to Gayle McCormick ("It's a Crying Shame") or Polly Brown ("Up in a Puff of Smoke").

But the unkindest cuts of all came from Lamont Dozier, Eddie Holland, and Brian Holland, Gordy's former star staff writers. Having left Motown in 1967 after bringing suit against the company, Holland-Dozier-Holland had debuted their Invictus label in 1970, with artists like the Chairmen of the Board and Freda Payne jockeying for chart position with their Motown counterparts. July 25, 1970, for instance, found Payne's "Band of Gold" adjacent to the Jackson 5's "The Love You Save" on the charts.

In 1971, Invictus's sister label, Hot Wax, unveiled the Honey Cone, a commercially potent female trio at least as soulful as the Supremes, and more sexually charged. The group's "Want Ads" and "Stick-up" (the latter was actually the blueprint for the former) hit big, participating in, if not actually causing, a wave of feminist pop, and follow-ups like "One Monkey Don't Stop No Show (Part 1)" and the Supremes homage "The Day I Found Myself" made the notion that men were superfluous endlessly entertaining. The Cone's Carolyn Willis, Chairmen of the Board chairman General Johnson, and Freda Payne are among the seventies' great unheralded voices.

Invictus and Hot Wax combined for eighteen Top 40 hits, but Holland-Dozier-Holland would have been very much in evidence even without their new venture. Covers of H-D-H Motown chestnuts like "Please Mr. Postman," "(Love Is Like a) Heat Wave," "How Sweet It Is (to Be Loved by You)," "Take Me in Your Arms (Rock Me a Little While)," and "This Old Heart of Mine" were everywhere. Even Motown occasionally went to the well. In 1972, at a time when Diana Ross could have been staking out new territory, she covered "Reach Out I'll Be There," the H-D-H–penned Four Tops hit, barely cracking the Top 30.

Thus ended the golden age of Hitsville U.S.A. Berry Gordy would continue to break new acts (like the Commodores) in the coming years, but Motown had begun the slow process of becoming just another big record label. Once in a while, a new release would summon the old days—Diana Ross and Marvin Gaye's "My Mistake (Was to Love You)" was a little slice of '66, eight years late—but increasingly Motown found itself following trends rather than initiating them. The post-Smokey Miracles' "Love Machine (Part 1)" was an obvious concession to disco, just as the Undisputed Truth ("Smiling Faces Sometimes") was Motown's attempt to find its own Sly & the Family Stone.

Wurlitzer stopped making jukeboxes in 1974, which was as good an indication as any that singles were on the wane. AOR (album-oriented rock) radio was helping LPs rack up unprecedented sales; faux-minstrel rockers Jethro Tull had eight albums certified gold between 1971 and 1975, and it certainly wasn't thanks to support from Top 40 stations. Acts like the Jackson 5, with their bell-bottomed stage wardrobe and underage fans, began to seem almost quaint. It would take another fifteen years for the 45-rpm format to peter out altogether, but the hit single—and Motown, the label that perfected it—would become less and less influential as the decade wore on.

THE SOUND OF PHILADELPHIA
Philly Soul

"I'll Be Around" • Spinners (Atlantic, 1972)
"Me and Mrs. Jones" • Billy Paul (Philadelphia International, 1972)
"If You Don't Know Me by Now" • Harold Melvin & the Bluenotes
(Philadelphia International, 1972)
"Zing Went the Strings of My Heart" • The Trammps (Buddah, 1972)
"TSOP (The Sound of Philadelphia)" • MFSB (Philadelphia International, 1974)
"When Will I See You Again" • The Three Degrees
(Philadelphia International, 1974)
"You Make Me Feel Brand New" • The Stylistics (Avco, 1974)
"Sideshow" • Blue Magic (Atco, 1974)
"You Little Trustmaker" • The Tymes (RCA, 1974)
"I Love Music (Part 1)" • The O'Jays (Philadelphia International, 1975)

I n mid-1971, scant months after its artists had dominated the annual Grammy Awards in almost every category, Columbia, the world's top record label, turned to the Harvard University Business School for help. The appeal seemed slightly absurd; with superstars like Bob Dylan, Barbra Streisand, Chicago, Santana, and Simon & Garfunkel under contract, what could Columbia Records possibly need to learn about the music business?

Plenty, as it turned out. Though Columbia had long since gotten over its fear of rock and roll, it had delved only tentatively into black music. The Grammy Rhythm-and-Blues categories, in fact, were the only ones in which the label had been shut out in March. Among all its successful acts, there was only one on the R&B side—a hitmaking, multiracial anomaly called Sly & the Family Stone. Columbia had a color void, and the label's wunderkind, Clive Davis, was growing tired of watching black labels like Stax, Motown, Atlantic, and Hi take the lion's share of the profits from the exponentially expanding (and increasingly album-oriented) soul market. He wanted a blueprint for black-market success.

In his 1975 autobiography, *Clive: Inside the Record Business,*

Davis glosses over the matter, saying simply, "I asked for some market research." In fact, the Harvard Report (as it became known) was much more than raw research: It was an explicit, stats-filled manifesto for R&B dominance in the seventies, including recommendations for TV and radio cross-promotion, a new "black" division at Columbia, and acquisition of relevant smaller labels. Davis had his blueprint; now he set about making things happen.

Step One was to enter into a partnership with Stax, one of the black "majors" and the birthplace of *Shaft*. The deal Davis negotiated with Stax owner Al Bell in 1972 (which included a $6 million advance) seemed like a blockbuster at the time, but its perceived importance faded quickly when Stax began to lose its commercial touch, finally folding in 1976.

The more successful second step involved a pitch by Davis to two Philadelphia-based writer-producers named Kenneth Gamble and Leon Huff, who by 1971 had already created hits for Jerry Butler ("Only the Strong Survive"), Wilson Pickett ("Don't Let the Green Grass Fool You"), Joe Simon ("Drowning in the Sea of Love"), Aretha Franklin ("Brand New Me"), Archie Bell & the Drells ("I Can't Stop Dancing") and fellow Philadelphians the Soul Survivors ("Expressway to Your Heart") and the Intruders ("Cowboys to Girls"). Under the proposed agreement, CBS, Columbia's parent company, would fund and distribute a new, Gamble and Huff–run label called Philadelphia International Records (PIR).

The rest is history. Over the next few years, PIR established itself as the premier black label of the seventies, rejuvenating the careers of vocal groups like Harold Melvin & the Bluenotes, the O'Jays, and the Three Degrees, and bringing up-to-the-minute production values to some timeless R&B sides. Clive Davis was fired by Columbia in May 1973 for alleged expense account improprieties (he went on to found Arista Records), but the effects of his PIR deal are still being felt today.

Philadelphia was an unlikely candidate to emerge as black music's new epicenter. For years it had labored musically in the shadow of nearby New York. With the exception of Solomon Burke, it had never produced a true R&B superstar, and was best known in pop circles as the birthplace of Dick Clark's *American Bandstand* and beach-movie idols like Fabian and Frankie Avalon. All that was about to change.

"Backstabbers," the menacing O'Jays hit that launched PIR in 1972, exemplified the mold into which many future Gamble-and-Huff productions would be poured. The upper elements consisted of big brass, bigger strings, loping Latin percussion, and jazzy chords, combined with a fierce, old-school soul vocal (Eddie Levert's) that seemed constantly on the verge of shattering the track's delicate equilibrium. Down below, there was the forward momentum of the airtight MFSB (Mothers Fathers Sisters Brothers) rhythm section.

All the big O'Jays hits were made in the image of "Backstabbers," particularly 1974's "For the Love of Money." Studio regular Anthony Jackson, who invented "Money" 's tough, Larry Graham–esque bass line, was given credit for cowriting the tune with Gamble and Huff, and deservedly so. On the lighter side were the chart-topping Amtrak-to-paradise anthem "Love Train" and "I Love Music," an ancestor of today's two-chord, minor-key house vamps and a hymn to the kind of intoxicating dance music PIR was producing.

Mass-producing, even. Gamble and Huff tallied more gold singles

during the seventies than any other producers, and fewer than half of those were O'Jays hits. Harold Melvin & the Bluenotes, whose fortunes improved when Teddy Pendergrass signed on as lead singer in 1970, scored several smashes before Pendergrass left again in 1975. "The Love I Lost" superimposed a bittersweet, downward-bending melody over an exhilarating, string-laden PIR romp. "If You Don't Know Me by Now," the definitive Gamble-Huff ballad, pitted the Bluenotes' tightly reined ensemble work against Pendergrass's raw, rambling leads. (The lack of this doo-wop–gospel dynamic is only one reason the 1988 Simply Red version pales by comparison.) "Wake Up Everybody" and "Bad Luck" featured the ordained Pendergrass warning against worldly excesses (smoking, drinking, blind faith in the GOP) while the propulsive abandon of the latter track contradicted every word.

"Bad Luck"'s groove deserves serious consideration as the best of the PIR era. MFSB bassist Ronnie Baker never played so hard—he sounded as if he might snap the neck of his instrument any second—and drummer Earl Young laid into his kit with everything he had, like Al Jackson on "Soul Man" without the Southern concision. "Bad Luck"'s only competition in the groove department was "TSOP (The Sound of Philadelphia)," the Grammy-winning, mostly instrumental 1974 hit that became the theme to *Soul Train*. Don Cornelius's long-running TV series never had it so good; "TSOP" was the rare disco tune that could make you feel like you were moving a thousand miles an hour even when you were standing still (as opposed to the reverse). It contained the requisite PIR contradictions: How can something designed to be disposable sound so memorable? How can something steeped in tradition sound so fresh? How can something so streamlined sound so funky?

The Three Degrees, who supplied the vocals for "TSOP," are remembered mostly for "When Will I See You Again," a mid-tempo ballad that sounded like Darlene Love and Lamont Dozier walking hand in hand across the Bridge of Sighs. It was a simple missing-you song, thematically different from most PIR material, and amid the funky clatter of late 1974, it recalled a disappearing tradition even as artists like Rufus, the Ohio Players, and Barry White were creating new ones.

Billy Paul addressed a more complicated situation on "Me and Mrs. Jones" (1972): a secret, going-nowhere affair that neither party had the strength to abandon. The track's leisurely swing and Paul's measured phrasing are the model of control, until the band suddenly stops, and our hero bubbles over emotionally: "Meee-eee aaa-aaand Mrs., Mrs. Jones, Mrs. Jones, Mrs. Jones, Mrs. Jones . . ." But this is Philadelphia International, after all, and as the gentle groove resumes, Paul collects himself.

Later odes to infidelity, like the Manhattans' "Kiss and Say Goodbye" (1976), lacked brilliant touches like those slippery violin figures that interrupted Billy Paul every time he seemed ready to tell you exactly what was "going on" with Mrs. Jones. PIR's strength was detail. Think of the tremolo effect on the guitar and electric piano on "Love Train" that made that sleek machine actually glimmer, or the one-step-up-two-steps-back opening bass figure in "Bad Luck" that describes the character's losing streak.

Gamble and Huff pursued their meticulous pop-soul aesthetic with the kind of reckless confidence that comes from knowing you're in the right place at the right time. Their agenda was not strictly musical—Gamble, in particular, was passionate about drawing attention to social issues and advancing a positive worldview—but their legacy is. People don't revisit the hits of Philadelphia International year after year for the *Message in the Music* (the title of a 1976 O'Jays LP); they're craving those distinctive voices, those slick arrangements, that big Sigma Sound sound.

The productions of Gamble-Huff cohort Thom Bell (the three have a joint publishing company called Mighty Three Music) were less politically charged but no less commercial; by the end of the decade, his sales figures and gold record totals had reached the same lofty heights as his friends'. He was more of a hands-on arranger than either Gamble or Huff, though, and he chose to work for various labels (Atlantic, Avco, Columbia, Philly Groove) in lieu of empire-building. Bell's approach to the rhythm section was less muscular—his signature groove was an easy canter like the one on the Spinners' "I'll Be Around"—and his hot period ended a few years sooner than PIR's precisely because his softer approach turned out to be less disco-compatible.

Bell had already tasted success with the Delfonics ("La-La Means I Love You") when he began producing the Stylistics, a fledgling vocal quintet whose chief asset was the haunting falsetto of Philly native Russell Thompkins. Starting in 1971, Bell and lyricist Linda Creed wrote a string of hit ballads for the group: "You Are Everything," "Betcha by Golly, Wow," "I'm Stone in Love with You," "Break Up to Make Up" (with Gamble) and "You Make Me Feel Brand New." These were dreamy, unapologetically romantic songs, brimming with emotion almost to the point of melodrama, but Thompkins's magical phrasing and Bell's perfect, soft-soul settings rescued them from the black-Bread status they sometimes courted. "You Make Me Feel Brand New," with its wedding-ready lyric and influential key change (to be revisited in Whitney Houston's 1985 debut "You Give Good Love"), was the most successful, but "I'm Stone in Love with You," at once simpler and more affecting, was probably the best.

If the Stylistics were Bell's house of love, the Spinners were his playground. The former second-tier Motown act had been given a new lease on life in 1972 by Atlantic, and their Bell-produced hits included "I'll Be Around"–style fare like "Could It Be I'm Falling in

Love" and "Then Came You" (with Dionne Warwick), as well as quirkier releases like the swinging "They Just Can't Stop It the (Games People Play)" and the just-plain-goofy "Rubberband Man." The love songs were vehicles for lead singer Phillippe Wynne, but the latter two songs split the vocal chores among the members in more traditional fashion—you may remember bass vocalist Pervis Jackson damaging your woofers with his solo lines on "Games People Play." Atlantic's other contributions to the Philly scene included "Love Won't Let Me Wait" by ex-Delfonic Major Harris, recorded at Gamble and Huff's Sigma Sound studio, and later recordings by the Trammps ("Disco Inferno") and Blue Magic ("Three Ring Circus").

Inevitably, the Spinners' distinctive rhythmic feel began to spread to other Philly soul hits. The Tymes, a mixed quintet that had notched a Number 1 record ("So Much in Love") on the local Parkway label in 1963, tied together two decades of Philadelphia hit-making when their "You Little Trustmaker" went to Number 12 in 1974. The song made conspicuous use of a Bell-style backbeat and PIR-derived orchestration. William DeVaughn, a D.C. native who recorded his only hit, "Be Thankful for What You Got," on a shoe-string budget in Philadelphia in early 1974, proved the formula could work without frills.

Direct offshoots of the Sigma scene included "Tossin' and Turnin' " (Bunny Sigler) and "You're the Reason Why" (the Ebonys), produced by Gamble and Huff; "Do It Any Way You Wanna" (People's Choice), written and produced by Huff; "Sideshow" (Blue Magic), produced by MFSB guitarist Norman Harris; "Armed and Extremely Dangerous" (First Choice), coproduced by Harris; "Ask Me" (Ecstasy, Passion & Pain), produced by MFSB pianist and arranger Bobby Martin; "Salsoul Hustle" (the Salsoul Orchestra), also featuring MFSB members, and "Zing Went the Strings of My Heart" by the Trammps, who were basically the MFSB rhythm section.

Elton John and David Bowie tapped the Philly groove, too. John's "Philadelphia Freedom" (1975), dedicated to tennis great and Philadelphia Freedoms coach Billie Jean King, was a catalog of Mighty Three mannerisms, from its prominent strings and brass to its unmistakably Spinners-style bed track. (Thom Bell later produced John's hit "Mama Can't Buy You Love" in the style of the Spinners' "One of a Kind [Love Affair].") When Bowie decided to reinvent himself as a white soul crooner, he came to Sigma Sound to record *Young Americans.* The album's biggest hit, "Fame" (1975), sounded more like Midwestern funk than Philly soul, but Sigma's presence was felt on other tracks like "Win" and "Right."

The Philly sojourns of Elton John and David Bowie were anything but acts of desperation; the two were peaking creatively and prolific as hell, with eight albums each since 1970. More likely, the two British superstars recognized that something extraordinary was happening in the City of Brotherly Love. Gamble and Huff had created their own private Motown-style hit factory and, like Berry Gordy, were using a single studio and a regular cast of musicians and arrangers to craft pop-soul classics whose influence would span decades. Thom Bell was having much the same effect with his multilabel approach. Philly soul ushered in an era of studio realism, saved some of the best voices of the era (Levert, Pendergrass, Thompkins, Wynne) from obscurity, and proved once and for all that a thirty-piece orchestra could groove like the dickens if you gave them the right stuff to play. (The lone sour note was the indictment of Gamble and Huff on payola charges; Gamble eventually paid a slap-on-the-wrist fine of $2,500.)

Philly soul didn't end in 1975—hits by Pendergrass, Lou Rawls, and McFadden & Whitehead still lay ahead—but in the late seventies, records from PIR and Atlantic's Philadelphia branch increasingly belonged to the larger classification of disco. If this new, mechanized dance music tended to coopt some of Gamble and Huff's best ideas (it's a pretty short walk from "TSOP" to "Fly, Robin, Fly"), at least the Philly groove survived at full strength long enough to influence Chic ("Good Times"), Donna Summer ("Last Dance") and the third coming of the Bee Gees ("Night Fever"). The best disco didn't suck, as all but the most hardcore Kiss fans now admit, and songs like "Bad Luck" can take credit for setting high standards in an often embarrassing genre. But the legacy is less important than the records themselves; even if Philly soul had disappeared after "I Love Music" dropped off the *Billboard* charts in early 1976, the stunning, soulful work of Gamble, Huff, and Bell would still rank among the best of the seventies.

WALKING IN RHYTHM
Seventies Soul

"Have You Seen Her" • The Chi-Lites (Brunswick, 1971)
"Whatcha See Is Whatcha Get" • The Dramatics (Volt, 1971)
"Let's Stay Together" • Al Green (Hi, 1971)
"Lean on Me" • Bill Withers (Sussex, 1972)
"Everybody Plays the Fool" • The Main Ingredient (RCA, 1972)
"Too Late to Turn Back Now" • Cornelius Brothers & Sister Rose
(United Artists, 1972)
"Midnight Train to Georgia" • Gladys Knight & the Pips (Buddah, 1973)
"Until You Come Back to Me" • Aretha Franklin (Atlantic, 1973)
"Fire" • Ohio Players (Mercury, 1974)
"Shining Star" • Earth, Wind & Fire (Columbia, 1975)

Soul is what happened when gospel collided with pop in the mid-fifties. It encompassed the work of giants like James Brown, Aretha Franklin, Otis Redding, Wilson Pickett, Sam Cooke, and Jackie Wilson. With its sacred origins and sexual content, it expressed rock and roll's essential duality. As a movement, it lasted from Ray Charles's first recordings until the Wattstax concerts in August 1972.

Wattstax, an all-star remembrance of the 1965 Watts riots, was organized by Stax Records boss Al Bell and his friend Jesse Jackson, and featured Isaac Hayes, the Staple Singers, Luther Ingram, and many other Stax/Volt artists in concert at the Los Angeles Coliseum. Later a film and multirecord set, Wattstax was evidence of the continuing relevance of soul, but it was also a last gasp of sorts: Redding, Cooke, Clyde McPhatter, and Little Willie John were already dead; Stax would go bankrupt within a few years; Atlantic was branching out into the rock market; and, most important, funk, disco, reggae, Philly soul, black rock, and various new strains of R&B would soon fragment soul forever.

Soul stars like James Brown, Aretha Franklin, Wilson Pickett, Joe Tex, Ike & Tina Turner, Jerry Butler, Johnnie Taylor, and the Isley Brothers continued to rack up hits during the early seventies, but not at the blinding pace they had in the sixties. Brown's biggest commercial successes—"Papa's Got a Brand New Bag," "I Got You (I Feel Good)," "Cold Sweat"—were behind him, and his Maceo Parker–led band had splintered in 1969. That didn't stop his legend from growing: He continued to jam on favorite subjects like sex ("Hot Pants [She Got to Use What She Got to Get What She Wants]") and his own bad self ("Super Bad") while occasionally tackling the hot topics of the day ("King Heroin"); he invented funk, supplying not only inspiration but personnel for Parliament/Funkadelic; and his 1974 single "The Payback," a Number 1 R&B hit, is frequently cited as the beginning of rap.

The throne of Aretha, Queen of Soul, remained inviolate (though not uncoveted) in the seventies. Franklin would never again have a year like 1967, when five of her first six Atlantic singles went Top 10, but new releases like "You're All I Need to Get By," "Spanish Harlem," "Rock Steady," "Oh Me Oh My (I'm a Fool for You Baby)," "Day Dreaming," "Angel," and "Until You Come Back to Me" refuted any and all Aretha-in-decline theories. "Rock Steady" (1971), an instance of its own doctrine, pulsed with a ferocity that could strike fear into the JBs. "Oh Me Oh My" (1972), a minor hit except on the R&B chart, where it reached Number 2, represented the other Aretha—the tender, giving, vulnerable one.

Somewhere in between was "Until You Come Back to Me" (1973), one of those rare pop singles that actually deserves the label "masterpiece." A decent missing-you song that recycled cowriter Stevie Wonder's "My Cherie Amour" chord progression to good effect, it was elevated to the level of surefire hit by Arif Mardin's arrangement, then to the level of truth by Aretha's vocal. Swooping, soaring, plunging, the voice (*the* voice) expressed, by turns, desperation, determination, resignation, and rapture. The way Franklin bent five consecutive syllables down into blue-note territory going into the final refrain was the kind of impossible, inspired choice that made other soul divas feel like soul Salieris (God is singing through her; why not me?). The electrifying, goosebump-inducing interjection that followed ("I got to cha-a-ange your view, baby") simultaneously conveyed fond hope and bittersweet surrender.

The R&B chart was also open to mere mortals, of course, but with artists like Aretha, Stevie Wonder, Gladys Knight, Al Green, and Marvin Gaye jockeying for position, serious talent was sometimes overlooked. Excluding three duets with Roberta Flack, silky-voiced soul man Donny Hathaway went largely unnoticed by the pop audience until his death in 1979. Millie Jackson's smoky pipes and explicitly sexual raps kept her following mostly underground after "Hurts So Good" (from the *Cleopatra Jones* soundtrack) left the charts in November 1973. Singer and guitarist Bobby Womack, who had written hits for Wilson Pickett, Janis Joplin, and the Rolling Stones, faded from the charts after one Top 10 hit of his own ("Lookin' for a Love"). Luther Ingram's "(If Loving You Is Wrong) I Don't Want to Be Right," an anguished "Me and Mrs. Jones"–style scenario, was the lone pop hit for the cowriter of "Respect Yourself." And the oft-covered R&B standard "I Can't Stand the Rain" outlived the career of its talented originator, Ann Peebles.

Even at the height of her success, Peebles played second fiddle to her Hi Records labelmate Al Green, the former gospel prodigy whose five-year gold streak (1971–1975) included unforgettable records like "Tired of Being Alone," "I'm Still in Love with You," and "Let's Stay Together" (no, it didn't come from *Pulp Fiction*). Green was the Otis Redding of romantic longing, a supremely gifted singer who chose the heart as his subject. With producer Willie Mitchell, he defined an intimate new strain of Memphis soul that coexisted briefly with Stax's more muscular style.

Stax was in flux at the time. The death of Redding in 1967 and the subsequent commercial decline of Sam & Dave and Booker T. & the MG's might have been a tidy conclusion to the label's story if not for the emergence in the early seventies of new stars like Isaac Hayes ("Theme from *Shaft*"), Jean Knight ("Mr. Big Stuff"), Shirley Brown ("Woman to Woman"), the Staple Singers ("I'll Take You There," "Respect Yourself") and the Dramatics ("Whatcha See Is Whatcha Get," "In the Rain"). These artists made some of the seventies' most vital music—the catchphrase-based tour de force "Whatcha See Is

Whatcha Get" alone was worth a round-trip ticket to Memphis—and forestalled the inevitable collapse of the Stax/Volt empire for about five years.

Motown, whose impact as a soul label had long since been eclipsed by its ability to court a broad, international audience, nonetheless enjoyed new credibility in the early seventies, releasing watershed albums by Marvin Gaye *(What's Going On)* and Stevie Wonder *(Talking Book)*. Wonder's singles ran the gamut from love songs like "You Are the Sunshine of My Life" to hard-edged grooves like "Superstition" (a song originally intended for Jeff Beck). The Temptations, collaborating with Norman Whitfield and Barrett Strong, specialized in social consciousness–raising material like "Papa Was a Rollin' Stone," "Take a Look Around," and "The Plastic Man." Meanwhile, Gladys Knight & the Pips became a top priority at Buddah Records, something they had never been at Motown, and a string of spectacular, from-the-heart soul ballads like "Best Thing That Ever Happened to Me" and "Midnight Train to Georgia" followed. (If all you remember is the "Whoo!-whoo!" of the Pips, you need to reinvestigate this stuff.)

Motown's Undisputed Truth ("Smiling Faces Sometimes"), Invictus's 8th Day ("She's Not Just Another Woman"), ABC's Rufus ("Once You Get Started") and UA's War ("Low Rider") were among the many quality Sly & the Family Stone–inspired acts to notch hits in the early seventies. Sly had made large, multiracial funk-rock bands attractive to record labels, and, by 1975, almost every label had one. Traditional vocal groups maintained their soul market share with harmony-rich hits like Cornelius Brothers & Sister Rose's "Too Late to Turn Back Now," the Main Ingredient's "Everybody Plays the Fool," and the Chi-Lites' "Have You Seen Her."

On the pop side, veterans like Diana Ross, Johnny Nash, and Dionne Warwick faced off against relative newcomers like Bill Withers, Roberta Flack, and Billy Preston. Withers, whose self-penned 1971 debut "Ain't No Sunshine" won a Grammy for Best R&B Song and featured backing by the MG's, had his greatest success the following year with the chart-topping buddies-for-life anthem "Lean on Me." (An early hip-hop version by Club Nouveau went to Number 1 15 years later.) Flack logged a total of twelve weeks at Number 1 with three MOR ballads: "The First Time Ever I Saw Your Face" (from the film *Play Misty for Me*), "Killing Me Softly with His Song" (written about Don McLean singing "Vincent") and the jazz-inflected "Feel Like Makin' Love." Preston, the fifth Beatle, was everywhere. His own records ("Nothing from Nothing," "Will It Go Round in Circles") were chart-toppers. He wrote "You Are So Beautiful," a Top 5 hit for Joe Cocker. He appeared on other artists' albums, both as a billed performer (on *The Concert for Bangla Desh*) and as a sideman (for Carole King, Barbra Streisand, and many others). He collected two Grammys. He toured with the Rolling Stones. He was a musical guest on the first-ever *Saturday Night Live* telecast in October, 1975.

Former Impression Curtis Mayfield was equally busy, and even more influential. His 1972 album, *Superfly*, went to Number 1 in *Billboard* and launched two searing singles, the title track and "Freddie's Dead." A unified, rhythmically complex song cycle masquerading as a blaxploitation soundtrack, *Superfly* sold in the millions. As an arranger, Mayfield was a peer of Isaac Hayes and Quincy Jones, juggling orchestral textures, Latin percussion, jazz leads, and funk grooves with ease. As a falsetto singer, he was rivaled only by the Temptations' Eddie Kendricks. He founded Curtom Records, Chicago's premier black label of the seventies, writing and producing hits for Gladys Knight ("On and On"), the Staple Singers ("Let's Do It Again") and Aretha Franklin ("Something He Can Feel"). His post-*Superfly* film scores included *Claudine* and *Let's Do It Again.*

Mayfield's early-seventies success had everything to do with the coming of age of the black album. Like Marvin Gaye's *What's Going On,* Sly & the Family Stone's *There's a Riot Goin' On,* Isaac Hayes's *Shaft,* Aretha Franklin's *Young, Gifted and Black,* and every Stevie Wonder LP from *Talking Book* to *Songs in the Key of Life, Superfly* was more than the sum of its singles—just as surely as the Rolling Stones' *Exile on Main Street* was bigger than "Happy" and "Tumbling Dice."

In effect, soul was now working with the same wide canvas rock had enjoyed since 1967. Apart from Earth, Wind & Fire and Prince, however, few late-seventies black artists took advantage of their new artistic freedom. Disco was as singles-driven as Motown had ever been, and the search for the next "Shake Your Groove Thing" took precedence over the search for the next *Innervisions.* But the soul album explosion had been real, and its best results evoked black experience in a way that *The Jeffersons* and *Sanford and Son* never could.

Meanwhile, funk, a rhythmically rigorous distillation of James Brown's late-sixties sides, was being defined by new bands like Parliament ("Up for the Down Stroke," "Chocolate City"), Kool & the Gang ("Jungle Boogie," "Hollywood Swinging"), the Ohio Players ("Fire," "Love Rollercoaster"), and Earth, Wind & Fire ("Shining Star," "Sing a Song"). Parliament, part of funk overlord George Clinton's "Parliafunkadelicament" empire, made extended, cosmically themed records for its almost entirely black, urban audience. Former jazzheads Kool & the Gang were party-anthem specialists. The Ohio Players, known for their explicit album covers *(Pain, Pleasure, Ecstasy, Climax, Honey),* were funk's Midwest branch office.

Earth, Wind & Fire had started in L.A. in the late sixties as a vehicle for former session drummer Maurice White's mystical pop songs. By 1974 (the year of their first Top 40 hit, "Mighty Mighty"), EWF had become the crossover Parliament/Funkadelic. Propelled by supernaturally funky arrangements that relied heavily on White's bass-playing younger brother, Verdine, the band outplayed, out-hooked, and generally outperformed competitors like the Commodores, Tower of Power, B.T. Express, and Average White Band. "Shining Star" was the funkiest record of 1975—sorry, KC—and the pilot for a series of intricate hit singles that promoted self-actualization while raising a funky stench. (The formula was perfected in 1977 with "Serpentine Fire.")

Maurice White's legacy is less audible today than George Clinton's; Parliament/Funkadelic's racially specific lyrics, bizarre stage antics, and ragged grooves are nineties-friendly, and EWF is, in a sense, the opposite of hip-hop. Still, many current pop stars learned what funk is from White—compare Lenny Kravitz's "It Ain't Over Til It's Over" (1991) to "That's the Way of the World" (1975)—and EWF's multi-platinum streak went a long way toward proving black superstars could sell albums in numbers comparable to their white counterparts.

After Wattstax, soul became harder to pin down than it had been in the days of "In the Midnight Hour" and "Knock on Wood." Latter-day nostalgia buffs attempting to get a handle on the music's pre-'75 second wave will encounter a baffling diversity of styles, and may well climb down from the Rollercoaster of Love muttering, "Say what?" Luckily for them, they will also run across some of the best music of our time.

GLOBAL VILLAGE
World Rhythms

"Oye Como Va" • Santana (Columbia, 1971)
"Funky Nassau—Part 1" • The Beginning of the End (Alston, 1971)
"The Lion Sleeps Tonight" • Robert John (Atlantic, 1972)
"Jungle Fever" • The Chakachas (Polydor, 1972)
"Suavecito" • Malo (Warner, 1972)
"Mother and Child Reunion" • Paul Simon (Columbia, 1972)
"I Can See Clearly Now" • Johnny Nash (Epic, 1972)
"Waterloo" • ABBA (Atlantic, 1974)
"Hooked on a Feeling" • Blue Swede (EMI, 1974)
"I Shot the Sheriff" • Eric Clapton (RSO, 1974)

Détente. To the French, it has always meant "relaxation." But for a time in the English-speaking world, it had a more specific meaning: cordiality among superpowers. Forced relaxation, on a global scale. Détente's finest hour was Richard Nixon's 1972 globetrotting; the president's visits to China and the U.S.S.R. couldn't have been better timed, what with the United States embracing Ping-Pong and panda bears, and Bobby Fischer and Boris Spassky going *mano a mano* for the world chess title. Nixon's cool-war diplomacy seemed a viable alternative to nuclear annihilation.

The music industry had less incentive to embrace détente—apart from Jimmy Page's guitar, there were no nuclear weapons involved—but by the mid-seventies, artists from Europe, Africa, and the Caribbean were infiltrating the American charts with increasing regularity. Funny thing was, no one knew it.

There was nothing particularly foreign-sounding about Golden Earring's "Radar Love," an extended rock shuffle with a driving-as-sex theme that dated back to Chuck Berry. Nor did Mouth & Macneal's gold-selling "How Do You Do?" sound like anything but good old American mainstream dreck. Surprise—both bands were Dutch.

Blue Swede's 1974 cover of B. J. Thomas's 1969 hit "Hooked on a Feeling" (featuring those immortal *"ooga-chaka"*s) was downright peculiar, but *Swedish?* The Chakachas' "Jungle Fever," while notable for its ecstatic moans and groans (malaria—yeah, right), didn't sound even vaguely Belgian. Giorgio Moroder ("Son of My Father") was Italian; the Pop-Tops ("Mammy Blue") were Spanish; Jigsaw ("Sky High") was Australian.

Still, in some cases, you could pick out the imports. If the lyrics weren't in English, as with Kraftwerk's "Autobahn" (Germany) or Mocedades' "Eres Tu" (Spain), well, that was a good clue. Harder to spot were artists alleged to have been singing phonetically in English, like Sweden's ABBA ("Waterloo") and Germany's Silver Convention ("Fly, Robin, Fly").

Giorgio Moroder went on to produce many of Donna Summer's biggest, most despised hits; to this day, his name is identified with the "Eurodisco" sound. Techno-patriarchs Kraftwerk will always be in vogue, at least as long as mind-numbing, synth-generated pop music has a place in the world. And "Radar Love" lives on wherever so-called classic rock is played. But the net effect of Western Europe's mid-seventies mini-invasion of the U.S. charts seems negligible today.

Conversely, reggae, one of the most important developments of the seventies, had relatively little commercial impact at the time. Bob Marley's songs were well known—Eric Clapton had a Number 1 hit with "I Shot the Sheriff," and Johnny Nash went to Number 12 with "Stir It Up"—but Marley himself never had a U.S. hit. Reggae was hypnotic, threadbare music, often politically charged, always rhythmically potent: not exactly a recipe for success in the lush seventies.

That's not to say Marley went unnoticed. U.S. sales of albums like *Burnin'*, *Natty Dread*, and *Rastaman Vibration* were healthy. But other reggae pioneers like Toots & the Maytals *(Funky Kingston)*, Peter Tosh ("Don't Look Back") and Jimmy Cliff *(The Harder They Come)* fared less well commercially. In fact, the most successful pop export from Jamaica during reggae's peak years was a strange, lo-fi 1971 single called "Double Barrel" by Dave and Ansil Collins, consisting of a basic reggae groove, a simple piano melody, and some proto-dub boasting buried in clamorous tape echo.

Pop artists had been up front about their fascination with world music at least as far back as 1968, when Paul McCartney made reference to Jamaican star Desmond Dekker in "Ob-La-Di, Ob-La-Da." Houston native Johnny Nash, a former teen star of the fifties, went one step further: He began recording in Jamaica in the late sixties. In addition to "Stir It Up," he hit pay dirt internationally with "I Can See Clearly Now" (1972), a song of bubbling, contagious optimism with exactly enough "rydim" to set the collective pelvis in motion. It was second-hand reggae, but reggae nonetheless. Paul Simon, who even then had his ear to the ground for emerging rhythmic structures, used a reggae feel (complete with percolating organ) to support the elemental sentiments of his first solo hit, "Mother and Child Reunion" (1972). Thus did Jamaican street music impact ever so slightly on the world of pant suits and Pet Rocks.

Regional styles were bubbling up all over the Caribbean. The Beginning of the End's "Funky Nassau—Part 1" was not only the most irresistible groove record of 1971, but an example of the brassy Bahamian junkaroo sound. "Chirpy Chirpy Cheep Cheep" was a borderline novelty record by an expatriate brother-and-sister team from Trinidad (Mac and Katie Kissoon). And though José Feliciano had

grown up in New York, his hit theme for the TV series *Chico and the Man* was infused with the rhythm and harmony of his native Puerto Rico.

Among the more familiar ethnic strains of the seventies were South African folk, via yet another version of "The Lion Sleeps Tonight" (or "Wimoweh," previously a hit in 1952 and 1961), this time by Robert John; George Harrison's Indian bent; and Carlos Santana's ongoing Latin rock experiment. The Mexican-born Santana enjoyed sustained success because he knew the first rule of pop fusion: Attach some memorable hooks to your musical hybrid. Whether working in Spanish ("Oye Como Va") or in English ("Everybody's Everything"), he managed to keep his audience, his creative momentum, and his Woodstock credibility—which, in the age of ABBA, was no mean feat. Interestingly, Santana competed with his younger brother Jorge (and Jorge's multiracial band, Malo) for airplay in the spring of 1972 when his "No One to Depend On" was outdistanced by Malo's lovable "Suavecito."

Central America, Africa, the Caribbean, Europe, Asia . . . American music was on a collision course with the rest of the world. Accordingly, by the mid-eighties, "world beat" had emerged as pop's best chance for relevance into the twenty-first century. Western artists including Talking Heads, Peter Gabriel, Sting, and Paul Simon were incorporating ethnic idioms into their work. The holier-than-thou critics who accused Simon et al. of panty-raiding the Third World were guilty of the worst kind of reverse discrimination, not to mention hypocrisy; were these pundits really listening to music from South Africa and Senegal and Zimbabwe in their spare time? Had they forgotten that their beloved Eric Clapton was among the first to plunder Bob Marley's catalog? Wasn't rock and roll itself a kind of cultural imperialism, containing as it did fragments of traditional African music? If so, leave room for Elvis, the Beatles, and the Stones on your list of cultural boycott violators. Or *ooga chaka* until you feel better.

WHAT'S SO FUNNY 'BOUT PEACE, LOVE, AND UNDERSTANDING?

Utopian Pop

"Imagine" • John Lennon/Plastic Ono Band (Apple, 1971)
"Peace Train" • Cat Stevens (A&M, 1971)
"Joy to the World" • Three Dog Night (Dunhill, 1971)
"I'd Like to Teach the World to Sing (in Perfect Harmony)" • The New Seekers
(Elektra, 1971)
and The Hillside Singers (Metromedia, 1971)
"Black & White" • Three Dog Night (Dunhill, 1972)
"Why Can't We Live Together" • Timmy Thomas (Glades, 1973)
"Love Train" • The O'Jays (Philadelphia International, 1973)
"Higher Ground" • Stevie Wonder (Tamla, 1973)
"If You're Ready (Come Go with Me)" • The Staple Singers (Stax, 1973)
"Why Can't We Be Friends?" • War (United Artists, 1975)

To hear the generation that came of age in the sixties tell it, the seventies were a wasteland of pop-cultural excess, an era devoid of meaning, a Sherwood Schwartz–ified desert island rerun with no hope of rescue. Those of us referred to as the Tail End of the Baby Boom (talk about a life sentence) have learned to listen politely, nod attentively, and hope someone more interesting comes by. Fact is, those nutty sixties visionaries folded up their tents and went home a long time ago; they don't like to talk about the seventies because the decade represents an awkward stage for them—a ten-year hangover that found them in funny clothes and saw them lurching from pacifism to passivism.

Their embarrassment about the era extends to AM radio and the popular view that Top 40 had lost all relevance by the early seventies. Despite this, seventies culture has rebounded, and those who have the most fun with retro-seventies schlock will be those who recognize within the ridiculous fashion trends and post-hippy platitudes a courageous unself-consciousness (hey, it took guts to wear those clothes!). While the boomers run for cover, it's worth noting that, although Tom Wolfe won the name-the-era contest with his "Me

Decade" moniker, and despite the fact that self-absorption replaced baseball as the national pastime, pop playlists during the early seventies still had plenty of room for artists who preferred the greater good to vain introspection.

Amidst headlines trumpeting the ongoing war in Southeast Asia, the Wacky White House Comedy Hour, terrorism, world hunger, and nuclear testing, an eclectic chorus of musical voices reacted with dreams of a better world—utopian sentiments often touching, sometimes ridiculous, in their naiveté. Either way, they were never insincere; not since the early seventies have statements like "form a love train" been made without irony.

Utopian pop represented the flip side of soul's grim new realism with its hopeful conviction that deliverance would come with positive thinking (the Staple Singers' "If You're Ready [Come Go with Me]" and Three Dog Night's "Black & White") or by harnessing the galvanizing power of music (the Coke-ad-turned-pop-song "I'd Like to Teach the World to Sing [in Perfect Harmony]" and the O'Jays' "Love Train"). The prototypical pop song of the utopian genre came from an ex-Beatle. "Imagine" (1971) wore its idealism on its sleeve; held together by a wonky piano track and an understated string arrangement, it was a spare, elegant recruitment song for the peace movement and one of the high points of John Lennon's solo career.

While ex-partner Paul McCartney was turning out hit after tuneful hit, Lennon's songwriting played second fiddle to his tireless efforts to promote world unity. He once called "Imagine" "a song for children," but its simple melodic plea touched adults and children alike, enticing listeners into envisioning a better world ("a brotherhood of man"). By using the inclusive pronoun "us," Lennon advocated collaboration, not confrontation. The more divisive "us and them" model that had defined the late sixties had played itself out.

Ironically, it was on March 6, 1972, shortly after Lennon asked us to imagine a world without countries, that U.S. Immigration authorities asked Lennon to imagine leaving theirs, revoking his visa. After a four-year legal battle and some Plan B house-hunting in Toronto, Lennon earned a permanent U.S. visa in 1976 and settled in the Dakota on New York's Central Park West. It's difficult to remember what it was like to hear "Imagine" without the pall of tragic irony that has haunted each listening since Lennon's death in 1980. The song will never be the same.

"Imagine" wasn't the only "song for children" that resulted from the early seventies' utopian fantasizing. Three Dog Night's 1972 hit "Black & White" (conceptual precursor to "Ebony and Ivory," the ingratiating Paul McCartney–Stevie Wonder duet recorded ten years later), featured a kiddy chorus sing-along and celebrated universal brotherhood as if it had already arrived. "Joy to the World" (1971), the Dogs' biggest hit and Hoyt Axton's biggest payday as a songwriter, was an all-purpose up-with-people (and fishes) anthem given some edge by Chuck Negron's ringing introduction of Jeremiah the bullfrog, his good friend and drinking buddy.

Stevie Wonder's "Higher Ground" (1973) moved us out of the rock-and-roll nursery. Despite its description of the planet's merry-go-round cycle of war and corruption, the song found hope in the individual's step-by-step (life-by-life) ascension to utopia—"the high-

est ground." Like Wonder's other keyboard-based hits in the early seventies ("Superstition," "Living for the City," "You Haven't Done Nothin'," "Boogie on Reggae Woman"), "Higher Ground" reached a mass audience in spite of its rhythmic and harmonic complexity. If the song's lyrics juxtaposed earthly and spiritual concerns, its musical vocabulary went one better, starting with an altered blues and incorporating strange new instrumentation and syncopated rhythms—a mixture that, at the time, amounted to pop science fiction. Wonder's cutting-edge pop music was rewarded with an unprecedented three Grammy Awards for Album of the Year in a four-year span from 1973 to 1976, prompting Paul Simon, who won the prize in 1975 for *Still Crazy After All These Years*, to thank Wonder for not releasing an album that year.

The O'Jays' "Love Train" (1973) brought salvation to the here and now: Let's not wait to be reincarnated two or three more times, let's join hands and form a conga line that girdles the globe. The core idea was sound—racial harmony—but the lyric conjured images of a bell-bottomed United Nations dance line breezing through the Middle East and ending two thousand years of religious strife with sheer good humor. The miracle was that with the absolute sincerity of their singing, the O'Jays got away with it. "Love Train" proved to be one of those pop songs that didn't need a completely credible lyric, just a thematic hint from the title and an irresistible, chugging groove. "Peace Train," the folk equivalent, had been a hit for Cat Stevens in 1971.

In the case of "I'd Like to Teach the World to Sing (in Perfect Harmony)," the title said it all. Based on a Coca-Cola jingle that featured a choral Christmas tree, two different versions of the song shared chart space, entering the Top 40 in December 1971 with Coke's "It's the real thing" slogan replaced by "That's the song I sing." One version was released by the New Seekers (evolved from the "old" Seekers, who scored with "Georgy Girl" in 1966), and another by the Hillside Singers (a nine-piece vocal ensemble formed by big band journeyman Al Ham). The two versions were interchangeable, and both eventually made it into the Top 20. (This wasn't the only early-seventies jingle to hit the charts; Sonny & Cher's 1972 hit "When You Say Love" was based on the "When You Say Bud" beer ad.)

Answers to questions like War's "Why Can't We Be Friends?" and Timmy Thomas's "Why Can't We Live Together" were not easy to come by. Simply by posing the questions, though, War and Thomas posited racial harmony as a social imperative. War, formerly the backup band for ex-Animal Eric Burdon, used the occasion to have some fun, singing in barroom unison, rhyming "CIA" with "Mafia" ("Ma-fie-ay"), and even leaving a glaring keyboard flub in the intro. Thomas, an organist with a number of Stax/Volt sessions under his belt, kicked off his desert-dry production with an unusually lengthy organ solo that wept and wailed, leading in to the first verse with a repeated high-note screech that begged "why" as eloquently as Thomas' silky singing.

The Staple Singers, never ones for asking questions, were far more interested in offering solutions (see "Respect Yourself," "I'll Take You There," "Touch a Hand, Make a Friend," even "Let's Do It Again"). Their Top 10 hit "If You're Ready (Come Go with Me)," released a year after "Why Can't We Live Together," worked almost as a direct answer to Thomas's song. Mavis Staples's sumptuous vocals and the track's soulful plea for racial harmony earned the Stapleses an instant pardon for the song's obvious repeat performance (the "Come go with me" refrain is a perfect rhythmic echo of "I'll take you there" from the earlier record).

Other releases from would-be utopians included Ocean's "We've Got a Dream," Carole King's "Believe in Humanity," and George Harrison's "Give Me Love (Give Me Peace on Earth)." But dreams of utopia weren't limited to the pop charts. Hollywood looked to its past in 1973, releasing a musical remake of Frank Capra's 1937 film *Lost Horizon,* the story of five survivors of an airplane crash and their discovery of a strange Tibetan Shangri-La, where health, long life, and peace hold sway (the score was written by Burt Bacharach and Hal David).

The same negative news headlines that inspired these utopian fantasies also inspired a less hopeful collection of dystopic pop songs: Steely Dan's "Black Friday" was an apocalyptic shuffle; Five Man Electrical Band's "I'm a Stranger Here" was a look at humankind from the point of view of a scolding extraterrestrial; Three Dog Night's "Family of Man" was a "four-level highway" nightmare; War's "The

World Is a Ghetto" was self-explanatory. David Bowie's *Diamond Dogs,* a concept album inspired by George Orwell's *1984,* was probably darkest of all.

Hollywood's dystopic visions included a successful series of five films inspired by Pierre Boule's science-fiction novel *Planet of the Apes,* a simian saga that made Hitchcock's *The Birds* seem like a walk in the park. A series of "you-can't-trust-anyone" films emerged around this time. The B-movie paranoia of fifties Red-scare parables (*The Invasion of the Body Snatchers* and *The Blob*) found new expression in conspiracy-touting films like *The Parallax View, Three Days of the Condor,* and *The Conversation.* These films had a gritty sophistication typical of Hollywood's short-lived early-seventies renaissance, and at the time they seemed credible and plausible.

That the world now seems further than ever from utopia has not dimmed the power of the best songs from this genre. In fact, they seem more urgent than ever. Even at its most childlike, at least here was a mainstream effort to slow the boomers' retreat into their suburban cocoons and to provide some grounding in an age when the nightly newscast often juxtaposed battlefront reports from Vietnam and a bizarre parade of manufactured "news."

It was such a piece of so-called news, a motorcyclist's 1974 attempt to leap over Montana's Snake River Canyon, that crystallized the era. The premature ejaculation of Bob "Evel" Knievel's Skycycle parachute just two-thirds of the way up the ramp that was to launch him into glory is a fitting symbol for the cynical disenchantment that billowed out of the Nixon years. As Knievel drifted into the canyon that Sunday afternoon, a human anticlimax in Captain America garb, news of President Gerald Ford's decision to pardon Richard Nixon was just beginning to spread. Ford had scooped Knievel, who touched down next to the Snake River with nothing more than a bruised ego. Betrayed by his too-eager safety gear, and upstaged by a more spectacular stunt in the nation's capital, Knievel went home to count his money.

It's pop music's dauntless utopians who deserve the last word here, however; if they could keep singing in the wake of that singularly strange Sunday—and they did—then theirs is the era's most heroic leap.

EARTH SHOES
Folk Pop

"You've Got a Friend" • James Taylor (Warner Bros., 1971)
"Take It Easy" • The Eagles (Asylum, 1972)
"Operator (That's Not the Way It Feels)" • Jim Croce (ABC, 1972)
"You Turn Me On, I'm a Radio" • Joni Mitchell (Asylum, 1972)
"Heart of Gold" • Neil Young (Reprise, 1972)
"Doctor My Eyes" • Jackson Browne (Asylum, 1972)
"Ventura Highway" • America (Warner Bros., 1972)
"Morning Has Broken" • Cat Stevens (A&M, 1972)
"American Tune" • Paul Simon (Columbia, 1973)
"Cat's in the Cradle" • Harry Chapin (Elektra 1974)

Like a Ford Country Squire station wagon with fake-wood paneling on the side, the singer-songwriters of the early seventies worked hard to maintain the appearance of rootsiness. Even as they set sales records, formed supergroups, and embraced pop, they clung to their voice-in-the-wilderness authenticity and troubadour mentality. The hippy-dippy image on the cover of Carole King's 1971 best-seller *Tapestry* gave no indication that the wool-and-denim-clad diva had spent the previous decade writing pop hits for nonfolky clients like Bobby Vee, Tony Orlando, and the Monkees. Nor did the sparse Joni Mitchell painting that adorned Crosby, Stills, Nash & Young's greatest-hits album *So Far* suggest that CSN (and sometimes Y) were a Grammy-winning commercial juggernaut. You didn't draw attention to your success in those days—not if you wanted more of it.

Folk's royal wedding, starring James Taylor and Carly Simon, was held in New York on November 3, 1972. By then, the pop-ification of folk was complete: Taylor, Simon, King, and Neil Young had all recorded Number 1 singles ("You've Got a Friend," "You're So Vain," "It's Too Late," "Heart of Gold"); the Eagles, Jackson Browne, and

Cat Stevens were rising stars; veterans Joan Baez and Arlo Guthrie were fading. Democratic presidential hopeful George McGovern welcomed fund-raising efforts by Taylor, King, and Simon & Garfunkel in 1972, not only because they were in his ideological neck of the woods, but also because they were among the biggest names in show business.

More than any other new act, America represented the corporate face of folk. The band, a trio of American army brats whose paths had crossed in a London high school in 1969, collected a Grammy award, two gold records, and three Top 10 hits within a year of moving back to the U.S.A. in 1972. That's a pace even a pop powerhouse like Three Dog Night might have found draining. "A Horse with No Name," featuring a nonspecific cast of "plants and birds and rocks and things," was America's first and biggest hit. "Ventura Highway," with its detailed acoustic guitar work and top-down atmosphere, was the best—it made you homesick for a place you had never been. Later releases like "Tin Man" and "Sister Golden Hair" (both produced by George Martin) did similarly big business but aroused little in the way of professional jealousy.

Especially from the Eagles, the other patriotically named folk-rock group on whom fortune was smiling. While Don Henley, Glenn Frey, and company waited until 1974 for their first gold certification (for *Eagles*), until 1975 for their first Number 1 single ("Best of My Love"), and until 1976 for their first Grammy award (a Best Pop Performance nod for "Lyin' Eyes"), they finished the seventies at the top of the rock-and-roll heap, having long since left competitors like America "chewin' on a piece of grass, walkin' down the road." Their early hits ranged from era-defining country sentiments like "Take It Easy" (the desert "59th Street Bridge Song") to funky, blue-balls entreaties like "One of These Nights."

The Eagles were at the center of the much-ballyhooed Southern California scene, a loose-knit, well-financed community of folk-, blues-, and country-based pop stars that also included Jackson Browne (who cowrote "Take It Easy"), Linda Ronstadt, Fleetwood Mac, Little Feat, Andrew Gold, and guitar messiahs Ry Cooder and David Lindley. Like all purportedly serious things from the left coast, SoCal rock was regarded by critics with deep suspicion; Lester Bangs coined the term "simper-whimper" for Ronstadt; Robert Christgau called the Eagles "slickshit" and said Browne's songs were as boring as Nixon's speeches. WEA, for whom all of the above recorded, cried all the way to the bank.

Browne got off one incredibly fresh pop single (1972's ebulliently fatalistic "Doctor My Eyes") before resigning himself to full-time singer-songwriter status. A singer-songwriter was more than just someone who sang his or her own songs (otherwise everyone from Paul Anka to Al Green would have fit the bill); a singer-songwriter wrote and sang songs that were serious, soul-searching, and really *about* something. Don McLean got inside Van Gogh's tragic genius in "Vincent." Harry Chapin sussed out the Oedipal ironies of father-son relationships in "Cat's in the Cradle." Janis Ian revisited the torture chamber called puberty in "At Seventeen."

Some singer-songwriters specialized. Randy Newman mastered the art of ironic detachment, sometimes confusing listeners (especially short ones) who thought he was saying what he meant. Tom Waits documented the lives of the downtrodden types he had met during his small-change days on the Sunset Strip. Little Feat's Lowell George recombined standard rock and blues images into compelling slices of backdoor Americana.

James Taylor and Joni Mitchell were the singer-songwriters most frequently taken to task for being "confessional." Admittedly, Taylor, a former junkie and mental patient, had plenty of personal demons to exorcise, but he had largely abandoned first-person purges by 1971's *Mud Slide Slim and the Blue Horizon,* and the best of his Columbia albums (1977's *JT* and 1988's *Never Die Young*) contain multiple points of view. Still, he seems unlikely to shed his image as the seventies' foremost whine expert.

Ironically, four of Taylor's five Top 5 hits were written by other people. But dismissing a songwriter of his magnitude on the basis of covers like "Mockingbird" and "How Sweet It Is" is like trashing the Beatles on the basis of "My Bonnie" and "Ain't She Sweet"; you're not getting the whole picture. Even when JT's covers were contemporary (Carole King's "You've Got a Friend"), the cover issue was misleading. Originals like "Sweet Baby James" and "Fire and Rain" were the core of his work.

To date, Joni Mitchell has never looked outside her own catalog for a single, though her songs have been hits for peers like Judy Collins ("Both Sides Now") and Crosby, Stills, Nash & Young ("Woodstock"). In the early seventies, she suffered under the confessionalist label even more than her sometime collaborator Taylor, partly because she mined her personal life for at least six full albums, and partly because people were more likely to interpret a woman's lyrics as personal statements. *Court and Spark* (1974) expanded Mitchell's palette noticeably, however, and subsequent albums, especially 1976's brilliant *Hejira,* staked out new musical and lyrical ground. In the meantime, hits like "You Turn Me On, I'm a Radio" (1972) and "Help Me" (1974) gave the AM audience keys to Joni's farther rooms.

If anyone doubted folk pop's commercial clout, they weren't listening to the radio. Cat Stevens (Yusef Islam to you) averaged two hits a year between 1971 and 1975, including bona fide folk constructions like "Moonshadow" and "Morning Has Broken." Jim Croce revealed his musical split personality by following the acoustic blues of "You Don't Mess Around with Jim" with the crafty emotionalism of "Operator (That's Not the Way It Feels)," both Top 20 hits. Hitmakers Loggins & Messina ("Danny's Song"), John Denver ("Annie's Song"), Gordon Lightfoot ("Sundown"), and Jonathan Edwards ("Sunshine") had roots in the folk and bluegrass scenes of the sixties.

So did Paul Simon, although his solo hits bespoke a willful eclecticism more than a folk background. His successful idiomatic experiments included "Mother and Child Reunion" (reggae), "Loves Me Like a Rock" (gospel), and "Me and Julio Down by the Schoolyard" (Latin). He collaborated with jazz musicians, world musicians, and traditional vocal groups, as well as with confrères Phoebe Snow and Randy Newman. Still, his dizzying early-seventies catalog was punctuated by folky guitar-and-voice fare like "American Tune" (Number 35) and "Duncan" (Number 52). These songs belonged with Simon's sixties hits only in a stylistic sense—lyrically, they were far less stuffy than "The Dangling Conversation" (1966)—but they allowed the public to keep Simon under the pliable "folk" heading. "American Tune," a moving, gloomy State of the Union address that was even more pertinent when it became a live hit in 1974 than when it was originally released in 1972 (before the Senate Select Committee on Presidential Activities had begun its hearings), remains one of Simon's best-ever songs.

Folk pop's strange mixture of traditional and commercial impulses was a reflection of forces at war in the culture at large: handmade candles, homegrown marijuana, Earth shoes, and *Watership Down* battled Merv Griffin, Quadraphonic sound, Tang, and subliminal advertising. In 1973 the lethal insecticide DDT was banned; 1973 was also a record year for shopping center construction. Nowhere was the gulf betwixt the bold and the bogus more apparent than on the pop charts, where Sammy Davis, Jr.'s "Candy Man" and Jimmy Castor's "Troglodyte (Cave Man)" could outmuscle Neil Young's "Old Man" and Graham Nash & David Crosby's "Immigration Man" (*Billboard,* June 10, 1972).

The folk-pop artists whose careers survived the early seventies must have seen the writing on the wall around 1975. Paul Simon and James Taylor veered toward pop's center. The Eagles became Hollywood's Greek chorus. Neil Young rocked with new fury. Joni Mitchell entered her unjustly maligned "jazz phase." In all cases, the results were spectacular, as even a cursory inspection of *Still Crazy After All These Years, JT, Hotel California, Rust Never Sleeps,* and *Hejira* will confirm. In the years that followed, Simon, Taylor, Young, Mitchell, and the solo Eagles remained commercial and/or artistic forces with which to be reckoned, but the peaceful, easy feeling of the early seventies slowly faded as grim, urban nightmares replaced the windswept landscape of "Ventura Highway." And folk left the pop charts, maybe for good.

RICHARD NIXON'S GREATEST HITS
Socially Aware Pop

"Signs" • Five Man Electrical Band (Lionel, 1971)
"Indian Reservation" • Raiders (Columbia, 1971)
"What's Going On" • Marvin Gaye (Tamla, 1971)
"Bring the Boys Home" • Freda Payne (Invictus, 1971)
"One Tin Soldier (The Legend of Billy Jack)" • Coven (Warner, 1971)
"Give Ireland Back to the Irish" • Wings (Apple, 1972)
"Dialogue (Part I & II)" • Chicago (Columbia, 1972)
"Dead Skunk" • Loudon Wainwright III (Columbia, 1973)
"You Haven't Done Nothin'" • Stevie Wonder (Tamla, 1974)
"Fight the Power Part 1" • The Isley Brothers (T-Neck, 1975)

E arly in the summer of 1971, the Cherokee Indians found themselves with some unlikely spokesmen: the Raiders, a squeaky-clean band better known as Paul Revere & the Raiders. "Indian Reservation" (subtitled "The Lament of the Cherokee Reservation Indian"), the band's first Number 1 record and, for a time, the biggest-selling single in Columbia Records history, spoke to the problems of Native Americans in the first person, bemoaning the loss of *our* language, *our* culture. Some tribespeople must have wondered, as they listened to the song's ersatz rain-dance rhythm and heavy-handed white liberal guilt-fest: Will this do more harm than good?

The social awareness that had crept into pop music via the folk scene in the sixties had become a mandatory component of pop stardom—part of the outfit, like platform shoes. Records like "Indian Reservation" appeared on first listen to be bucking the status quo but, by 1971, they *were* the status quo. The music industry had figured out that political integrity was a selling point for the rock audience, and the sense of purpose that had once accompanied protest music was gone.

Things hadn't always been so cynical. Buffalo Springfield's "For

What It's Worth (Stop, Hey What's That Sound)" (1967), the Young-bloods' "Get Together" (1969), and dozens of other protest songs had been integral to the peace movement at a time when bands still felt their music could provoke change. But the "statement" songs that opened the seventies often aimed to succeed within the system while merely creating the appearance of subversion.

Five Man Electrical Band's "Signs," hailed at the time as an anti-establishment anthem, posited a world in which landowners, restaurateurs, churchgoers, employers, and other sign-posters had it in for young freethinkers. The song's success had little to do with its populist pretensions, however. It had everything to do with learning those deliciously self-righteous couplets and trying to yell "Ugh!" in the right spot. (For those who still haven't hit it, it's on the last eighth note before the guitar solo.)

A less general and hence more constructive version of the youth-versus-establishment standoff could be seen every Monday night from 1971 to 1979 on Norman Lear's groundbreaking sitcom *All in the Family*. Rob Reiner's "Meathead," the long-haired freaky person in the equation, went head-to-head with Carroll O'Connor's Archie Bunker, his reactionary father-in-law, on all manner of issues— racism, feminism, birth control, the corruptibility of presidents. Reiner and O'Connor were the TV yin and yang of the generation gap, and in making the two sides flesh and blood they went one better than the "Signs" stereotypes.

Meanwhile, Richard Nixon's lunch-meat presidency (Spamelot) was nearing its expiration date. Five burglars funded by contributions to the Nixon campaign were arrested while trying to bug the Democratic National Headquarters at the Watergate Hotel complex in Washington, D.C., on the evening of June 17, 1972. On June 23, in a taped phone conversation that would force his resignation just over two years later, Nixon discussed with top aide H. R. Haldeman the idea of using the CIA to obstruct the Watergate investigation. In November, the Nixon-Agnew ticket won forty-nine states (way to go, Massachusetts) in a landslide reelection, even as the scandal widened. Responding to John Dean's damning 1973 Watergate testimony, Nixon asserted, "I am not a crook." The remark was quoted widely. Eventually, the White House was compelled to release subpoenaed tapes of the president's Watergate-related phone calls. Along with many colorful expletives, the tapes featured suspicious gaps, one long enough to accommodate the entire album version of "In-A-Gadda-Da-Vida."

At this late date, it is almost easier to remember Rich Little doing Nixon on *The Tonight Show* than it is to remember Nixon himself, but Tricky Dick's impact on pop culture extends well beyond impersonators. Neil Young referred to Nixon by name in "Ohio," his searingly direct response to Kent State. Freda Payne's heartrending "Bring the Boys Home" was a plea for the commander in chief to retreat from the morass of Vietnam. "You Haven't Done Nothin'," Stevie Wonder's blistering, clavinet-driven sequel to "Superstition," was interpreted as an open letter to the White House. And consider: When Loudon Wainwright III stuck his nose in the air and penned "Dead Skunk," the best song ever written about roadkill, was the stench coming from the direction of Pennsylvania Avenue?

Career Nixon-haters Chicago (see 1971's "Song for Richard and His Friends") used a point-counterpoint format to tackle some big questions on "Dialogue (Part I & II)", a minor hit by the band's usual standards. Guitarist Terry Kath played the angry young man to Peter Cetera's spoiled college kid, and, while that may sound about as interesting as Jack Klugman and Tony Randall facing off on *The $20,000 Pyramid,* the musical debate did throw off a few sparks. What about the war? asks the angry young man. What about hunger, urban blight, student apathy? The fortunate son answers: What about it? The song might have maintained more dramatic tension if it hadn't been so clear from the outset that we were to regard one character as a well-informed progressive and the other as a clueless greenhorn who trusted the president.

Chicago would take another oblique shot at Nixon with the ironically intended "Harry Truman" in 1975. But in light of the band's penchant for lovey-dovey lyrics, many listeners (especially those employed as rock critics) found its political forays less than credible. Ditto Neil Sedaka's plea for racial tolerance ("The Immigrant"), the Isley Brothers' incendiary funk anthem ("Fight the Power"), the Spinners' ode to hypocrisy ("They Just Can't Stop It the [Games People Play]"), Seals & Crofts's antiabortion statement ("Unborn

Child"), and Paul McCartney's BBC-unfriendly response to the Bloody Sunday massacre in Northern Ireland ("Give Ireland Back to the Irish"). In McCartney's case, the critics' reaction was simple type-casting: John was supposed to write the angry, socially redeeming stuff, not Paul.

The seventies antiwar statement that's easiest to pick on is "One Tin Soldier," the song that took the "gory" out of "allegory." A hit in 1970 for the Original Caste and in 1971 for Coven, it was short on soul but long on plot: Bloodthirsty valley people covet treasure belonging to peaceful mountain people; valley people issue warning, invade, take no prisoners; treasure turns out to be simple message ("Peace on earth"). Can you dig it? Accompanying the fairy tale are a military fife-and-drum motif and some very cheesy horn parts. This was the antiwar effort as MOR fodder—silly, yes, but significant as an example of the mainstreaming of the sixties' radical politics.

Even *Rolling Stone* magazine, the house organ of the counter-culture, adapted its combative style to the commercial realities of the seventies. By adding color and general-interest cover stories, *RS* flirted with mass circulation, anticipating the era of celebrity journalism that would begin in earnest in 1974 with the launch of *Peo-*

ple. Meanwhile, a new streak of pseudo-sixties awareness was emerging as far down the journalistic ladder as the children's book (Dr. Seuss's 1971 classic *The Lorax* was an environmental statement) and the lowly comic book, where masked men in tights were collaring drug pushers and corporate polluters, dishing out controversial subject matter in easy-to-swallow portions.

Most rock stars liked to think they had more in common with Che Guevara than with the Green Lantern, but it was getting harder and harder to find *truly* revolutionary voices on the radio. Often songs that appeared to be taking a hard stand contained an underlying message of impotence, or confusion, or both. Ten Years After's "I'd Love to Change the World" had the atmosphere of a call to arms, but was in fact an admission of powerlessness: "I'd love to change the world / But I don't know what to do." "You Haven't Done Nothin' " expressed weariness and frustration without suggesting alternatives. And the apathetic student being cross-examined in "Dialogue" didn't sound likely to change his stars and stripes any time soon.

Marvin Gaye's "What's Going On," for all its passion, posed a question to which Gaye's audience already knew the answer. There was too much going on. Too much to understand, too much to fight. With families being shattered and picket lines fostering only hatred, Gaye argued, communication was urgently needed, and his song's seductive arrangement provided a model of constructive dialogue by meshing call-and-response gospel vocals, slick jazz-rock textures, free-form sloganeering ("Solid!" "Right on!") and straight-ahead soul crooning. But real solutions were harder to come by.

One school of thought maintains that the mainstream's coopting of sixties stances signaled not defeat, but victory; formerly fringe concepts like Native American rights and pacifism found their way into the pop-cultural agenda. But even nonmusical gestures like Marlon Brando's rejection of his 1972 Best Actor Oscar for *The Godfather*, in which Native American actress Maria Cruz ("Sacheen Littlefeather") read Brando's commentary on the portrayal of Indians in the cinema, probably raised awareness more effectively than four months of "Indian Reservation" airplay. And Freda Payne's entreaties didn't perceptibly expedite the end of the war; the United States didn't fully withdraw from Southeast Asia until 1975.

Sadly, the point is moot. By the end of the seventies, high-minded records like "What's Going On" had disappeared into a sea of singles-bar sexuality, where the only "Signs" were astrological. Richard Nixon was in San Clemente, *All in the Family* was in syndication, and Marlon Brando was in *Superman*. Later, with the advent of a new generation of singer-songwriters (Suzanne Vega, Tracy Chapman, et al.), it would once again become cool to have a message. But for the moment, popular music's social conscience was missing in action.

CARNAL KNOWLEDGE
Sexual Revolution

"Stay Awhile" • The Bells (Polydor, 1971)
"Pillow Talk" • Sylvia (Vibration, 1973)
"Touch Me in the Morning" • Diana Ross (Motown, 1973)
"Feel Like Makin' Love" • Roberta Flack (Atlantic, 1974)
"Do It ('Til You're Satisfied)" • B.T. Express (Roadshow, 1974)
"I Don't Like to Sleep Alone" • Paul Anka (United Artists, 1975)
"Lady Marmalade" • LaBelle (Epic, 1975)
"One of These Nights" • The Eagles (Asylum, 1975)
"Chevy Van" • Sammy Johns (GRC, 1975)
"Love to Love You Baby" • Donna Summer (Oasis, 1975)

Five days before Christmas 1975, chart virgin Donna Summer entered the Top 40 with a virtual-reality studio orgasm that combined "Jungle Fever"–style moaning with a throbbing dance groove. "Love to Love You Baby," the "Hey Jude" of hyperventilation, peaked at Number 2 on Valentine's Day 1976.

"Love to Love You Baby" felt like nothing more than a disco novelty hit ("Disco Duck" with one letter changed). It gave no hint of the multiple hits that lay in store for Summer, but it did provide a climax to the pop foreplay that had been going on since 1970, when Stephen Stills had decided to love the one he was with.

This was the pre-AIDS, post-Pill era. Sex was safe and, Charlie Rich's modesty aside, it was out from "behind closed doors." *The Joy of Sex* hit the best-seller list for the first time in 1972. The fashion industry advocated near nudity, with halter tops, string bikinis, and hot pants making the scene. Edible underwear was introduced, bringing new meaning to the phrase "Fruit of the Loom." ABC's *Love, American Style* featured a wacky "rep" company of actors and guest stars that celebrated the new permissiveness with three or four playlets per episode. (The show, which gave birth to the long-running series *Happy Days* with a 1972 segment called "Love and the Happy Days" starring Ron Howard and Anson Williams, was Friday-at-ten o'clock fare, discreetly scheduled to follow the bedtimes of the Brady-Partridge audience.) *The Match Game,* featuring host Gene Rayburn, took game-show sexual innuendo to new heights. Charo shook herself silly all over the prime-time dial. A love-starved stewardess juggled boyfriends in 1973's *Superchick. Deep Throat,* deemed "irredeemably obscene" in 1973 by a New York criminal court, became the first mainstream porn flick. Hollywood had sex on the brain: In *Carnal Knowledge* sex was a game; in *Last Tango in Paris* it was a purging but impersonal act; in *Shampoo* it was a second career for a playboy hairdresser (played by Warren Beatty).

Pop's sexual awakening encompassed the macho soul of Barry White and Isaac Hayes ("I'm Gonna Love You Just a Little More Baby" and "Theme from *Shaft*"), the funky lasciviousness of the Ohio Players and the Average White Band ("Sweet Sticky Thing" and "Cut the Cake") and the feminist ire of Jean Knight and the Honey Cone ("Mr. Big Stuff" and "Want Ads"). The Bells' "Stay Awhile," a quivering, ecstatic duet that made listeners feel like Peeping Toms, initiated soft rockers into the new promiscuity. Paul Anka admitted he didn't like to sleep alone. Marilyn McCoo (of the 5th Dimension) didn't get to sleep at all. Diana Ross missed waking up with a partner, as her lush soul ballad "Touch Me in the Morning" made clear.

Sylvia Robinson, billed with Cher-like simplicity as Sylvia (she had been half of the '50s duo Mickey and Sylvia) actually invited the listener between the sheets with 1973's "Pillow Talk." Sung in a breathy hiss of anticipation that would have made Dr. Joyce Brothers blush, this proto-phone-sex rant amounted to a hands-on defense of her favorite hobby. If you didn't get the message from the "I'll-have-what-she's-having" inhaling, the "aye-yi-yi-yi-yi"-ing, and the "nice Daddy" coaching, you just weren't listening (or you were still wet behind the ears). Sylvia, seemingly as interested in her supine position as her position in the Top 40 ("Pillow Talk" made it to Number 3, by the way), would later write and produce Shirley and Company's "Shame, Shame, Shame" and head up influential Sugar Hill Records ("Rapper's Delight"). But in 1973, she was the one doing the talking, and her lone solo hit nudged pop's boudoir door open a few more inches.

Donna Summer would eventually kick that door right off its hinges, but in the meantime, LaBelle's rip-roaring ode to a French Quarter prostitute named "Lady Marmalade" had deejays scurrying for their French-English dictionaries. "Voulez-vous coucher avec moi ce soir?" went the $50 question. Patti LaBelle sang the song with a mix of contempt and solicitude, and breathed life into the story of a middle-class man haunted by a French Quarter tryst. The dictionaries left no doubt as to the meaning of the chorus's overture—it translates as "Do you want to sleep with me tonight?"—but were useless when it came to deciphering the accompanying phrase, "Gitchy, gitchy, ya-ya, da-da." Some things transcend the need for literal translation.

Country rock's forays into pop sexuality seemed a trifle tame compared to the from-the-gut lewdness of LaBelle, but songs like the Eagles' "One of These Nights," the Amazing Rhythm Aces' "Third Rate Romance," and Sammy Johns's "Chevy Van" (all from 1975) nonetheless fared well on the charts. "One of These Nights" dates better than the rest (despite its use of the phrase "pretty mama") because by mid-decade the Eagles had shaken off their C&W shackles and were looking to R&B for inspiration. "Third Rate Romance" was a clear-eyed morning-after account of a "low-rent rendezvous," but the Amazing Rhythm Aces were kidding themselves if they thought they were kings of the cheap date: Johns's "Chevy Van" was a *no*-rent rendezvous starring a seventies everyman and a seductive small-town hitchhiker in a no-strings scenario worthy of *Penthouse* (check out Tom Waits's brilliant "Burma Shave" for the obverse). Johns got lucky one more time when his hit was turned into *The Van,* a 1976 movie.

B.T. Express (originally "Brooklyn Trucking Express") also saw one of their hits adapted to another medium; their Dionysian disco anthem "Do It ('Til You're Satisfied)" (1974) was used briefly to sell Oh! Henry bars ("Chew it, chew it . . . "). "Do It," a Philly-style rave-up that advocated hedonism at all costs, was a stylistic and thematic cousin of "Do It Any Way You Wanna" by People's Choice. By 1975, Donna Summer was taking both songs literally, raising eyebrows if not consciousness.

After "Love to Love You Baby," pop artists began to search for more direct expressions of sexuality. The mellow sensuality of "Feel Like Makin' Love" gave way to the robotic vulgarity of "In the Bush" ("Push, push, in the bush!"). When Philip Roth published *Portnoy's Complaint* in 1969, the "real struggle" had been "to be bad and enjoy it"; now, it seemed, the challenge was merely to offend. For all the off-color excitement, though, the forces of conservatism were gathering strength. In the midst of disco's gay abandon, former *Girls on Probation* star Ronald Reagan was emerging as a genuine presidential contender. Reagan would miss the Republican nomination in 1976, but get it in 1980, and right around that time "Bush" began to sound less sexy.

I AM WOMAN
Feminist Pop

"Want Ads" • The Honey Cone (Hot Wax, 1971)
"Mr. Big Stuff" • Jean Knight (Stax, 1971)
"Women's Love Rights" • Laura Lee (Hot Wax, 1971)
"Clean Up Woman" • Betty Wright (Alston, 1971)
"I Am Woman" • Helen Reddy (Capitol, 1972)
"You're So Vain" • Carly Simon (Elektra, 1972)
"Woman Is the Nigger of the World" • John Lennon/Plastic Ono Band (Apple, 1972)
"Free Man in Paris" • Joni Mitchell (Asylum, 1974)
"Tell Me Something Good" • Rufus (ABC, 1974)
"You're No Good" • Linda Ronstadt (Capitol, 1974)

When Lesley Gore caught Johnny with Judy in 1963's "It's My Party," she didn't want revenge. She didn't want respect. She just wanted to cry. In the early sixties, the standard female pop persona simply didn't allow for a more assertive response.

All this changed for good later in the decade when Aretha Franklin reset the table, turning the sex-on-demand lyric of Otis Redding's "Respect" on its head. Aretha's version was a kickass call-to-arms that literally spelled out its terms (the classic "R-E-S-P-E-C-T" break is credited to Franklin's sister Carolyn) and allowed "women's lib" its first look at the pop charts. Cry if you want to, Aretha said, I'm going to *haul some butt.*

The early seventies were a breakthrough period for women's issues (*Roe v. Wade* was handed down in 1973), and, as usual, pop culture was quick to reflect the societal change. Gloria Steinem founded *Ms.* magazine; best-sellers like Germaine Greer's *The Female Eunuch* and Erica Jong's *Fear of Flying* advocated female empowerment; National Women's Political Caucus founder Shirley Chisholm campaigned for the Democratic presidential nomination; TV's most popular single woman, Mary Richards, leapfrogged her way up WJM's male-dominated ladder on *The Mary Tyler Moore Show;* tennis star Billie Jean King made Bobby Riggs (1939 Wimbledon champ and male chauvinist pig *du jour*) eat his words by winning their so-called "mixed singles" match in Houston in 1973; and Helen Reddy, accepting the 1973 Best Pop Vocal Performance Grammy for the bra-in-flames anthem "I Am Woman," referred to God as "She."

Although it's that song (and Reddy's paradoxically tame delivery) that most people remember as the archetypal feminist hit, "I Am Woman" was a stylistic aberration within the genre; it was soul singers like Jean Knight, Laura Lee, and the Honey Cone who picked up where "Respect" had left off. With Aretha's proclamation ringing in their ears, they made equality in the sexual arena their top priority. Songs like "Mr. Big Stuff," "Women's Love Rights," and "Want Ads" provided a cold shower for male counterparts like Barry White who were taking sexual boasting to new heights, and this inspired, if unintentional, Top 40 dialogue between the sexes resulted in some of the best records of the era. On the men's side, the arguments ran the gamut from playful lights-out pedantry (Johnny Bristol's "Hang On in There Baby") to cynical advice for the lovelorn (Cornelius Brothers & Sister Rose's "Treat Her Like a Lady"). In the latter, considerate treatment of the woman was recommended only as a means to sexual conquest.

On the women's side, there was unity born of pain. Refusing to get lost in Shaft's formidable shadow, the women flouted their philandering lovers mercilessly, often with the aid of full-frontal grooves that perfectly complemented the righteous indignation of the lyrics. Although it stopped short of the sweeping change Helen Reddy was espousing, this was a grassroots, you-gotta-start-somewhere feminism that took no prisoners.

Jean Knight, for one, was showing her hulking male opponent no mercy. "Mr. Big Stuff," her lone hit and one of the top-performing R&B records of the seventies, turned male-bashing into an art form. In it, the New Orleans–bred Knight tauntingly refuses the advances of a career ladies' man as her rhythm section backs her up musically and, if necessary, physically. She lets the air out of Mr. Big Stuff's balloon until he is reduced in the listener's mind from the larger-than-life dude who appeared on the *Mr. Big Stuff* album cover to a Huggy

Bear–sized huckster left only with the deflated symbols of his potency ("fancy clothes" and "a big, fine car") as cold comfort.

Knight's defiance was typical of the new breed of R&B songstress, and the repercussions could be seen in other media. Flip Wilson's prime-time drag performances as the feisty Geraldine Jones spoofed the new soul woman broadly. Geraldine coined the catchphrase "What you see is what you get!" and fended off all macho come-ons, albeit with the threat of her boyfriend, "Killer." Before long, even the burgeoning blaxploitation film boom had waived its no-girls-allowed policy. Tamara Dobson karate-chopped her way to camp immortality in the title role in 1973's *Cleopatra Jones* and the 1975 sequel *Cleopatra Jones and the Casino of Gold.* Pam Grier played a nurse taking revenge on pushers in 1974's *Foxy Brown* (violent even by blaxploitation standards), accompanied by some tough ad copy: "Don't mess aroun' with Foxy Brown / She's the meanest chick in town / She's brown sugar and spice / But if you don't treat her nice / She'll put you on ice." The phenomenon moved to the small screen in 1974 with ABC's *Get Christie Love,* starring Teresa Graves.

It was a Supremes-style trio from L.A. that finally laid down the law. The Honey Cone was part of the Holland-Dozier-Holland Hot Wax stable that out-Motowned Motown in the early seventies; their killer hooks and seasoned vocal delivery made their two-year winning streak one of the era's musical highs. In "Want Ads," sex suddenly became for the female singer what it had long been for the male singer: something to be enjoyed. Leader Carolyn Willis sang of her plans to advertise for a new man (standard practice in today's personals, but an unusual threat in 1971) and pitch her former lover's lipstick-and-perfume-soiled laundry right out the door. In the follow-up, "Stick-up," a stolen-heart metaphor is playfully extended until the song's feminist credibility disappears with the old-world scenario of its last verse: "I'll wear a smile down the aisle / 'Cause he's the father of my child." This time, rather than being turfed out, the reluctant male is trapped into marriage.

Another artist seeking good loving on her terms was former Chess Records signee Laura Lee. Her "Women's Love Rights" started with a thank you to her fellow "women's libbers," then took listeners through a list of her love demands. Built on a Honey Cone–style groove but sung with the husky determination of a woman who had been messed around with one too many times, the track left no room for compromise. Lee was seeking nothing short of equality in the bedroom. In "Rip Off" she planned a Grinch-who-stole-Christmas departure from her mean mistreater, threatening to take the carpet, wallpaper, and phone with her.

Pop feminism's total solidarity was illusory, of course. An amazingly mature-sounding seventeen-year-old named Betty Wright warned against taking the equality thing too far in "Clean Up Woman." Here, the heroine's frequent nights out allow another woman to come in and "clean up," making off with her man. The love triangle is mirrored in the rhythm-guitar interplay: first, the dotted-eight-based part (let's call it Betty) enters, followed by the busier, picked part (the man) and finally, entering as she is first mentioned, the third part, sly, sneaky, gliding wantonly up and down the fretboard . . . who else but the Clean Up Woman? This counterpoint describes the conflict so eloquently that it is allowed four full repetitions between the first chorus and the second verse, an unheard-of practice in the era of the three-minute pop song. "Clean Up Woman" inspired a paranoid follow-up by Wright about another intrusive household rival, this time, the "Baby Sitter," and a dismissive answer song from Laura Lee called "If You Can Beat Me Rockin' " ("Now, the Clean Up Woman may be a threat . . .").

In 1974, Chaka Khan and her band, Rufus, swept away the last vestiges of female passivity on the charts with "Tell Me Something Good." (Legend has it new fan Stevie Wonder dropped in on a Rufus session and wrote the song on the spot.) The group's biggest hit— slow, syncopated, and grinding, with Khan on top— "Tell Me Something Good" was edgy enough to require a new classification: "funk rock." It was more than Khan's astonishing vocal chops that were a revelation at the time; she was singing from a position of total sexual authority.

Soul's crash course in female assertiveness training soon began to infiltrate pop's middle of the road (where Helen Reddy was directing traffic), with artists like Linda Ronstadt ("You're No Good," 1974) and Jessi Colter ("I'm Not Lisa," 1975) expressing various levels of dissatisfaction with their men. Carly Simon's biggest hit, "You're

So Vain," drips with sarcasm as it mocks an unidentified male ego—said to be Warren Beatty's, but Simon has denied that the lyrics are about any particular real-life person—and her "That's The Way I've Always Heard It Should Be" is an elegiac study of a woman questioning the traditional assumption that happiness can only be derived from marriage. (From the unlikely-couple department: Listen for ego almighty Mick Jagger on "Vain" 's chorus.)

Joni Mitchell's gutsy "Free Man in Paris" was sung from the point of view of a man reminiscing about his salad days. The lyrics were printed in quotation marks on the album cover, but the delivery was definitely first-person; somewhere, George Eliot was smiling. Mitchell's lyrical prowess was accompanied by a musical daring that would lead her further and further into the jazz realm in the coming years.

John Lennon's self-explanatory "Woman Is the Nigger of the World" (1972) demonstrated that musical feminism could appear where you least expected it (from a male rock star), but, by and large, men were useful to the movement only as foils. As the women's movement gathered steam in the coming years, a diversity of artists would conspire to make Lesley Gore's "Party" a distant memory, including an Ike-less Tina Turner, Rickie Lee Jones, Kate Bush, Annie Lennox, Sinead O'Connor, Queen Latifah, Tori Amos, Jane Siberry, Liz Phair, and, okay, Madonna. Aretha, "Queen of Soul," burst back onto the charts in the eighties with nine Top 40 hits, including a feminist duet with Lennox ("Sisters Are Doin' It for Themselves"). By then, she didn't need to ask for it, demand it, or spell it out. She had the respect she deserved.

SHAFTS
Macho Soul

"Theme from *Shaft*" • Isaac Hayes (Enterprise, 1971)
"Drowning in the Sea of Love" • Joe Simon (Spring, 1971)
"A Natural Man" • Lou Rawls (MGM, 1971)
"I Gotcha" • Joe Tex (Dial, 1972)
"Let's Get It On" • Marvin Gaye (Tamla, 1973)
"Show and Tell" • Al Wilson (Rocky Road, 1973)
"Can't Get Enough of Your Love, Babe" • Barry White (20th Century, 1974)
"Hang On in There Baby" • Johnny Bristol (MGM, 1974)
"Lookin' for a Love" • Bobby Womack (United Artists, 1974)
"Love Machine (Part 1)" • The Miracles (Tamla, 1975)

He's wearing a silk shirt, some impressive gold jewelry, and a splash of fetid, pheromone-based cologne. He's whispering sweet some-thangs in your ear. And he's got a small string section backing him up.

It's 1973, and you're trapped in the lair of a seventies love god. Don't panic—first, check out the supremely soulful groove he's laying down. Sure, he's begging for sex, but what about that hypnotic drum pattern, that "Afro-disiac" orchestration, that pleasantly scratching wah-wah guitar? You're listening to a whole new strain of highly polished R&B. So lie back and enjoy . . . at least until he reaches for that fourteen-karat zipper.

Stax songwriting guru Isaac Hayes was the first true practitioner of macho soul. His soundtrack for *Shaft*, the film that started the blaxploitation craze, was a full-blown concept album that synthesized the best aspects of soul, funk, jazz-rock, and traditional film scoring. In addition to spawning a hugely influential single ("Theme from *Shaft*"), it was nominated for seven Grammys (winning two) and even captured an Academy Award, making Hayes the first black composer to earn the distinction. Hayes's performance of "Shaft" at the

1972 Oscars was an unforgettable moment in black popular culture, at least as electrifying as Michael Jackson's moonwalk at the Motown twenty-fifth-anniversary celebrations: Here was the bald, bearded Chocolate Chip himself, bedecked in a chain-link shirt, singing of his sexual prowess to the unsuspecting Academy.

"Theme from *Shaft*" was a major achievement, both instrumentally and as the opening salvo for a new chapter in pop, during which pre–rock and roll skills like string arranging would once again become useful. Unfortunately, the inspired work of artists like Hayes, Curtis Mayfield *(Superfly)*, Joe Simon *(Cleopatra Jones)*, and Bobby Womack *(Across 110th Street)* will forever be associated with the garish brutality of blaxploitation; macho soul's street beats and sexual posturing jibed perfectly with the films, which featured Action Jackson prototypes battling slave traders *(Shaft in Africa)*, weapons traffickers *(Superfly T.N.T.)*, and the mob *(Shaft's Big Score!)*. Hayes's image was so well suited to the genre that the casual fan could be excused for confusing him with supercop John Shaft himself. (Shaft was actually played by Richard Roundtree; Hayes played the title role in 1974's *Truck Turner.*)

Any hit as big as "Theme from *Shaft*" was bound to inspire spin-offs; "Son of Shaft" by the Bar-Kays (1972) and "Superfly Meets Shaft" by John Ernest (1973) quickly materialized to fill the pop-cultural vacuum. The latter, a "who-would-win-if" fantasy, was co-produced by novelty pioneer Dickie Goodman. More importantly, Hayes's Shaft persona paved the way for other baritone Casanovas like Barry White.

White's infamous half-spoken, half-sung seductions ("Can't Get Enough of Your Love, Babe," "I'm Gonna Love You Just a Little More Baby," "Never, Never Gonna Give Ya Up," "You're the First, the Last, My Everything") brought new meaning to the phrase "verbal intercourse," and his operatic physical proportions were fitting, given the astonishing vocal depths he was able to reach. His protégées, Love Unlimited, whose 1972 hit "Walking in the Rain with the One I Love" featured their producer's deep-throated "Barry-tone" and some rainy sound effects, also got billing on the breathtaking instrumental standard "Love's Theme." Barry White was, for better or worse, one of the artists who made the seventies the seventies.

Another key macho soul hit betrays White's influence, but the credit for "Hang On in There Baby"—maybe the most underrated record of the decade—is all Johnny Bristol's. The track is a masterpiece of tension and release that transcends its make-out agenda and cheesy, kitten-poster title phrase. In a reverse of the old "Teach Me Tonight" scenario, the singer is doing the teaching, and he guides his "sweet virgin of the world" through what is—judging from the slow build and multiple peaks of the arrangement—a great experience for both teacher and pupil. Bristol, an ex-Motown staffer, wrote, arranged and produced "Hang On in There Baby," a quickie at just 3:25, as a soul "Bolero," a musical approximation of great lovemaking: Even as the track careens toward its fade, wah-wah working overtime, there is a triumphant key change, one last euphoric surprise in a record that is chock-full of them.

A publicity photo of soul man Bobby Womack from around this time—all wily grin, open shirt, and gold medallion—announced Womack's participation in the Charge of the Love Brigade. The medallion wasn't quite the hardware Isaac Hayes had sported on Oscar night in April 1972, but it fit right in with Womack's new single, "Lookin' for a Love" (originally cut in 1962), a song as suggestive of finding a good housekeeper as it was of finding a good mate. (Marrying for laundry was, of course, an outdated concept, and "Lookin' " was Womack's last hit as a solo artist.) Among the other love gods: Marvin Gaye, whose chart-topping "Let's Get It On" was the beginning of a succession of sex-themed singles that would include "I Want You," "Got to Give It Up (Pt. I)," and "Sexual Healing"; Joe Simon, whose "Drowning in a Sea of Love" was the last independent production of Philly soul kingpins Kenneth Gamble and Leon Huff; Mel and Tim, whose "Starting All Over Again" featured that immortal rap about "Barbara"; Major Harris, whose "Love Won't Let Me Wait" features the quiet, desperate moaning of an anonymous companion; Lou Rawls, whose "A Natural Man" celebrated his mellow brand of hedonism; and Al Wilson, the man who made "Show and Tell" an adults-only game.

"Show and Tell," like most of these songs, was all about mutual consent. The true seventies love god didn't force himself on anyone; as Gaye sang in "Let's Get It On," "we're all sensitive people." Still, with so much testosterone in the air, things were bound to get out of hand, and Joe Tex, the Earth-X James Brown, staged a minor comeback in 1972 with "I Gotcha," a song that seemed to be espousing nothing short of date rape. "Gotcha" 's grinding funk groove was hard to resist—it eventually gyrated its way to Number 2 for two weeks—but its content was pretty despicable, even by 1972 standards. True macho soul might leave you slightly embarrassed (as if your mother had overheard you reciting George Carlin's "Seven Words You Can't Say on Television"), but it never involved coercion.

Some of the top musical minds of the seventies participated in this sub-genre. With *Shaft*, Isaac Hayes created the rhythmic prototype for disco, expanded the scope of R&B orchestration, and set the tone for just about every post-1971 cop show soundtrack, from *Starsky and Hutch* to *NYPD Blue*. Marvin Gaye continued to explore the spirituality of sex until his death in 1984. Barry White is, naturally, still recording—lust never sleeps—and his "Can't Get Enough of Your Love, Babe" was exhumed in 1994 by Taylor Dayne.

The last great thrust of macho soul's golden age was "Love Machine (Part 1)", a 1975 hit for the Miracles (sans Smokey), built, presciently, on a chugging disco groove. Soon, dance songs with sexy titles would become pop's stock-in-trade, and the late seventies' wham-bam approach to romance would leave sensitive studs like Al Wilson and Johnny Bristol behind. But macho soul had already made its point: In an era of big hair, big shoes, big cars, big stadiums, and big money ("Broadway" Joe Namath's 1973 salary was $400,000), size mattered.

PLANET OF THE APES
Hard Rock

"Brown Sugar" • The Rolling Stones (Rolling Stones, 1971)
"Black Dog" • Led Zeppelin (Atlantic, 1972)
"School's Out" • Alice Cooper (Warner, 1972)
"Smoke on the Water" • Deep Purple (Warner, 1973)
"We're an American Band" • Grand Funk (Capitol, 1973)
"Smokin' in the Boy's Room" • Brownsville Station (Big Tree, 1973)
"Sweet Home Alabama" • Lynyrd Skynyrd (MCA, 1974)
"Rock and Roll, Hoochie Koo" • Rick Derringer (Blue Sky, 1974)
"Can't Get Enough" • Bad Company (Swan Song, 1974)
"Rock and Roll All Nite" • Kiss (Casablanca, 1975)

Back in high school, we had a name for people who lived for the hard stuff. Hanging out in packs, smoking at the back of the school, they wore lumberjack jackets, rock-and-roll T-shirts, and steel-toed work boots (laces flying). They fancied themselves rebels, but they weren't dangerous in the way metal-detected high school students are today; in a crowd, they might have played the bully or picked fights, but it was just for effect. One-on-one, they were surprisingly good-natured. In common parlance, they came to be known as "headbangers"; our name for them was inspired by their too-stoned-to-care pronunciation of "man" ("Ay, mon, howzitgoin?"). We called them *mons.*

In the early seventies, before hëavy mëtal's hostile takeover, hard rock produced some bona fide classics for mons and closet mons alike. Musically, it retained a controlled toughness that metal, in its decibel-mongering fury, would all but abandon. Lyrically, it catered almost exclusively to the angry-young-mon demographic with an unholy trinity of popular subjects: sex, drugs, and rock and roll.

Brownsville Station's 1973 anthem "Smokin' in the Boy's Room," with its unfiltered teen angst and rebelliously misplaced apostrophe,

Don's drawing of a "mon," completed in Mr. Reid's geography class, 1978.

typified the ethos of the struggling male mon. *Girlfriend, teachers . . . on case . . . must cut class, hang out in washroom . . . smoke . . . unhhh . . .* Fortunately, the song's rebel-rousing sentiments were accompanied by a very convincing rock shuffle. But Brownsville Station's only other hit would be "Kings of the Party" (1974).

Alice Cooper, too, knew how to sniff out teen spirit. "School's Out," his antischolastic 1972 opus, was sung in a vicious growl—he sounded psychotic, but was actually just celebrating the arrival of summer (two whole months without "teachers' dirty looks"). Cooper probably represents the exact moment when fame and infamy became one and the same. He was hard rock's Tiny Tim (substitute a live python for the ukulele), and his outrageous appearance, highlighted by stringy black hair and cadaverous makeup, was carefully

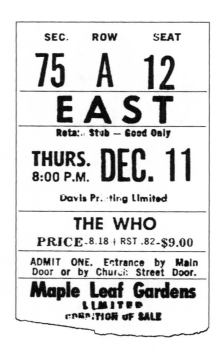

SEC. ROW SEAT

75 A 12

E A S T

Retai.. Stub — Good Only

THURS. **DEC. 11**
8:00 P.M.

Davis Printing Limited

THE WHO
PRICE-8.18 + RST .82-$9.00

ADMIT ONE. Entrance by Main
Door or by Church Street Door.

Maple Leaf Gardens
LIMITED
CONDITION OF SALE

calculated to disturb parents. For a time in the early seventies, he was the world's top concert draw, his stage antics luring curious mons from smoky suburban toilet stalls all over North America. Cooper's star has never set; his twenty-two LPs span twenty-five years, with no gap greater than three years. Call him Rebel without a Pause. His "Eighteen" (a kind of hard rock retelling of *The Graduate*) went to Number 21 in early 1971, more than a year before his after-school special cracked the Top 10.

It was right around this time that "party" became a verb, the only one worth conjugating if you were part of hard rock's loyal listenership. For them, "to party" meant smoking pot, listening to tunes, and making out with "your best girlfriend" (in the inimitable words of Brownsville Station). The reality often fell far short of that Platonic ideal, as many washroom-puffing mons could have told you. Hard rock allowed them to dream, though.

Grand Funk's 1973 cock rock classic "We're an American Band" was allegedly inspired by a Baton Rouge barroom almost-brawl with bluesy Brits Humble Pie, in which the not-so-humble Grand Funk drummer Don Brewer stood up and patriotically pronounced, "We're an American Band!" That hand-on-hearts statement became one of the early seventies' hard rock classics (on a gold-vinyl 45, too!). Its "Honky Tonk Woman" cowbell and crunching air-guitar-inspiring riffs led the charge as vocalist Mark Farner, still adrenalized from the band's clash with the Pies, related the perks of rock stardom—a hotel room trashing, booze aplenty, and an eager Arkansas groupie. (I party, you party, he parties, she parties, they party.)

Rick Derringer, fresh from production and guitar work with both Edgar and Johnny Winter, hit with a similar classic—"Rock and Roll, Hoochie Koo" (1974). Celebrating sex ("Gonna' do it to you"), drugs ("high all the time") and rock and roll (a four-nighter at the "old Town Hall"), the song is a desert-island choice for anyone interested in preserving hard rock's hedonistic quintessence.

Hiding behind elaborate makeup derived from Alice Cooper and garb derived from superhero comics (their footwear put steel-toed mons to shame), Kiss partied all the way to Number 12 in 1975 with their first Top 40 hit, a live version of "Rock and Roll All Nite." With Gene Simmons's tongue threatening to tear up its roots and attack the planet like some B-movie alien, the band was poised for five very big years. Appealing almost exclusively to early-teen boys, their product (that's what it was) represented a move away from the rock-essentials honesty of Derringer and company, and steered the genre toward the crass commercialism of the late seventies.

Adding a touch of raunchy class to the early-seventies proceedings were the Rolling Stones, who occasionally steered into hard-rock territory with kickass material that stayed true to their considerable legacy. In "It's Only Rock 'N Roll (But I Like It)" (1974) they showed us why we should like it too; in "Tumbling Dice" (1972) they slowed down their standard blues-rock approach; and in "Brown Sugar" (1971) Mick Jagger snarled his way through some Top 40 interracial sex ("Yeah, yeah, yeah, woooooh!").

Other hard rockers who got themselves all hot and bothered included Bad Company, who shared hooks with Barry White ("Can't Get Enough") and Roberta Flack ("Feel Like Makin' Love"); Golden

Earring, whose protagonist was ensured first-strike capability by a "Radar Love" that signaled him whenever his girlfriend was in the mood; ZZ Top, who were looking for some "Tush"; Aerosmith, who penetrated the Top 40 with "Sweet Emotion," their rock-and-roll euphemism for sweet something else; and glam rocker Marc Bolan of T. Rex, who made banging a gong seem much more fun than Chuck Barris did a few years later on TV's talent contest from hell, *The Gong Show*.

Hard rock's self-congratulatory tradition was rampant with songs like "Ballroom Blitz" (Sweet's hard-edged follow-up to "Little Willy"), "Cum On Feel the Noize" (Slade's Number 1 U.K. hit), and "Rock and Roll" (Led Zeppelin's cacophonous blast from the past). Finally, there was Deep Purple's "Smoke on the Water," featuring Ritchie Blackmore's preschool guitar riff, which even nonmusicians could play after a few beers. The song was an apocalyptic elegy inspired by the incineration of Switzerland's Montreux Casino during a Frank Zappa show on December 3, 1971.

Hard rock, apart from containing the seeds of punk (Patti Smith, Iggy Pop, the Ramones), encompassed a variety of sub-genres like glam rock (David Bowie, Roxy Music, the New York Dolls), theatrical rock (the Tubes, Frank Zappa), heartland rock (Bruce Springsteen, Bob Seger), and, most notably, Southern rock. The latter's signature tune was "Sweet Home Alabama" (1974), a musical response to Neil Young's caustic "Southern Man," courtesy of Lynyrd Skynyrd (the band was named after the members' high school gym teacher, Leonard Skinner). With its popping guitar riff as Exhibit A, the song was a convincing defense of life in Alabama, particularly considering the band was from Jacksonville, Florida. Also part of Southern rock's alumni: the Allman Brothers Band, whose guitarist Duane Allman (killed in a 1971 motorcycle accident) was eulogized in Lynyrd Skynyrd's classic "Free Bird" (1975) and who themselves hit paydirt with "Ramblin Man" (1973); Black Oak Arkansas ("Jim Dandy," 1974); the Ozark Mountain Daredevils ("If You Wanna Get to Heaven," 1974); the Marshall Tucker Band ("Fire on the Mountain," 1975); and Wet Willie ("Keep on Smilin'," 1974).

Just in case all those debauched hard-rock heroes were giving the wrong impression, they showed us a sensitive side, risking mon backlash with a series of power ballads that inspired late-seventies successors like Foreigner and Journey. Nazareth weighed in with the tortured vocal of "Love Hurts"; Styx beat Kenny Rogers and the Little River Band to the popular song title "Lady"; and Kiss stopped shouting it out loud for a moment with its bittersweet "Beth."

If heavy metal (the phrase was first used in William Burroughs's *Naked Lunch*) has thrived in the years since the early seventies, it is because hard rock paved the way. It upped the ante in the volume department and renewed rock and roll's rebellious spirit (waking up with little Susie in a movie theater was *nothing* compared to partying with groupies). Led by album-oriented guitar bands like Led Zeppelin ("Black Dog," "D'yer Mak'er"), Black Sabbath ("Iron Man"), Uriah Heep ("Easy Livin' "), and Foghat ("Slow Ride"), hard rock was as much an FM force as it was an AM one. In fact, the genre's crowning glory was Led Zeppelin's "Stairway to Heaven," a hugely popular album cut that the band refused to release as a single.

In 1974, right around the time hard rock's metal offspring were preparing to take over, "Sensurround" hit the movie theaters. A film fad in the tradition of 3-D glasses, it first appeared as—sorry, Charlton—the main character in *Earthquake* (1974). The new craze (last felt in 1977's *Rollercoaster*) sent out a low-frequency hum during the "quake" scenes that had audiences shaking all over. For hardrock fans, the sensation was like a cheap aftershock; anyone who had attended an arena concert had already experienced it. Paul McCartney immortalized in loving detail the rock concert ritual with "Venus and Mars/Rock Show" (1975).

Even the Osmonds (bet you didn't think you'd see *them* in this chapter) scraped the bubblegum off their shoes for a couple of ill-advised attempts at hard rock, taking both "Hold Her Tight" and the incomprehensible "Crazy Horses" to Number 14 in 1972. If lightweight popsters like the Osmonds could be tempted into the hard-rock fray, it's interesting to speculate what might have happened if a hard-rock band like Led Zeppelin had tackled bubblegum. None of us will likely ever hear Robert Plant lending his searing pipes to "One Bad Apple," but in 1975 a friend of ours experienced the next best thing. Just weeks after the release of *Physical Graffiti*, he stumbled upon a Zep-mad mon stashing some "weed" in a school locker and quietly singing the final verse of "Billy Don't Be a Hero," a bubblegum story song that no mon would ever admit to liking. When Dean (not his real name) realized he had been caught, he said nothing, but a silent covenant was forged (even now, on the strength of Dean's wordless threat, we feel it necessary to use a pseudonym).

That 1975 incident was a revelation; despite the dope, the Sabbath T-shirt and his subscription to *Creem,* Dean liked "Billy Don't Be a Hero." And like everyone else, he was embarrassed about it. The power of early-seventies pop was laid bare; hard rock's unified front was a sham. Slamming his locker door shut, Dean hummed loudly as he headed out to the back of the school for a "butt." He was humming Jimmy Page's guitar solo from "Stairway to Heaven." Note perfect.

EWWWWW!
Bad Taste

"Timothy" • The Buoys (Scepter, 1971)
"My Ding-A-Ling" • Chuck Berry (Chess, 1972)
"Follow Your Daughter Home" • The Guess Who (RCA, 1973)
"(You're) Having My Baby" • Paul Anka (United Artists, 1974)
"Don't Eat the Yellow Snow" • Frank Zappa (Discreet, 1974)
"Rock and Roll Heaven" • The Righteous Brothers (Haven, 1974)
"Werewolf" • Five Man Electrical Band (Polydor, 1974)
"Only Women" • Alice Cooper (Atlantic, 1975)
"Shaving Cream" • Benny Bell (Vanguard, 1975)
"Squeeze Box" • The Who (MCA, 1975)

Leisure suits.
Roller derby.
The Happy Hooker.
Burt in *Cosmo.*
Sensurround.
Count Chocula.

Accusing the early seventies of bad taste is too easy. You feel like you're picking on a defenseless loser. You feel like you should just leave the poor geek alone.

And yet, it must be done.

The word "innovator" has seldom been applied to Rupert Holmes, composer of 1979's "Escape" (a Number 1 hit about consuming piña coladas), but Holmes single-handedly initiated the bad-taste revolution of the early seventies with the song "Timothy" (a Number 17 hit about consuming human flesh). Moreover, he did it deliberately. Holmes has admitted that "Timothy" was intended to attract controversy for the Buoys (the band took its name from Lifebuoy soap), and that the idea for the song came to him when he overheard *The Galloping Gourmet* in the next room while tinkering with Tennessee Ernie Ford's coal-mining classic "Sixteen Tons."

Just in case you've forgotten the plot: Three pals (the narrator, Timothy, and "hungry" Joe) are trapped in a mine after a cave-in, and food and water are scarce. Joe starts eyeing Tim, and before long he's having one of those Looney Toons hallucinations where your buddy begins to look uncannily like a roast turkey. Just then our humble narrator blacks out. The next thing he knows, he and Joe are being pulled from the wreckage, tummies full as can be. Odd . . . Where's Timothy? Confused . . . Can't think . . .

Well, that's some story. They never found Timothy, you say? Hmmm. Do you think it might be because YOU ATE HIM?

"Timothy" was groundbreaking, not only by virtue of its taboo-busting depravity and its uncanny foreknowledge of world events (in 1972, a Uruguayan soccer team whose plane had crashed in the Andes would resort to cannibalism), but for the way in which it re-futed "Bridge Over Troubled Water." Just a year earlier, Simon & Garfunkel's somber hymn to friendship had spent six weeks at Number 1, but the Buoys were serving notice that all that warm, fuzzy stuff was over. Sure, those bastards ATE TIMOTHY, but in the egocentric, looking-out-for-Number-One seventies, *that's what friends are for.*

"Eaters of raw flesh" is the literal meaning of the word "Eskimo," and it has, accordingly, fallen into disuse in the nineties. "Inuit" is the term now preferred by people indigenous to the Arctic. Nevertheless, "Eskimo" was still accepted terminology when Frank Zappa set his immortal hit "Don't Eat the Yellow Snow" in the far north. The song's disjointed story involved hand-to-hand combat between a young Eskimo lad (Zappa's alter ego) and a cruel, baby-seal-bludgeoning trapper who could be temporarily blinded by snow soaked in husky urine. As Zappa waxed scatalogical in 7/4 time, mixing his trademark poo-poo humor with elements of rock, blues, and twentieth-century chamber music, he answered the question that would inform his whole career: Does humor belong in music?

It does, but songs like Benny Bell's "Shaving Cream" make you wish it didn't. Already thirty years old when it became a surprise novelty hit in 1975, "Shaving Cream" was to "s——" what the Ohio Players' "Fopp" was to "f——." Each verse would set up an "it" rhyme, then defy the listener's expectations by launching into the refrain: "SHaving cream / Be nice and clean . . ."

"My Ding-A-Ling", Chuck Berry's only Number 1 and his last hit save for a live remake of "Reelin' & Rockin' ", was a nudge-nudge song in the "Shaving Cream" mold. Actually a cover of a prerock record by the influential New Orleans producer Dave Bartholomew, it was recorded in England using an early version of the Average White Band. A four-minute penis joke may not have been an appropriate coup de grâce for the true king of rock and roll, but "My Ding-A-Ling" 's bawdy charms were enough to take it to the top of the charts for two weeks while worthy challengers like "Freddie's Dead," "Tight Rope," and "Everybody Plays the Fool" fell short. Audiences in 1972 reacted strongly to the song because they were not yet accustomed to hearing superstars serenading their genitalia—a similar song would surely produce little in the way of shock waves today. In any event, Berry's comeback was short-lived; 1975 found him playing to a paltry audience of forty at a New York show.

Pete Townshend, another rock legend not above a little sexual wordplay, joined the bad-taste fray in 1975 with "Squeeze Box." Taken from the excellent *Who by Numbers* album, the song was crystal clear in its innuendo—no one really thought it was a tribute to an accordion-playing couple—but it overshadowed other, better cuts like "Slip Kid" and "Blue Red and Grey."

The trick may have been not to have other, better cuts to overshadow. Supporters of Paul Anka's "(You're) Having My Baby" claimed the song was a glorification of women, but its detractors maintained it was a misogynist anthem that defined women strictly as childbearers and, worse, suggested childbearing was a tribute to the father. Even giving the well-intentioned composer the benefit of the doubt (Anka has four daughters), you'd have to admit the song pushed the bad-taste envelope. The next time you hear it on the radio, though, don't lunge at your dashboard to change the station; listen to the whole song, and marvel at just how much mutant sentiment the early seventies could tolerate.

As it happened, Alice Cooper's "Only Women Bleed" entered the charts exactly nine months after "(You're) Having My Baby." The song turned out to be the most controversial of his many attention-seeking hits. Though its title was abbreviated to "Only Women" for the single release, the tune immediately created trouble for Cooper (né Vincent Furnier), the self-appointed menstrual minstrel. But public outrage was misdirected. Had "Only Women" 's critics examined it more closely—they gave it the same once-over Ronald Reagan gave "Born in the U.S.A." before brandishing it as a campaign slogan in 1984—they would have realized its message was entirely *pro*-female. The loutish husband was the villain, and the blood thing was mostly metaphorical. Rock critic Robert Christgau was clued in; he called "Only Women Bleed" "the most explicitly feminist song to hit the top forty since 'I Am Woman,' " and, with Loretta Lynn's "The Pill" fizzling at Number 70 on the pop charts, he was probably right. In the end, Alice Cooper's only real crime against women was the way he looked in lingerie.

Not surprisingly, "Only Women Bleed" didn't change the world. Hard rock's concept of women continued to find expression in sensitive numbers like ZZ Top's "Tush" and Aerosmith's "Walk This Way"; Alice Cooper's Top 40 clout faded after *Welcome to My Nightmare* was milked for two more singles. But unlike Helen Reddy ("I Am Woman") and Aretha Franklin ("A Natural Woman"), Cooper wasn't preaching to the converted; "Only Women Bleed" infiltrated that most sacred enclave of sexism, the bedroom of the *National Lampoon*–thumbing teenage boy, and may even have changed a few attitudes along the way (or not).

Teenage boys were also the core audience for the early seventies' werewolf boom. Flicks like *Werewolves on Wheels,* comic books like *Werewolf by Night,* cartoon characters like Weirdo Wolfie, face-smothering hairstyles like Gregg Allman's muttonchops, and the omnipresent Wolfman Jack were all part of the phenomenon. The soundtrack of the movement was "Werewolf," a 1974 story song by Five Man Electrical Band that made "Monster Mash" seem like a masterpiece of subtlety. In it, a rural father goes after his lycanthropic son with the traditional silver bullet, but ends up getting mauled to death. Fair enough, but did Mom have to be so darned happy about it ("Mama smiled and said, 'Betcha Billy got him' ")?

Lest we conclude that seventies fathers had it in only for their furry sons, we have the Guess Who's "Follow Your Daughter Home,"

a strangely cheerful track in which a creepy, overprotective dad shadows his daughter with stalkerlike precision, wondering aloud, "Is she still a virgin?" In light of lead singer Burton Cummings's other misogynist pronouncements (like the foulmouthed live version of "American Woman"), "Daughter" can be seen as part of a larger pathology, but that spoils the fun, doesn't it? Better instead to groove to that flute solo and hum along with the generic calypso melody.

Cummings's traditionalism went beyond sexual stereotypes; he was also a rock-and-roll preservationist. From "Clap for the Wolfman" to *Rockin'* (with its covers of "Sea of Love" and "Running Bear"), he was possessed by the spirit of '59. He may even have liked "Rock and Roll Heaven," the 1974 Righteous Brothers reunion hit that memorialized dead pop stars from Bobby Darin to Jim Croce. It was, in spite of its morbid subject, a hard record not to like. A crash course in the lost art of building to a chorus, it put blue-eyed-soul veterans Bill Medley and Bobby Hatfield in a comfortable neo-Spector setting, and flourished in an extremely competitive summer. In the end, its pop appeal outweighed its questionable lyric, though not by all that much.

For later elegies, check out the Commodores' "Nightshift" (1985) and the string of early-eighties tributes to John Lennon that culmi-

nated with Paul Simon's excellent "The Late Great Johnny Ace."
Simon also dealt briefly with the passing of his peers in *One-Trick Pony*. The 1980 movie featured a scene in which journeyman folk-rocker Jonah Levin (played by Simon) and his band pass the time en route to a gig playing a game called "rock-and-roll deaths": you ante up, you take turns naming deceased rockers, and the last one in wins all the money. It's exactly what you'd expect, cinematically, from Paul Simon—that is, it's more verbal than visual—and it's at once more unsettling and more poignant than "Rock and Roll Heaven." It's also a great illustration of the difference between 1980 and 1974: *One-Trick Pony* is ultra-self-conscious; "Rock and Roll Heaven" is virtually guileless.

The hallmark of many seventies hits, in fact, was their oblivious-ness to their own weirdness. Yes, in the case of Loudon Wainwright III's "Dead Skunk" (1972), the artist knew his work was funny-peculiar, but can the same be said of America's "Muskrat Love" (1973), Cher's "Half-Breed" (1973), Sister Janet Mead's "The Lord's Prayer" (1974), Elvis Presley's "Burning Love" (1972), Hot Butter's "Popcorn" (1972)? Irony is now the everyday language of pop, but in the early seventies, it belonged only to outsiders: Randy Newman, Steely Dan, David Bowie, Bryan Ferry. Rank-and-file popsters were as earnest as could be, and that's why the Generation-X'ers currently revisiting the seventies find it so easy to laugh at everything—they aren't used to pop culture that wants to be taken at face value. Instead of David Essex's "Rock On" (1974), they have grown up with R.E.M.'s deconstructionist "Drive" (1992). In place of *The Midnight Special*, they have the wise-cracking, self-referential MTV. Their Scooby Doo is Beavis and Butthead.

The records in this chapter were in bad taste in the seventies; now the decade itself is in bad taste. The seventies are back in style, to be sure, but only for their camp value; the typical latter-day ironist would rather take an easy shot at ABBA than give Frank Zappa any credit. Someday, the gloom-mongering nineties may be judged even more harshly, if only because the stakes were higher—reveling in fin-de-siècle political, moral, and cultural collapse is perhaps more serious than singing a few naughty songs—but for now, the seventies remain a defenseless geek people just can't leave alone.

JIFFY POP
Novelty Records

"Brand New Key" • Melanie (Neighborhood, 1971)
"Troglodyte (Cave Man)" • The Jimmy Castor Bunch (RCA, 1972)
"The Cover of 'Rolling Stone' " • Dr. Hook & the Medicine Show (Columbia, 1972)
"Playground in My Mind" • Clint Holmes (Epic, 1973)
"Kung Fu Fighting" • Carl Douglas (20th Century, 1974)
"Spiders & Snakes" • Jim Stafford (MGM, 1973)
"Life Is a Rock (But the Radio Rolled Me)" • Reunion (RCA, 1974)
"Don't Call Us, We'll Call You" • Sugarloaf/Jerry Corbetta (Claridge, 1974)
"No No Song" • Ringo Starr (Apple, 1975)
"Mr. Jaws" • Dickie Goodman (Cash, 1975)

As decades go, the seventies are a novelty, a plastic bubble surrounding a multitude of bizarre fads, gimmicks, and gadgets that, like John Travolta in the 1976 made-for-TV movie, would never survive a day on the outside. A patchwork of novelty humans (Evel Knievel), novelty house pets (Pet Rocks), novelty nuptials (Sly Stone onstage at Madison Square Garden), novelty combat (kung fu), and novelty presidents (who else?), the decade also provided shelter for that musical equivalent of the whoopee cushion, the novelty record. Don't try to pin down a specific style; the novelty classification is defined less by a sound than by a mind-set, an affable willingness to be silly.

The novelty renaissance was most likely a reaction to the sheer intensity of late-sixties rock. People who only a few years earlier had been serious about Iron Butterfly entered the seventies in a joking mood, and hallowed subject matter like psychedelic drugs and free love became novelty's fodder. The void between Ringo Starr's "No No Song," in which the ex-Beatle refuses a variety of recreational drugs, and the hallucinogenic landscape of his former band's "Lucy in the Sky with Diamonds" is as deep and wide as Snake River Canyon.

Compare the celebratory public lovemaking at Woodstock with the crude sexuality of the Jimmy Castor Bunch's funky "Troglodyte (Cave Man)", in which a troglodyte (cave man) hunts down his woman in a masturbatory frenzy while repeating his mantra: "Gotta find a woman, gotta find a woman, gotta find a woman . . ."

Despite the strong chart performance of many novelty records, they rarely spawned extended careers. While a pop curio like Daddy Dewdrop's lascivious "Chick-A-Boom (Don't Ya Jes' Love It)" might give an otherwise not-likely-to-succeed new artist two minutes and forty seconds of fame, more often than not a big novelty hit hurt the career of a promising newcomer whose dopey debut masked more serious musical aspirations. Call it the novelty-killed-the-radio-star syndrome.

Record labels, in their dubious wisdom, often saw novelties as first hits that would inspire many more, but novelty resists repetition, and the follow-ups usually failed. Carl Douglas was denied the opportunity for a more interesting vocal career when his "Kung Fu Fighting," originally intended as a B-side, was catapulted to Number 1 by a Fu-hungry audience that hadn't had enough of David Carradine on TV (*Kung Fu*) or Bruce Lee in the movies (*Enter the Dragon*). The doomed repeat attempt in his case was a dawn-of-disco concoction called "Dance the Kung Fu." Better have a lot of room on the dance floor.

Another artist who might have earned some respect as an R&B singer had he not been held back by an instant hit was Clint Holmes, whose "Playground in My Mind" was part feel-good pop, part nursery school sing-along. The song's childlike "I got a nickel" chorus, performed by producer Paul Vance's son, overshadowed Holmes's unremarkable but sound performance. Holmes understood the pitfalls of typecasting; he later admitted to Bob Gilbert and Gary Therous (authors of *The Top Ten*): " 'Playground' hurt me. It branded me as a novelty singer." Failing to recognize that novelty hits rarely spawned successful follow-ups, though, someone made the decision to keep Holmes in the novelty universe with another kiddy tune called "Shiddle-ee-Dee." It stiffed. (ABC Television might have had its own nursery-style hit with the *Schoolhouse Rock* classic "Conjunction Junction [What's Your Function?]" had it chosen to release it from cartoon limbo into the world of Top 40; for those of us who munched Froot Loops in the TV room every Saturday morning, "Conjunction" remains as familiar as many Top 40 favorites.)

A childlike approach informed Melanie's songwriting and she, too, experienced the paradox of a career that stalled at the instant of her biggest hit. Her Number 1 swan song, "Brand New Key," sounded like a children's record, but was actually a variation on Freud's *The Interpretation of Dreams:* something about a pair of roller skates and a key fitting together. Was this the same Melanie who had serenaded a candle-carrying throng during Woodstock's famous downpour? It was, and the hipness she had acquired in 1969 was evaporating even as her sweet, sassy vocal on "Brand New Key" attracted over 3 million buyers.

The sexual revolution produced more than a childish double entendre and a horny troglodyte. Jim Stafford, one of the few artists to score multiple hits in the novelty genre, gave us "My Girl Bill," a gender-bending, one-joke love song, and "Spiders & Snakes," wherein a Jim Carrey–esque protagonist woos his girl by trying to gross her out. This icky approach, akin to stealing the girl's hat at recess (a courting ritual that was still in vogue in our peer group circa '74), prompts Stafford's heroine to state the obvious: She "don't like spiders and snakes" and, indeed, "that ain't what it takes" to love her. Stafford's string of hits (which also included drug-themed ditties like "Wildwood Weed" and "I Got Stoned and I Missed It") lasted over two years, climaxing in a summer replacement TV series in 1975. In novelty terms, that's longevity. Maybe not immortality, but enough to set Stafford, the pride of Eloise, Florida, apart from mono-novelteers like Napoleon XIV, whose 1966 hit "They're Coming to Take Me Away, Ha-Haaa!" resurfaced briefly in 1973.

Dickie Goodman, a career novelty man who defied the one-hit nature of his craft, had invented the "break-in" record in 1956 with "The Flying Saucer (Parts 1 & 2)". On that record, clips of current pop songs were cut into a mock radio broadcast for comic effect. Goodman's method was basically unchanged when he was tempted back into the fray in 1973 by the Watergate scandal. "Watergrate"—note the extra "r"—stalled at Number 42, but the Godfather of Droll finally struck gold in 1975 with "Mr. Jaws," a spoof of Steven Spielberg's record-breaking film.

Other early-seventies spoofs of note included the Delegates' "Convention '72" (an election-year Goodman-style laff riot), Martin Mull's "Dueling Tubas" (after "Dueling Banjos," the theme from *Deliverance*), Grand Canyon's "Evil Boll-Weevil" (after a certain Skycycle-riding daredevil), *National Lampoon*'s "Deteriorata" (after "Desiderata," featuring Max Ehrman's mellow words of wisdom), Ray Stevens's "The Streak" (one of over thirty records on the topic), and Dr. Hook & the Medicine Show's "Cover of 'Rolling Stone' " (a Shel Silverstein song that was to seventies rock stardom what *This Is Spinal Tap* was to eighties rock stardom).

"Cover" actually got Dr. Hook on the cover of *RS,* but the most notable novelty success story was the comedy duo Cheech & Chong. They were quoted even more widely than contemporaries like George Carlin and Richard Pryor, their stoner-comedy albums *(Cheech & Chong, Big Bambu, Los Cochinos, Cheech & Chong's Wedding Album)* had rock-and-roll sales figures, and, unbelievably, their singles were bona fide hits. "Sister Mary Elephant (Shudd-Up!)," "Basketball Jones Featuring Tyrone Shoelaces," and "Earache My Eye Featuring Alice Bowie" all went to Number 25 or higher on the pop charts. The charmingly spaced-out pothead disappeared as a type around the same time as the charmingly incoherent drunk (see *Arthur 2: On the Rocks*), but the irreverent, stash-flushing antics of Cheech & Chong will never die (they're chemically preserved).

Jerry Corbetta and Sugarloaf had to their credit one AM-radio classic (1970's "Green-Eyed Lady") when they turned the travails of an up-and-coming glitter rock band into "Don't Call Us, We'll Call You" in 1975. Featuring musical references to the Beatles and Stevie Wonder, a Wolfman Jack interjection, and some snazzy push-button telephone effects, the song was a catalog of current keyboard technology; Corbetta supplements the power guitar riff with electric piano, organ, clavinet, and synthesizer. A valuable mid-seventies time capsule, "Don't Call Us" lives on wherever young musicians are put on hold by monolithic record labels.

Some novelty hits—Hurricane Smith's "Oh, Babe, What Would You Say?," Pete Wingfield's "Eighteen with a Bullet," Billy Swan's "I Can Help"—earned the distinction simply because they *sounded* funny. Reunion's "Life Is a Rock (But the Radio Rolled Me)" was a pastiche of song titles, lyric quotations, artists, producers, and record labels delivered in rapid-fire plainsong, every so often giving way to the anthemic chorus. The ability to accurately sing along was certainly an indication that you had too much time on your hands, but the words did fall trippingly off the tongue: "B.-B. Bumble and the Stingers, Mott the Hoople, Rachel Singers . . ." Billy Joel used the same gimmick on his 1989 compendium of world news references, "We Didn't Start the Fire." Unlike Joel, Reunion was not destined for any more hits, but their nostalgic, affectionate tribute to pop radio has become an all-oldies staple.

The novelty muse normally strikes in the same place only once (heard from Rick Dees & His Cast of Idiots lately?), and many a musical prankster found temporary asylum in the seventies' plastic bubble. To this day, behind that protective coating, singular novelty hits like "Saturday Morning Confusion" (1971) and "Coconut" (1972) hold their own alongside the odd accoutrements of the seventies: Pillsbury Dough dolls, toe socks, black-light posters, Charlie perfume—to some, a definition of hell. The early seventies produced much that was genuinely funny, including great television *(Monty*

Python's Flying Circus, Saturday Night Live), movies *(Love and Death, Blazing Saddles, M*A*S*H)*, stand-up comedy (Bill Cosby, Richard Pryor, Robert Klein) and prose *(Breakfast of Champions, Metropolitan Life)*, but it's hard to think of them as a great period for humor when you're confronted with a dated contrivance like "Kung Fu Fighting." Maybe the hits of the novelty resurgence would have weathered better if they had provoked laughter instead of merely being laughable.

UNSUNG HEROES
Instrumentals

"Melting Pot" • Booker T. & the MG's (Stax, 1971)
"Outa-Space" • Billy Preston (A&M, 1972)
"Popcorn" • Hot Butter (Musicor, 1972)
"Frankenstein" • The Edgar Winter Group (Epic, 1973)
"Dueling Banjos" • Eric Weissberg & Steve Mandell (Warner, 1973)
"Love's Theme" • Love Unlimited Orchestra (20th Century, 1973)
"The Entertainer" • Marvin Hamlisch (MCA, 1974)
"Pick Up the Pieces" • Average White Band (Atlantic, 1974)
"The Rockford Files" • Mike Post (MGM, 1975)
"Autobahn" • Kraftwerk (Vertigo, 1975)

Stax Records keyboard wiz Booker T. Jones coaxed many exotic textures from his Hammond organ during his ten-year reign as the king of instrumental pop, but none was more evocative than the shimmering heat haze of "Melting Pot." As funky and familiar as it was hypnotic and otherworldly, the single (from the album of the same name) was a perfect soundtrack for the dog days of summer 1971. It would prove to be the last true Booker T. & the MG's hit—the group disbanded later that year, and plans for a 1975 reunion album were abandoned when drummer Al Jackson was shot to death in his Memphis home—but a new era of high-tech instrumentals was beginning, and Jones's torch would be carried into the new decade by an army of qualified studio hounds.

Billy Preston, for one, found the early seventies extremely receptive to his frenetic organ-and-clavinet workouts. The honorary fifth Beatle, still busy with his Liverpudlian buddies (he was one of the "friends" on George Harrison's *The Concert for Bangla Desh*) had signed with A&M and was poised for a commercial hot streak. "Outa-Space" (Number 2, 1972) and "Space Race" (Number 4, 1973) brought Preston galaxy-wide success, and joined other space-

themed records like "Rocket Man," "Space Oddity," and "Also Sprach Zarathustra (2001)" in making the known universe totally cool.

Space exploration was the stuff of front-page headlines: Soviet cosmonaut Viktor Patsayev and the crew of *Soyuz 11* had suffocated during reentry in 1971; unmanned missions to Mars and Jupiter were being planned, and NASA's ongoing exploration of the moon was reaping major scientific rewards. Keeping track of the *Apollo* missions that followed Neil Armstrong's excellent adventure in '69 was not unlike trying to follow the sequential release of Chicago albums (NASA at least used arabic numerals), but *Apollo 15* was more memorable than most in that it featured astronauts roaming the moon's surface in a battery-powered dune buggy called the Lunar Rover— picture the Banana Splits in one-sixth gravity. If the dream of finding a full-size Lunar Rover under the Christmas tree eluded many an aspiring Rocket Robin Hood (the authors included), Billy Preston's funky interstellar excursions provided at least some consolation.

Though the real *Apollo* program would eventually be discontinued after seventeen round trips, British keyboardist and arranger Tom Parker dubbed his 1972 faux-classical studio project Apollo

100. The group's rock version of "Jesu, Joy of Man's Desiring" (Number 6, 1972), complete with thematically unrelated guitar break, must have sent J. S. Bach into a perpetual gravespin, but proponents of the "Hooked on Classics" approach argued that it fostered tolerance for the classics in young people. (Yes, but at what cost?) Felix Mendelssohn was spared Bach's fate when Apollo 100's follow-up single, "Mendelssohn's 4th (2nd Movement)," peaked at Number 94 and disappeared after only three weeks. Still, music lovers weren't out of the woods yet, as Walter Murphy's discofied "A Fifth of Beethoven" (1976) lay in wait.

Other instrumentals from the legit side of the pop spectrum included movie and TV themes like Peter Nero's "Theme from *Summer of '42*," John Williams's "Theme from *Jaws*," Henry Mancini's "Theme from *Love Story*," Nino Rota and Carlo Savina's "Love Theme from *The Godfather*," Herb Alpert & the Tijuana Brass's "Last Tango in Paris," Michel Legrand's "Brian's Song," Hagood Hardy's "The Homecoming," Rhythm Heritage's "Theme from *S.W.A.T.*," and, most notably, Mike Post's "The Rockford Files." Peaking at Number 10 in mid-1975, "Files" was a departure from the standard soundtrack hit in that its melody was assigned not to violins or softly tinkling piano, but to a strange combination of harmonica and whining synthesizer. Uptempo and almost cloyingly cheerful, it would have been a perfect free-standing hit in the summer of Tennille (it reached Number 10 in August), except that for most transistor-toting teens it was already associated with *The Rockford Files*, a detective show their parents watched. Post, who had cut his teeth as musical director for *The Andy Williams Show* and *The Mac Davis Show,* is still a TV presence today—check the credits on *E.R.*

Synth-based "main themes" represented only the tip of the techno-instrumental iceberg. The robotic novelty hit "Popcorn," with its droning opening note, water-torture melody, flatulent sequence, and Pong-style lead, was an oddity that could only have come from the seventies. "Popcorn" creator and Moog-manipulator Stan Free was certainly successful in conjuring the depressing inertia of a movie snack-bar lineup—the record's two minutes and thirty seconds feel like an eternity—but there was no Milk Duds payoff at the end, only a growing sense that pop music was becoming more and more automated. Hot Butter, the "band" behind the "song," seemed to have been named with the foreknowledge that "Popcorn" would be an unrepeatable novelty; follow-ups like "Percolator," "Pipeline," and "Apache" fell on deaf (plugged?) ears. (Does anyone else have the recurring nightmare that, even now, Stan Free is sitting somewhere, like the man behind the curtain in *The Wizard of Oz*, noodling with the next wave of musical gadgetry? Run, Dorothy! Run like the wind!)

Kraftwerk, the Düsseldorf duo that achieved art-rock celebrity by using Hot Butter–style trickery for up to twenty-two minutes at a stretch, hit the U.S. jackpot in 1975 with a substantially edited version of its album-side opus "Autobahn" (German for "highway"). The single sounded as if it could have been extracted from just about anywhere in the full-length version, but it contained all the key "Autobahn" elements: the monotonic chanting, the three-chord vamp, the ambient electro-kazoo textures. Kraftwerk's style-over-substance breakthrough might seem less offensive in retrospect if it hadn't helped unleash the flock of haircuts that dominated popular music throughout the eighties.

"Popcorn" and "Autobahn," two records that pushed listeners' tolerance for open-format radio to the breaking point, weren't fair demonstrations of the synthesizer's potential. Stevie Wonder's one-man-band hits showed the new technology could contribute to, even spearhead, biting grooves and soulful balladry. Ex–Roxy Musician Brian Eno used synthesizers and tape loops for pop song construction *(Another Green World)* and early new age experiments *(Discreet Music)*. Weather Report keyboardist Joe Zawinul coaxed a rainbow of colors from his arsenal of gear on fusion albums like *Heavy Weather* and *Mr. Gone*.

The Edgar Winter Group's "Frankenstein," named for the many cuts it received when it was reduced from a lengthy band feature to a 3:28 single, featured bubbling synth effects that added a B-movie laboratory atmosphere to Ronnie Montrose's monster guitar work. "Frankenstein" was jazz rock masquerading as hard rock; its complex riffing and time changes required virtuosity well beyond the range of most muscle bands. Today's fans, whose standards have been systematically lowered by hard rock's offspring, grunge and metal, might be shocked to learn that a bona fide rock classic like "Frankenstein" could feature substantial melody and a saxophone in its quest for total heavy-osity. Three Edgar Winter Group graduates went on to solo success: Montrose's eponymous rock quartet struck platinum with its 1973 debut; Dan Hartman reinvented himself as a pop star with "I Can Dream About You" (1984), and Rick Derringer's smash album *All American Boy* (1973) contained his signature tune, "Rock and Roll, Hoochie Koo." (Derringer was also a top-flight session guitarist, contributing to Steely Dan's *Katy Lied* LP, among many others.)

The advent of synth-pop didn't completely exclude traditional instruments from the charts. Marvin Hamlisch's piano adaptation of a seventy-one-year-old ragtime classic called "The Entertainer" (for George Roy Hill's hit movie *The Sting*) was improbable Top 5 company for Paul McCartney, the Jackson 5, and the Stylistics, but don't tell that to the millions of piano students who labored over every note. To this day, Hamlisch, who also contributed to Woody Allen's *Bananas* and Sydney Pollack's *The Way We Were* and won the Pulitzer Prize for the Broadway musical *A Chorus Line*, is remembered by many late boomers as the father of the modern piano lesson. (Banjo players were required to learn "Dueling Banjos," the 1973 remake of a 1955 hillbilly romp that became a Number 2 hit for Eric Weissberg & Steve Mandell and the signature tune of hyperextended families everywhere when it was featured in the harrowing Burt Reynolds buddy-film-gone-awry *Deliverance*; fledgling flautists were stuck with "The Hustle"; trumpet players cut their chops on Maynard Ferguson licks.)

R & B artists were responsible for the best work in many of the Watergate years' musical sub-genres, and the instrumental category was no exception. Subsonic luuuv guru Barry White had written "Love's Theme" as an overture to Love Unlimited's debut album, but club support of the track soon necessitated a full album project for the Love Unlimited Orchestra. Originally a kind of symphonic Pips for the female trio, the White-directed group-within-a-group was ultimately credited with the Number 1 single. It was easier to imagine White reclining in an Orgasmatron (from Woody Allen's *Sleeper*) than conducting a forty-piece studio orchestra, but "Love's Theme" was proof he was more than the sum of his part. In fact, if there's one instrumental hit that sounds like the seventies (no one actually presumed to write "Theme from the Seventies," so we'll have to choose one), it's "Love's Theme," with its tender refrain, rhythmic guitar interplay, swooping French horn line, and carefully planned peaks and valleys. During the opening moments of the record, as the strings fall all over themselves trying to be the first to reach that exultant nineteen-second high A, the decade's eager-to-please spirit shines through.

Former Motown session guitarist Dennis Coffey (and his Detroit Guitar Band) took full advantage of the "What's your sign?" craze—the phrase was on the lips of every bar-hopping Mr. Goodbar in the free world—by naming his new cycle of instrumental R&B jams after the signs of the zodiac. "Scorpio" (Coffey's own sign), with its jagged, sheet-metal guitar riff, was the most popular, at Number 6, followed by "Taurus" (Number 18). Drummer Paul Humphrey, yet another studio pro from Detroit, scored with "Cool Aid."

Like a steaming plateful of haggis and chitlins, the Scottish soul of the Average White Band—singer Bonnie Bramlett is credited with suggesting the band's ironic monicker—invaded North America in late 1974. AWB's "Pick Up the Pieces," a killer funk-disco-soul-jazz-pop-rock track that crossed more musical lines than the Nixon administration did ethical, went to #1 and quickly became a staple for any bar band with a sax player.

More than any other musical trend, the wave of instrumental hits that mounted the charts during the first half of the seventies epitomized the era's eclectic spirit. From the zany glam pop of Gary Glitter's future sports anthem "Rock and Roll" to the hard funk of the Commodores' onomatopoeic "Machine Gun," the sheer number of new wordless hits suggested a retreat from the proselytizing lyrics of the late sixties. "Love's Theme," "Outa-Space," "Rock and Roll," and "Pick Up the Pieces" were unapologetically apolitical; they were updates of vintage party records like "Sleep Walk" (1959), "Telstar" (1962), "Wipe Out" (1963), and "Yakety Sax" (1963).

Pop for pop's sake may have seemed a dubious philosophy with the sweet, serious stink of Woodstock still in the air, but mainstream rock's responses to earthly crises like Watergate and the ecology were sounding altogether too pat. A little trip to "Outa-Space" was probably in order. Truth was, the seventies' new instrumentalists were more interested in changing a guitar string than the world.

PLAY MISTY FOR ME

Jazz Pop

"Go Down Gamblin' " • Blood, Sweat & Tears (Columbia, 1971)
"One Fine Morning" • Lighthouse (Evolution, 1971)
"Saturday in the Park" • Chicago (Columbia, 1972)
"You're Still a Young Man" • Tower of Power (Warner, 1972)
"Reeling in the Years" • Steely Dan (ABC, 1973)
"Also Sprach Zarathustra (2001)" • Deodato (CTI, 1973)
"Midnight at the Oasis" • Maria Muldaur (Reprise, 1974)
"People Gotta Move" • Gino Vannelli (A&M, 1974)
"Chameleon" • Herbie Hancock (Columbia, 1974)
"Operator" • The Manhattan Transfer (Atlantic, 1975)

The seventies produced many unlikely combinations: cattle and buffalo ("beefalo"); gas and alcohol ("gasohol"); ice cream and *Apollo 13* (Baskin-Robbins's "Lunar Cheescake"). But the decade's strangest bedfellows may have been the musical genres of jazz and rock.

To begin with, the arguments against jazz rock seemed pretty sound. Jazz was serious. Rock was fun. Jazz was art. Rock was entertainment. Jazz was cerebral. Rock was visceral. Moreover, to many, jazz represented the traditional musical values that rock was supposed to have replaced.

On the other side, there was the fact that proven innovator Miles Davis, who had been a key player in the bebop revolution of the mid-1940s and had invented modal jazz in 1959, had also kicked off jazz rock with his electric-jam album *Bitches Brew* in 1969. Davis's instinct for the next wave was the stuff of legend; if he was doing it, it was worth doing.

In the wake of *Bitches Brew,* "fusion" acts like Return to Forever, Weather Report, and Herbie Hancock (many featuring Davis alumni) began to achieve crossover success with groove-driven, improvisa-

```
┌─────────────────────────────────┐
│   BOX      ROW      SEAT         │
│                                 │
│   17       F        5           │
│   E A S T                       │
│   Retain Stub -- Good Only      │
│  No Exchange — No Refund        │
│                                 │
│  MON.    OCT. 31                │
│  8:00 P.M.                      │
│                                 │
│   Davis Printing Limited        │
│                                 │
│      CHICAGO                    │
│  PRICE-7.73+RST .77-$8.50       │
│                                 │
│  ADMIT ONE. Entrance by Main    │
│  Door or by Church Street Door. │
│                                 │
│  Maple Leaf Gardens             │
│       LIMITED                   │
│    CONDITION OF SALE            │
│  Upon refunding the purchase    │
│                       may       │
└─────────────────────────────────┘
```

tional material. Hancock, in particular, seemed to have the commercial touch, pulling a successful single ("Chameleon") from his now-platinum *Headhunters* album. By 1975, jazz-related instrumental artists could claim a handful of other minor hits like the Crusaders' "Put It Where You Want It," Quincy Jones's "Money Runner," Bob James's "Feel Like Makin' Love," Chuck Mangione's "Chase the Clouds Away," the Brecker Brothers' "Sneakin' Up Behind You," and one bona fide smash, Brazilian arranger Eumir Deodato's supremely funky adaptation of Richard Strauss's *Also Sprach Zarathustra* (1973). These records represented a new wrinkle in the fabric of pop in that they fell outside the usual territory of instrumental hits (surf music, movie themes, R&B riffs).

Jazz pop, the mellower younger brother of jazz rock, traces its lineage not to Miles Davis, but to Blood, Sweat & Tears and Chicago. These two large, brass-driven outfits, both Columbia signings from the Clive Davis era, combined scaled-down big-band arrangements and conventional pop melodies with a groovy, up-to-the-minute lyrical bent.

Chicago would prove to be jazz pop's longest-running success story, racking up twenty-two Top 40 hits during the seventies (second only to Elton John and Paul McCartney). Its signature sound, an impossibly crisp three-horn unison with James Pankow's trombone at its center, punctuated songs whose easy charm belied their complex structures. "Saturday in the Park" changes key eleven times in under four minutes, skittering from a rock feel to a shuffle then back again, yet comes off as downright relaxing. Later feel-good hits like "Feelin' Stronger Every Day," "Call On Me," and "Old Days" were similarly ambitious—and effective.

Overnight, brass instruments regained the cachet they had lost in the mid-fifties. While rock remained guitar-dominated (emptying your spit valve will never be as cool as messing with your wah-wah pedal) there was a sudden proliferation of Chicago wannabes. Bill Chase, a blazing lead trumpeter who had interned with Woody Herman and Stan Kenton, scored in 1971 with "Get It On," a furiously paced, wad-blowing extravaganza whose unrelenting energy lent credibility to its sexual braggadaccio. (Chase, a Best New Artist Grammy nominee for 1971, never got to fully explore his new direction, as he and three members of his band were killed in a plane crash in 1974.)

Tower of Power, saxophonist Emilio Castillo's Oakland-based funk group, held down the R&B end of the jazz pop spectrum for most of the decade. The majestic ballad "You're Still a Young Man" became its signature tune, but later hits like "Down to the Nightclub" and "What Is Hip?" were more typical of the T.O.P. precision-funk aesthetic. The band's renowned horn section was occasionally farmed out to high-profile clients.

The Canadian entry in the horn-band sweepstakes was Lighthouse, a Chicago-size ensemble augmented by two full-time string players. Lead singer Bob McBride sounded a lot like David Clayton-Thomas, which invited comparisons to Blood, Sweat & Tears. The group's Stateside hits included "Sunny Days" and "Pretty Lady," but Lighthouse is best remembered for "One Fine Morning" (1971), a soaring, uptempo workout driven by—of all things—a guitar riff.

A jazz flavor pervaded many other early-seventies records. The Manhattan Transfer revived the jazz vocal quartet tradition, starting with "Operator." Seals & Crofts used a swing feel on "Diamond Girl." Carole King enlisted top reedman Tom Scott for "Jazzman." Bette Midler camped up the Andrews Sisters' classic "Boogie Woogie Bugle Boy" for her Grammy-winning 1973 debut album. As often as not, jazz cropped up in a singer's phrasing, as with Maria Muldaur's sultry "Midnight at the Oasis," Joni Mitchell's acrobatic "Help Me," Natalie Cole's full-tilt "This Will Be," and Minnie Riperton's dreamy, proto-Mariah "Lovin' You."

Through much of this, the early twentieth century's jazz greats endured. Duke Ellington, for one, lived until 1974, which means it's at least possible that he heard Steely Dan, his musical grandchildren. What the world's greatest jazz composer would have thought of wiseass Dan songwriters Donald Fagen and Walter Becker is hard to guess, but we know the two were influenced by Ellington and other jazzmen like Miles Davis, Sonny Rollins, Wynton Kelly, Clifford Brown, and Bill Evans.

While Steely Dan's dark lyrical themes made them a natural for the burgeoning FM rock market, their melodic chops also ensured a handful of hit singles. "Do It Again," the first of these, used a hypnotic Latin groove to introduce now-familiar Steely Dan themes like violent revenge and romantic betrayal. The followup, "Reeling in the Years", may have been the freshest-sounding record of the era. Fagen's joyously sneering vocal, the track's freewheeling shuffle, and Elliott Randall's one-for-the-ages guitar solo charted lower than later smashes like "Rikki Don't Lose That Number," but amounted to jazz pop's first masterpiece.

If slick improvisations, war-era song structures, and vintage jazz harmony seemed like a strange recipe for a rock band, that was fine with Fagen and Becker. They were overtly hostile to the trappings of rock stardom, expressing in interviews their disdain for hippie culture, large-scale touring, and image-driven behavior in general. To date, their faces have never appeared on the front of a Steely Dan album cover. They flaunted their literary credentials, not least by naming their band after a sex toy in the William Burroughs novel

Naked Lunch. And in 1973, the year the American League adopted the designated hitter rule, Steely Dan began using what would become a long line of studio DHs in lieu of a steady rhythm section.

All of this left Fagen and Becker free to concentrate on their harmonically intricate, pointillist pop tunes. They became full-time studio hounds in the age of quad, answering only to themselves (and like-minded producer Gary Katz) and frequently running up huge production bills in the process. Oddly, the results were anything but claustrophobic—the great irony of these obsessively crafted records is that often they gave the feeling of release and spontaneity.

Steely Dan's legacy is hard to locate in these "alternative" music nineties ("alternative-*to*-music" would be a better phrase), but the duo undeniably expanded the palette of subjects available to pop songwriters—anybody else out there release a single about safe sex in 1976 ("The Fez")?—and paved the way for nonrock rock hits like Joni Mitchell's "Free Man in Paris," Gino Vannelli's "People Gotta Move," and Ace's "How Long." Compare the guitar solo in the latter to the one in "Do It Again" for eye-popping proof.

Louis Jordan, Chuck Berry, and most of the progenitors of rock and roll could swing like mad. But the artists who put jazz elements (like swing) back into the rock mainstream in the early seventies were and are the subjects of frequent critical derision. *Creem* editor Lester Bangs wrote at the time that Chicago's horn arrangements sounded "like Stan Kenton charts played backwards," and he didn't mean it as a compliment. In most rock histories, Steely Dan and their ilk represent not innovation but soulless complacency, the kind punk rock would shatter a few years later.

It's no coincidence that the term "laid-back" officially entered the English language in 1974, around the time jazz pop was peaking. Radio- and Grammy-friendly, the music followed a kinder, gentler muse and lacked rock's anger and brashness, ingredients essential for lasting acclaim. Top 40 auteurs Steely Dan, who by mid-decade still had their best work ahead of them, were beneficiaries of an open-door policy at radio stations that has long since disappeared. As Fagen and Becker put it in the song "Pretzel Logic": "Those days are gone forever / Over a long time ago."

ART ATTACK
Progressive Rock

"**Lucky Man**" • Emerson, Lake & Palmer (Cotillion, 1971)
"**Living in the Past**" • Jethro Tull (Chrysalis, 1972)
"**Roundabout**" • Yes (Atlantic, 1972)
"**Nights in White Satin**" • The Moody Blues (Deram, 1972)
"**Money**" • Pink Floyd (Harvest, 1973)
"**Evil Woman**" • Electric Light Orchestra (United Artists, 1975)
"**Fame**" • David Bowie (RCA, 1975)
"**Killer Queen**" • Queen (Elektra, 1975)
"**Love Is the Drug**" • Roxy Music (Atco, 1975)
"**Bloody Well Right**" • Supertramp (A&M, 1975)

lassical music and rock and roll make as odd a couple as Felix Unger and Oscar Madison. One is meticulous and compulsively structured; the other is unkempt and imprecise. One attends Lincoln Center in the company of subscribers; the other attends Madison Square Garden in the company of imbibers. And yet like Neil Simon's unlikely buddies, classical and rock music did live together, for a time, in the same apartment.

Progressive rock began in the late sixties, soon after the string section was hired for "Eleanor Rigby," and thrived throughout the seventies. The new genre encouraged both crap-meisters and adventuresome originals to take advantage of the long-playing field that FM stations, rock critics, record labels, and sophomoric teenagers gave them. Most of what resulted was confined to the new world of "album rock," but enough of it found its way to the Top 40 to warrant discussion here.

Not surprisingly, the most pretentious of these bands came off best on their single releases. The 45's confines kept the nonsense to a minimum and allowed Yes, for example, the opportunity to illustrate that when their energies were channeled (and their opera

edited), they could actually pump out some memorable music. Never hearing "Roundabout" again would be no cruel punishment, but its circular keyboard riff, unfettered Jon Anderson vocal, and straight-ahead rock feel combined to make Yes sound almost spontaneous—a true rarity. As time steadily erodes their place in pop history, Yes may eventually be remembered best for those Roger Dean album covers. (Dean's nifty "Yes" logo and sci-fi landscapes dripping with color date-stamp the band as a post-psychedelia phenomenon, but as album covers went, they were pretty cool.)

All the effort being expended on making "important" music led some prog-rockers to the conclusion that serious music had to be glum. Living up to their name, the Moody Blues went to Number 2 in 1972 with "Nights in White Satin," a hollow ballad that was a belated release from their 1968 magnum dopus *Days of Future Passed*. The first word in the song's title referred to night-time, but

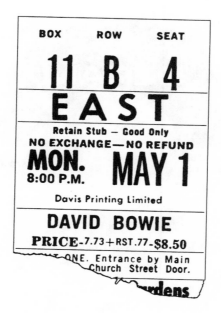

BOX   ROW   SEAT

11 B 4

E A S T

Retain Stub — Good Only
NO EXCHANGE—NO REFUND
MON. 8:00 P.M. **MAY 1**

Davis Printing Limited

DAVID BOWIE

PRICE-7.73+RST.77-**$8.50**

ONE. Entrance by Main Church Street Door.

rdens

if you didn't see it in print, the title evoked images of knights standing around in billowy white satin, swords at the ready. That interpretation didn't make much literal sense, but progressive rock was known to dabble in dungeons, dragons, castles, kings, and God-knows-what-all, so a knight in white satin didn't seem especially unusual. Like Yes, the Moody Blues were better off when held in check by more obvious attempts at hitmaking. "The Story in Your Eyes" (1971), for example, sported an ambitious, skittering melody and added the concept of "hook" to the band's musical vocabulary.

(Keith) Emerson, (Greg) Lake, and (Carl) Palmer were hookless, by and large; "Lucky Man" (Number 48, 1971) and "From the Beginning" (Number 39, 1972) were their only "hits." Like most in the genre, though, these guys were more into writing albums than songs, and ELP fans probably think of *Works,* a two-record set that allowed each band member a side of his own, as their greatest hit. Led by Keith Emerson's virtuoso keyboard work, the band did manage on occasion to stretch rock in some new and lasting ways.

Jethro Tull, named after an eighteenth-century agriculturist (not

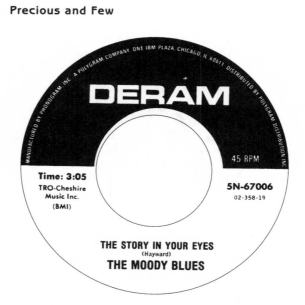

Jethro from *The Beverly Hillbillies*, as it turns out), peppered over-ambitious concept albums like *A Passion Play, Thick as a Brick,* and *Aqualung* with some interesting songwriting, but finding it meant a lot of filler-digging. With a sound grounded in traditional folk and hard rock, blowhard flautist and lead singer Ian Anderson flouted convention, establishing for his silver "third arm" the status that Hendrix, Clapton, and Beck had found for their guitars (Lester Bangs called Anderson "the Eric Clapton of wind"). Now and then, his band descended from its high-*flutin'* conceptual perch with a single or two; "Living in the Past" (1972) and "Bungle in the Jungle" (1974) both flirted with the Top 10. But Anderson's grand gestures were better suited to the LP.

Queen and the Electric Light Orchestra found their place in the prog-rock firmament with a sort of progressive pop that allowed them full access to the charts. The late glam rocker Freddie Mercury fronted Queen, bringing an operatic sensibility to the band's melodic fare. The heavily multitracked "Killer Queen" (1975) was only a prelude to later Queen smashes like "Bohemian Rhapsody" (1976) and "We Are the Champions" (1977). ELO began their chart run with "Can't Get It Out of My Head" and Ee-"Evil Woman" (both 1975), two songs typical of the band's claustrophobic, pseudo-symphonic music. Later, ELOverlord Jeff Lynne would put his sonic stamp on records by the Traveling Wilburys (1988), Tom Petty (1989), and the Beatles (1995).

Critic Dave Marsh wrote that progressive rock's "would-be classicists" (Procol Harum recorded a live album with the Edmonton Symphony Orchestra in 1971) "enjoyed the sniffs of their own nattily arranged album-length farts." If that sweeping swipe is easy to accept in connection with Yes or Jethro Tull, it's way wide of the mark for bands like Pink Floyd (named after Georgia bluesmen Pink Anderson and Floyd Council) and Supertramp (named after a 1938 novel called *The Autobiography of a Supertramp*), who stuck closer to their rock roots and avoided affectation in favor of thoughtful, organic detail. When it worked, as it usually did in the case of these two bands, progressive rock challenged shrinking attention spans and rewarded repeated listenings.

And repeated buyings; Pink Floyd's *Dark Side of the Moon* album, for example, stayed on *Billboard*'s album chart for an incredible fifteen and a half *years* (by far the longest stay for any record on any chart) with the help of only one Top 40 single. That song, "Money" (1973), with its cash register percussion track, didn't *feel* like a single, though; it worked best within *Dark Side*'s broader context. By the time of their follow-up album, 1976's *Wish You Were Here,* Pink Floyd was more or less at the creative mercy of bassist-vocalist Roger Waters. Lucky for them. Pre-Waters Floyd is unessential, while post-Waters Floyd is, as real fans know, not actually Floyd—just a few blokes imitating their former selves with pseudo-Waters lyrics and a spectacular light show. Minus Waters's darkly literate ruminations on the British class system, the horrors of war, and the fickle world of rock celebrity, Pink Floyd is a clone of itself.

Supertramp's *Crime of the Century* (1974) did better in the U.K. and Canada than it did in the U.S.—stateside success was still five years away. But *Crime*'s fully explored arrangements, Ken Scott's supernaturally crisp production, Richard Davies's percussive Wurlitzer playing, and the Lennon/McCartney-style interplay between Davies and Roger Hodgson became the band's hallmarks. While toying with an expanded palette, Supertramp's music felt firmly connected to pop music tradition; note the Motown-esque handclaps and the soulful sax that punctuated the band's first Top 40 hit, the heavy and unmistakably British "Bloody Well Right" ("Quoite roit!"). In addition to typical progressive rock themes ("School," "Bloody Well Right," and "Hide in Your Shell" are explorations of Roger Waters–like territory), the band celebrated melody (just try *not* singing along to "Dreamer," which became a Number 15 single six years after *Crime*'s release).

Some of progressive rock's finest moments could be found in the early-seventies work of former adman David Bowie, who changed his surname from Jones because Davy Jones of the Monkees beat him to a career (as if anyone could confuse squeaky-clean Davy with cross-dressing David, included on Mr. Blackwell's Worst-Dressed List in 1974 and described as "a cross between Joan Crawford and Marlene Dietrich"). Bowie's hits were usually more stylish than substantial ("Fame" and "Golden Years"), although on "Young Americans," which cracked the Top 30 in 1975, he managed one of rock's all-time style-*and*-substance, full-steam-ahead vocal rants. Albums like *Hunky Dory* (1971), *The Rise and Fall of Ziggy Stardust and the Spiders from Mars* (1972), and the apocalyptic *Diamond Dogs* (1974) are powerful reminders that long before his hollowed-out eighties personae and his nineties Tin Machine experiment, Bowie was first and foremost a songwriter.

More than any other pop music form, progressive rock emphasized the concert, making full use of props, projections and far-out new instrumentation (double-necked guitars, walls of synthesizers— that sort of thing). The bands brought new levels of theatricality to the live ritual: Pink Floyd inflated a giant pig during the *Animals* tour; Bowie featured a set straight out of expressionist cinema on the *Diamond Dogs* tour; Supertramp perfected rear projection; and Genesis spotlighted costumed chameleon Peter Gabriel playing a host of bizarre characters (when he left in 1975, the band turned to laser lighting). No doubt, these are the theatrics Rob Reiner had in mind when he directed his eighties mock-umentary *This Is Spinal Tap,* featuring an earnest hard rock band whose concerts featured giant pods and a miniature Stonehenge prop (the result of faulty specs scribbled on a napkin). Spinal Tap's inability to keep a drummer spoofed legendary rock deaths, but also hinted at progressive rock's tendency toward lineup changes. Yes has changed its personnel more than twenty times since 1971, hosting prog-rock all-stars like Rick Wakeman, Bill Bruford, and Steve Howe.

In addition to the bands already mentioned, Gentle Giant, Triumvirat, Nektar, Hawkwind, Roxy Music, the Tubes, and Frank Zappa enjoyed a wide-open window of opportunity in the seventies, thanks largely to the advent of FM rock radio, which started when San Francisco deejay Tom Donahue bought failing station KMPX and began featuring tapes, test pressings, and "album cuts." By the time progressive rock fell out of vogue, Igor Stravinsky had died (of embarrassment?) in 1971, and innovators like Brian Eno, David Bowie, and Peter Gabriel had moved on to other styles, leaving behind a strange collection of hits and near hits that only hinted at the pomposity that had been.

GOD HELP US
Religious Pop

"Put Your Hand in the Hand" • Ocean (Kama Sutra, 1971)
"Mighty Clouds of Joy" • B. J. Thomas (Scepter, 1971)
"Superstar" • Murray Head and the Trinidad Singers (Decca, 1971)
"I Don't Know How to Love Him" • Helen Reddy (Capitol, 1971)
"Everything's Alright" • Yvonne Elliman (Decca, 1971)
"I'll Take You There" • The Staple Singers (Stax, 1972)
"Amazing Grace" • The Royal Scots Dragoon Guards (RCA, 1972)
"Day by Day" • Godspell (Bell, 1972)
"Speak to the Sky" • Rick Springfield (Capitol, 1972)
"The Lord's Prayer" • Sister Janet Mead (A&M, 1974)

Long before Jimmy Swaggart took to weeping in public, long before Jim Bakker met Jessica Hahn, long before Oral Roberts claimed God was holding him for ransom, there was the "plastic gospel" of the early seventies.

Andrew Lloyd Webber and Tim Rice dragged Christianity into the pop-culture arena in 1970. Their blockbuster rock opera *Jesus Christ Superstar* spawned multiple hit singles and earned Grammy nominations for Album of the Year in both 1971 and 1972—for the London and Broadway casts, respectively. Suddenly, the Savior was everywhere: on T-shirts, on black-light posters, on drug paraphernalia, but mostly, on the radio. In 1973, a *Top Hits* survey showed pop songs about religion increasing from a one percent share in the mid-to-late sixties to a 17 percent share in the first three years of the seventies.

It's tempting to attribute this increase to "Jesus freaks," the counterculture Christians who attracted much media attention (including a *Time* cover) in those days. But the reality is more complex; religious pop came from all walks of life. The artists included an Australian nun (Sister Janet Mead), a Scottish military ensemble (the

Royal Scots Dragoon Guards), another Broadway musical cast *(God-spell),* a high school dance band (Ocean), and an ex-Beatle (George Harrison). Together they challenged the secular bent of most rock-era popular music and, in the process, often made the sublime ridiculous.

Sister Janet Mead was already famous for her "rock masses" in Australia when her toe-tapping version of the Lord's Prayer became an international hit in 1974. Mead was following in the footsteps of Sister Luc-Gabrielle (the Singing Nun, whose "Dominique" was America's favorite song for four weeks in 1963), *The Sound of Music,* and the TV series *The Flying Nun* (starring Sally Field) in debunking the traditional image of nuns. But "The Lord's Prayer" was a singular achievement. It may have been the most unintentionally weird record of the seventies.

Think back: Mead's colorless vocal floats above a limp rhythm track so devoid of energy that the robotic prayers that began each day in Catholic grammar schools seem almost funky by comparison. So what was "The Lord's Prayer" doing at Number 4 on the *Billboard* chart? Well, for starters, it had built-in sing-along potential—middle America already knew the words. It also provided an antidote to the "evil" implications of "Tubular Bells," Mike Oldfield's haunting theme from *The Exorcist,* which was on the charts at the same time.

Mostly, "The Lord's Prayer" was there because radio had yet to be fully "formatted." Formatting is the practice that would, by the mid-eighties, fragment non-talk radio into CHR (Contemporary Hit Radio), AOR (Album-Oriented Rock), AC (Adult Contemporary), and a host of other stiflingly narrow classifications. Futurist Alvin Toffler had anticipated the trend in his runaway 1970 best-seller *Future Shock,* positing a world in which groups such as doctors, lawyers, and accountants would have their own radio networks. But in 1974, with *Future Shock* in its umpteenth printing, radio was still open to anomalies like "The Lord's Prayer." The main question on a programmer's mind as he auditioned a new release was not "Does this suit our format?" but "Is this interesting?" Certainly, Sister Janet Mead was interesting. She was the very model of a one-hit wonder—an outsider to the American star system who momentarily tapped into the strange personality of her time.

If the commercial success of "The Lord's Prayer" seemed far-fetched, it was only the icing on the cake. Since 1971, Top 40 berths had been occupied by the pre-born-again B. J. Thomas's "Mighty Clouds of Joy" (the first Vegas gospel tune), the Royal Scots Dragoon Guards' "Amazing Grace" (the first bagpipe "Cross"-over hit) and Ocean's "Put Your Hand in the Hand" (the musical equivalent of cheery door-to-door pamphleteers). Ocean keyboard player Greg Brown has said of the band's hit song (which went to Number 1 in his native Canada), "I wouldn't say that we felt strongly about the religious angle."

Putting aside, for the moment, the question of what other angle there could possibly be on a song that uses specific biblical references to recruit new followers of Jesus Christ, the implication is that the band's apparent Christian convictions were only a commercial convenience. This is surprising only if you're naive enough to think that message is anything more than peripheral to Top 40 radio. Religion was a hot topic for singles in the early seventies in the same way the Twist was in the early sixties. Many religious hits had as much to do with genuine faith as the ubiquitous Happy Face button had to do with genuine happiness.

Though *Jesus Christ Superstar* had been a hit in London in 1970, it wasn't until the next year that Murray Head, Yvonne Elliman, and Helen Reddy brought three of its songs to the U.S. charts. Head's "Superstar" maintained the energy of the original cast recording and then some, Elliman's "Everything's Alright" was as serene as anything in 5/4 time could ever be, and Reddy's "I Don't Know How to Love Him" was a middle-of-the-road meditation on flesh versus spirit. A medley from the show, by the Assembled Multitude, also cracked the charts briefly in 1971.

In its best moments, *Superstar* was a minor revelation, a rethinking of the New Testament for the modern world; in its worst it was an exercise in studied grooviness: the Easter-a-Go-Go. Of course, in the early seventies it was hard to go wrong with a story of long-haired, anti-establishment types living communally and doing a lot of soul-searching—film critic Pauline Kael wrote that *Superstar* portrayed Jesus Christ "as a misunderstood kid"—but the show's strange combination of fuzz guitar and fuzzy theology has not withstood the test of time especially well.

Nevertheless, *Superstar* succeeded in both its Broadway and Hollywood incarnations. The American response to it was Stephen Schwartz's *Godspell*, a sort of heavenly *Hair* in which Jesus sported clown makeup and a Superman T-shirt. Its Grammy-winning soundtrack was represented on the charts by "Day by Day," whose three prayers were repeated in various tempi and keys until the tambourine level on the single became so oppressive that a fourth prayer was added to the list: Oh, God, please let this record fade. Other *Superstar* contemporaries included the Hollies ("He Ain't Heavy, He's My Brother"), Glen Campbell ("I Knew Jesus [Before He Was a Star]"), Judy Collins ("Amazing Grace"), Sweathog ("Hallelujah") and, most ominously, Curtis Mayfield ("[Don't Worry] If There's a Hell Below We're All Going to Go").

Some artists ascribed an almost religious significance to music itself. Songs like the Doobie Brothers' "Listen to the Music," Gallery's "I Believe in Music," Kiki Dee's "I've Got the Music in Me," the O'Jays' "I Love Music," and Dobie Gray's "Drift Away" all treated music as a healing force, a protector and source of bliss.

The Beatles began an alternate stream of pop spirituality in 1967 when they visited the Maharishi Mahesh Yogi in India for a spiritual retreat. Following the media blitz that accompanied the pilgrimage, accoutrements of Eastern mysticism—incense, meditation how-to books, sitar music—became hip talismans for the middle class, and George Harrison's "My Sweet Lord," surely the climax of the trend, spent a full month at Number 1 in 1970–71. Fitting that in a world of religion-for-sale, Harrison's musical inspiration for his hymn to Krishna proved to be less than divine: He was convicted in 1976 of plagiarizing the Chiffons' lightweight girl-group classic "He's So Fine." (Harrison's nonmusical good works, like his spearheading of the 1971 Concert for Bangladesh, proved more worthwhile.)

Pop's divine phase produced exactly one masterpiece: the Staple Singers' "I'll Take You There." The song, a five-minute jam that used call-and-response gospel vocals but avoided preachy exhortation, was from the Al Bell–produced Stax album *Be Altitude: Respect*

Yourself. With three simple ingredients (Mavis Staples's gutsy leads, the repeated title line, and a downright hypnotic two-bar vamp) it put a slice of real Memphis R&B into the mainstream at a time when the designation "black music" included Sammy Davis, Jr.'s "Candy Man." (The *Willy Wonka and the Chocolate Factory* theme song knocked "I'll Take You There" out of the Number 1 spot in June 1972.)

Alas, as the seventies wore on, more and more artists forsook the high road in favor of the disco inferno. Musical theater embraced kitsch *(Grease, The Rocky Horror Picture Show),* and pop's spiritual ambitions began to fade as songwriters turned their attention back to earthly matters like sex, dancing, and sex. Soap-opera star Rick Springfield, whose 1972 hit "Speak to the Sky" urged listeners to pray, would be heard nine years later lusting after "Jessie's Girl." For whatever reason—the death of Mahalia Jackson? the end of the Jesus Movement? Reverend Sun Myung Moon?—Top 40's holy heyday was short-lived.

SOCIALIST RADIO
Canadian Pop

"Sweet City Woman" • The Stampeders (Bell, 1971)
"Rain Dance" • The Guess Who (RCA, 1971)
"Absolutely Right" • Five Man Electrical Band (Lionel, 1971)
"You Could Have Been a Lady" • April Wine (Big Tree, 1972)
"Painted Ladies" • Ian Thomas (Janus, 1973)
"Wildflower" • Skylark (Capitol, 1973)
"Raised on Robbery" • Joni Mitchell (Asylum, 1974)
"Takin' Care of Business" • Bachman-Turner Overdrive (Mercury, 1974)
"Brother and Me" • Fludd (Attic, 1974)
"Million Dollar Weekend" • Crowbar (Epic, 1974)

Leonard Cohen, in accepting his trophy for Male Vocalist of the Year at the 1993 Juno Awards (the Canadian equivalent of the Grammys), remarked that only in Canada could he get an award for his singing. The joke smacked not of ingratitude, but of truth. Cohen is more poet than singer; his vocal range is negligible (the "Theme from *Jaws*" would be a stretch), and his low-key delivery makes Leon Redbone sound hyperactive. The award had more to do with Cohen's living-legend status than his recent work. He had not made anything resembling a pop record in the thirty-year history of the Junos, but the voters figured it was time he had something for his mantel.

In the early seventies, Cohen was part of an elite corps of Canadian songwriters that included Joni Mitchell, Neil Young, Gordon Lightfoot, Ian & Sylvia Tyson, Bruce Cockburn, Murray McLauchlan, Buffy Sainte-Marie, Kate & Anna McGarrigle, and the Band's Robbie Robertson. In addition to their own recordings, these writers supplied hits for U.S. counterparts like Crosby, Stills, Nash & Young, Judy Collins, Joan Baez, Tom Rush, Peter, Paul & Mary, Linda Ronstadt, and Glen Campbell. Canada might have been playing catch-up in the rock-and-roll department, but it was a veritable breeding ground for folkies.

Exactly why is debatable. It may have been the relative absence of black culture in Canada, the lingering influence of British and Celtic traditions, or the predominance of wilderness over cities. Critic Wilder Penfield III writes, "In Canada, where the distances between paying gigs were so great, the survivors were . . . solo, mobile, flexible, affordable performers"—meaning singer-songwriters whose equipment could fit into a cardboard guitar case.

Ironic, then, that so many of Canada's folkies had to set up shop south of the border before anything big happened. The McGarrigles went to New York separately; Joni Mitchell went to New York via Detroit; Neil Young went to L.A. in a hearse (seriously). Much of their initial credibility came from the above-mentioned American covers.

The Canuck singer-songwriter brigade was responsible for some of the most influential and commercially successful music of the decade. Joni Mitchell's brilliant *Court and Spark,* the favorite of the 1974 *Village Voice* Critics' Poll and a Number 2 *Billboard* album, spawned three hit singles ("Help Me," "Free Man in Paris," and "Raised on Robbery") and made a lasting impression on future stars from Rickie Lee Jones to Prince. And 1972's *Harvest,* the quintessential "soft" Neil Young album and the home of Young's best-known song, "Heart of Gold," still receives multiplatinum recertification every so often. Gordon Lightfoot's "Sundown," from the album of the same name, was an unplugged miracle during disco's first blush and one of five *Billboard* Number 1s by Canadians in 1974.

The other '74 chart-toppers—Terry Jacks's "Seasons in the Sun," Paul Anka's "(You're) Having My Baby," Andy Kim's "Rock Me Gently," and Bachman-Turner Overdrive's "You Ain't Seen Nothing Yet"—were all by artists whose careers were well under way when the "Canadian content" era began in 1971. Jacks had been half of the Poppy Family ("Which Way You Goin' Billy?"), Anka had been mining gold since 1957's "Diana," Brill Building vet Andy Kim had written smashes for himself ("Baby, I Love You") and the Archies ("Sugar,

Sugar"), and Randy Bachman had co-written the Guess Who's biggest hits, including "American Woman," before founding BTO.

The year 1971 represents a dividing line in the history of Canadian pop. In January, a federal regulatory agency called the Canadian Radio Television and Telecommunications Commission (CRTC) imposed its "Canadian content ruling" on AM radio. The ruling stated, in essence, that at least 30 percent of the music broadcast by a station during peak hours should be "by a Canadian." It drew immediate criticism from radio-industry insiders who felt there was not enough Canadian pop out there to fulfill the CanCon quota, or, as the gripe went, how many times can you play "Snowbird" in a twenty-four-hour period?

At first, the nay-sayers were right. Canada had little in the way of musical infrastructure (recording studios, record labels, industry organizations) in place to keep up with the sudden demand for product. But soon enough, new studios, domestic signings by major labels, and the founding of the Canadian Academy of Recording Arts and Sciences improved things. Regionally known bands were able to take advantage of national airplay; careers were made overnight. For pop radio, new artists like Gino Vannelli, Lighthouse, Rush, April Wine, and the Stampeders provided alternatives to the venerable but overfamiliar Guess Who. In the space of a few years, Canada had grown a music industry (one that today includes Alanis Morissette, Crash Test Dummies, Bryan Adams, Sarah McLachlan, Shania Twain, and Barenaked Ladies). Accordingly, the trade mag *RPM Weekly* rechristened its annual Readers' Poll honors the "Juno Awards" after CRTC chairman and CanCon patron saint Pierre Juneau.

Juno results from 1971 to 1975 indicated that old habits die hard—Gordon Lightfoot and Anne Murray still dominated—but in the CanCon–assisted Top 40, the list of new stars was growing. Bachman-Turner Overdrive may have done little to combat America's image of Canadians as well-meaning clods, but it was hard to argue with their success. Including "You Ain't Seen Nothing Yet," they scored six Stateside hits, the most memorable being a classic rock lifestyle anthem called "Takin' Care of Business." But the *Billboard* chart performance of these songs (average position: 14) was nowhere near the Canadian (average position: 2), and several additional BTO singles, including "Quick Change Artist" and "Blue Collar," were hits in Canada only.

This was typical. The Stampeders, known in the United States for the banjo-driven hook-fest "Sweet City Woman" (a truly singular single), were something of a hit factory in their home and native land, where their singles ran the gamut from country ("Carry Me") to hard rock ("Wild Eyes"). April Wine's "You Could Have Been a Lady" (1972) stalled at Number 32 in *Billboard*, but opened the door for five Canada-only hits by the band before 1975 (including the definitive version of Elton John's "Bad Side of the Moon"). Terry Jacks, the death's-doorstep singer behind "Seasons in the Sun," notched domestic hits with wife Susan in the Poppy Family ("Where Evil Grows"), with the Hood (" 'Cause We're in Love"), and under his own name ("If You Go Away").

Other acts whose Canadian careers were more extensive than their U.S. stats might indicate included Ian Thomas ("Painted Ladies"), brother of *SCTV* star Dave Thomas; R. Dean Taylor ("Indiana Wants Me"), a former Motown staff writer; Skylark ("Wildflower"), producer David Foster's first bid for immortality; Lighthouse ("One Fine Morning"), the Canadian Chicago; Edward Bear ("Last Song"), the Canadian Bread; and Dan Hill ("Sometimes When We Touch"), the Canadian Lobo.

The Guess Who stepped up production in the face of this new competition, averaging an album every six months until their demise in late 1975. Singer Burton Cummings was on a roll, crafting pop-y song cycles that emphasized his piano playing and retro sensibilities. The best of these was 1972's *Rockin'*, but anything up to the overly ambitious *Power in the Music* (1975) was worth a listen. Hits like "Albert Flasher," "Rain Dance," "Star Baby," and "Dancin' Fool" outdistanced the rest of the Canuck pack (with the ironic exception of BTO) and kept the franchise alive and well in the United States. Only when Cummings got too specifically Canadian ("Running Back to Saskatoon") or too pretentious ("Glamour Boy") did new Guess Who releases miss the *Billboard* charts entirely.

Invisible not only in the United States but in much of anglophone

Canada were artists from the province of Quebec. Then as now, Quebec had an autonomous star system in which French-speaking artists could attain Beatles-like status without making concessions to English tastes, and bands like Beau Dommage, Offenbach, and especially Harmonium (all based in Montreal) were a far better argument for Quebec's distinctness than any of the political ones we've heard lately. Harmonium's orchestral folk-pop excursions, especially the 1976 double album *L'Heptade,* rank with the best progressive rock of the seventies.

Crossover was possible if you sang *en Anglais*—Michel Pagliaro's McCartney-esque "Lovin' You Ain't Easy" went Top 10 in Toronto and elsewhere—but most Quebec acts simply weren't interested. That cannot be said of Gino Vannelli, the Quebec-born singer-songwriter whose legendary self-confidence ("Yes I know / How much you love me," he sang on the 1975 single "Love Me Now") led to a direct signing with A&M, tours with Stevie Wonder and Gladys Knight, an appearance on *Soul Train,* and a few U.S. hits: "People Gotta Move," "I Just Wanna Stop," and "Living Inside Myself." Albums like *Powerful People* and *Storm at Sunup* were original as only the work of a megalomaniac can be. Vannelli, a self-styled pop-fusion auteur and purveyor of gorgeous, soul-searching erotica, had a fatal flaw: He overestimated the public's willingness to search for substance behind his hairy-chested, Don-Juan-de-Montreal image. For him, the price was high—to say he was reviewed unfavorably is like saying Fat Albert was prone to the occasional between-meal snack—but for the pop audience at large, the price was even higher. The best mid-seventies Vannelli is in a class with mid-seventies Elton John and Earth, Wind & Fire, but will likely never be widely recognized as anything more than semi-funky dross. Your loss.

One of the complaints regarding CanCon was its tendency to encourage knockoffs—that is, "This band is the Canadian equivalent of [insert name of famous international artist here]." "Painted Ladies" was the sound of Ian Thomas imitating America imitating Neil Young. "Heartbeat—It's a Lovebeat" by the DeFranco Family proved that Osmond-like behavior was not confined to Utah. Klaatu, the anonymous Beatles clone band named "hype of the year" by *Rolling Stone* in 1977, raised mimicry to high art on their debut album and the even better *Hope.*

Sometimes a Canadian artist would scoop the originator of a new song, using Canada's legislated airplay quota to outmuscle the legit version with a cover. As far as Canada's pop audience knew, Leo Sayer's "Long Tall Glasses (I Can Dance)" was by Shooter; Rhythm Heritage's "Theme from *S. W.A. T.* " was by the THP Orchestra; Todd Rundgren's "It Wouldn't Have Made Any Difference" was by Tom Middleton; and Chicago's "Anyway You Want" was by Charity Brown. CanCon fodder also crowded out the odd American release entirely, most often an R&B title like the Spinners' "Mighty Love" or the Stylistics' "Break Up to Make Up." Canada's own R&B scene was in its infancy—still is—with only a handful of artists (Shawne Jackson, Sweet Blindness, Mandala) working in the genre.

The upside to the CRTC's tampering with the musical free-market system is obvious to anyone who grew up in Canada during the mid-seventies. Homegrown hits like Fludd's "Brother and Me," Jackson Hawke's "You Can't Dance," A Foot in Coldwater's "(Make Me Do) Anything You Want," Bearfoot's "Passing Time," and Crowbar's "Million Dollar Weekend" may have failed to make a dent in the *Billboard* charts, but they constitute a style of Canuck pop-rock that was as much a part of the teenage landscape as "chopper" bicycles, tight corduroy pants, and *Mad* magazine. If Canadians still spent too much time thinking about their neighbors to the south—Toronto broadcaster Gordon Sinclair's editorial "The Americans (A Canadian's Opinion)" was a smash in 1974—at least they were developing a canon of domestic pop music that didn't need U.S. approval.

CANCON AWARDS
(Featuring Gratuitous References to Other Famous Canadians)

Peter Jennings Award for Best News-Related Song
"The Wreck of the Edmund Fitzgerald," Gordon Lightfoot

Rich Little Award for Best Impression of Another Artist
"Sub-Rosa Subway," Klaatu (The Beatles)

Lorne Michaels Award for Funniest Title on a Million-Selling Single
"Put the Bone In," Terry Jacks (B side of "Seasons in the Sun")

David Cronenberg Award for Scariest Song Title
"Fire, Baby I'm on Fire," Andy Kim

Margaret Atwood Award for Best Musical Metaphor
"You Turn Me On, I'm a Radio," Joni Mitchell

Robert Goulet Award for Singer Even Canadians Didn't Know Was Canadian (tie)
David Clayton-Thomas (Blood, Sweat & Tears)
John Kay (Steppenwolf)

Pierre Trudeau Award for Hippest Political Statement
"Ohio," Crosby, Stills, Nash & Young (Neil Young, composer)

Leslie Nielsen Award for Self-Parody
"Sour Suite," The Guess Who (Burton Cummings, composer)

Dan Ackroyd Award for Best Blues Record
"Flip, Flop and Fly," Downchild Blues Band

Maynard Ferguson Award for Highest Sound Generated by a Male
Tony DeFranco

Bobby Orr Award for Best Hockey Reference
"Raised on Robbery," Joni Mitchell ("A little money riding on the Maple Leafs")

Tommy Chong Award for Best Stoner Song
"Getting High," Gino Vannelli

Douglas Coupland Award for Single with Lowest Attention-Span Requirement
"Absolutely Right," Five Man Electrical Band (2:12)

Yosuf Karsh Award for Best Portrait of a Famous Person
"Free Man in Paris," Joni Mitchell (David Geffen)

William Shatner Award for Best Science-Fiction Concept Album
2112, Rush

Amazing Kreskin Award for Best Psychic Theme
"If You Could Read My Mind," Gordon Lightfoot

Chief Dan George Award for Best Single About a Native Canadian (tie)

"He's an Indian Cowboy in the Rodeo," Buffy Sainte-Marie
"Then Came the White Man," The Stampeders

Mike Myers Award for Song Best Suited to 8-Track Players

"Roll On Down the Highway," Bachman-Turner Overdrive

THE MAUDLIN SQUAD
Self-pity Pop

"Rainy Days and Mondays" • The Carpenters (A&M, 1971)
"I Ain't Got Time Anymore" • The Glass Bottle (Avco Embassy, 1971)
"Alone Again (Naturally)" • Gilbert O'Sullivan (MAM, 1972)
"Without You" • Nilsson (RCA, 1972)
"Rocket Man" • Elton John (Uni, 1972)
"Seasons in the Sun" • Terry Jacks (Bell, 1974)
"Feelings" • Morris Albert (RCA, 1975)
"At Seventeen" • Janis Ian (Columbia, 1975)
"Rocky" • Austin Roberts (Private Stock, 1975)
"All By Myself" • Eric Carmen (Arista, 1975)

You wouldn't even let your best friend go on like this. Wallowing in misery, infatuated with despair, uninterested in solutions, and using you as a sounding board. No—after a couple of minutes, you'd force-feed your friend some borrowed bromides: "You're not the first person this has happened to"; "Time heals"; "Everything happens for a reason." If that didn't work, you'd suggest a program of vigorous exercise or professional counseling, but you wouldn't just sit there and listen. And you wouldn't *pay* to hear it, right?

How, then, to explain the commercial appeal of the Maudlin Squad, an all-star lack-of-glee club who would happily bleed the life right out of you for the sake of one more moribund verse and chorus? What good would your armchair psychology be against these melancholy babies? How are you going to talk Gilbert O'Sullivan down from the ledge? Or get Janis Ian picked for the basketball team? Or find a little company for Eric Carmen?

Most important, how are you going to get those damn melodies out of your head?

Sorting through the regret, despair, and loneliness that permeates

so much early seventies pop can be a little like sitting in on one of Dr. Bob "Newhart" Hartley's group therapy sessions, minus the jokes. It's with a huge sense of relief that the realization comes: *I'm not like them!* That "It-could-be-worse-I-could-be-Morris-Albert" catharsis is one reason for the huge popularity of these gloomy tunes. The other is the vicarious appeal of the lyrics for people who *are* Morris Albert and who *do* have feelings (whoa, whoa, whoa, feelings).

Maybe Tom Wolfe was listening to America's "Lonely People" when he coined the phrase "the Me Decade" in 1975. Certainly, the pap music professionals of the early seventies were as self-involved a bunch as has ever taken up residence on the charts. Question is, were they symptom or cause? Wolfe wasn't wrong; narcissism rose to new heights in the seventies, what with the popularity of "finding yourself," "getting your head together," "getting in touch with your feelings," and mood rings. Whatever color the culture's ring was registering (black meant doom), Morris Albert and his friends found responsive, lint-covered muses lolling in their fascinating navels, and sold a few records in the process. They even had a mascot: a free-thinking seagull named Jonathan Livingston who was a hit at the box office, on the best-seller lists, and, thanks to Neil Diamond's "Be" (from the movie), on the pop charts.

For better or worse, these are the songs of the Maudlin Squad. These are self-pity's best ditties.

Gilbert O'Sullivan risked critical scorn when he invoked two legendary composers by changing his first name from Raymond (this was a little like someone calling himself Lennon O'McCartney sometime in the middle of the next century). Nevertheless, he spent six weeks at the top of the charts with "Alone Again (Naturally)." The song begins with the narrator promising, with singsongy good cheer, that he will "treat" himself by climbing to the top of "a nearby tower," so that he can—What? Take in the view? Catch some fresh air? Get some perspective on his problems? No, so that he can *throw himself off.* Those dark opening lines are sung against a bouncy piano-based arrangement that will have you gently rocking your head from side to side, never once registering the lyric's morbid undercurrent. This guy's living in his miserable past—his girlfriend deserted him, God followed her lead, and he lost both parents. But it's the inclusion of "naturally" in the title that really puts this one over the top; the resignation in that one word lends the song an air of self-fulfilling prophecy. And yet, for all of this, it's still the world's catchiest suicide note.

Former Raspberry Eric Carmen slipped into the murk of self-pity in 1975 with "All By Myself," based on a Rachmaninoff composition. We're spared the addition of "Naturally" in the title (although it's there in spirit), but then, the song doesn't have a chipper melody to battle its dreary sentiments. Carmen's mumbled delivery of the verses suggests that he doesn't even have the energy to properly articulate his sorrow, and his pinched, upper-register singing of the choruses inspires sympathy for the first time (and for all the wrong reasons). His next hit "Never Gonna Fall in Love Again" was also borrowed from Rachmaninoff, but this time the title was 83 percent Bacharach-David.

Other denizens of the Heartbreak Hotel included: the Glass Bottle, whose "I Ain't Got Time Anymore" contained the Maudlin Squad's definitive lyric, "It takes up all my time just trying to be alone"; Nilsson, whose "Without You" represented a departure for the composer of "Me and My Arrow," "Coconut," and the theme song to *The Courtship of Eddie's Father;* Three Dog Night, whose "Pieces of April" ended the band's reign as "one of the heaviest bands in America today" (so they were introduced on tour); and Janis Ian, whose "At Seventeen" was lifted above the level of generic moping by a sharply detailed lyric.

Songs about death raised the stakes in the I'm-lonelier-than-you-are game. Austin Roberts's "Rocky" is two-thirds happily-ever-after love song and one third *Love Story*–style melodrama. Rocky and his wife have set up housekeeping with their first child when suddenly— a key change. Uh-oh. Before long, Mrs. Rocky is singing, "Rocky, I've never had to die before." But die she does, even making an appearance from beyond the grave to bolster Rocky's spirits.

If "Rocky" seemed a sad statement, it was only following in the footsteps of "Seasons in the Sun," Terry Jacks's deathbed farewell to friends and family. The Jaques Brel–Rod McKuen song, which did for dying what "(You're) Having My Baby" did for being born, was supersaturated with saccharine sentiment. When the narrator admits to "Pa-*pa*" (emphasis on second syllable) in a repentant, defeated voice that he was "the black sheep of the family," you have to wonder just how much of a bad seed this starfish-collecting, bird-watching, tree-climbing nature boy could have been.

Released at the beginning of 1974, "Seasons" stayed on the charts for twenty weeks (including three at Number 1), extending the February blahs well into May. By then, David Bowie's space-walking "Major Tom" and Elton John's anonymous "Rocket Man" (the seventies' ultimate loners) had already been floating in space for over a year. "Space Oddity" and "Rocket Man" measured the distances between people in light-years and put the era's terrestrial sob stories to shame. Not only were these characters dealing with nagging questions like how to find a good school on Mars, they had no one to talk to about it. What could be lonelier than the solitary confinement of a tiny space capsule plummeting, Apollo 13–style, into the existential void?

"Rocket Man" and "Space Oddity" succeeded at least in part because of their larger-than-life settings (Houston, these guys actually *did* have a problem). More often, lonesome-loser pop appeared to be making mountains out of molehills. The Carpenters may have felt a little sorry for themselves when those "Rainy Days and Mondays" came a-knockin', but Helen Reddy's agoraphobic heroine "Angie Baby" was actually living her life by the songs she heard "on the rock and roll radio," and if those songs were anything like "Alone Again (Naturally)," she was in big trouble. Austin Roberts's pre-"Rocky" hit "Something's Wrong with Me" was another pity ditty that got a little strange. Sounding remarkably like Cher in the track's most intense moments, Roberts stopped short of shutting his protagonist away in a bedroom, but instead had him "hanging around" a woman who didn't seem to know he existed. Watching her "on the street" with another man, he eventually reached the title epiphany, "Something's wrong with me." Yes, *you're a stalker.* I'm okay, you're *not* okay, all right, pal?

"Something's Wrong with Me" was similar in spirit to "I'd Love You to Want Me," Lobo's obsequious follow-up to "Me and You and a Dog Named Boo." Roland Kent Lavoie's stage name was Spanish for "wolf" but, on the evidence of his ultra-low-key delivery, some might have interpreted it as an abbreviation of "lobotomy." At least "Want Me" 's hero had the guts to talk to the object of his affection, though you were a little embarrassed for the poor guy. Likewise, Dave Loggins's "Please Come to Boston" showed us a man pleading with his home-town Tennessee girlfriend to join him in Boston, Denver, and Los Angeles, each time receiving the answer no. Mercifully, the song ends before we have to hear Loggins pitch her on any more of the country's major sports markets.

Perhaps someone should have dragged Angie, Rocky, Major Tom, et al. off to Dr. Bob Hartley's office for a little soul-searching:

The session begins. Tales of loss, betrayal and tragedy are shared. Humble pie is passed around. Slowly, mood rings begin to turn blue (happy). Dr. Bob tells the group he's pleased with its progress.

The lonely-hearts club adjourns. Angie heads back to her bedroom. Rocky goes home to his daughter. And Major Tom, the high-flying spiritual leader of the group, climbs back into his capsule. He dons his space suit, takes a belt of Tang, and tries once more to reach Ground Control. No response. Our hero is alone again. Naturally.

THE ENERGY CRISIS
MOR

"Daddy Don't You Walk So Fast" • Wayne Newton (Chelsea, 1972)
"Song Sung Blue" • Neil Diamond (Uni, 1972)
"Candy Man" • Sammy Davis, Jr. (MGM, 1972)
"Say, Has Anybody Seen My Sweet Gypsy Rose" • Dawn featuring Tony Orlando (Bell, 1973)
"The Morning After" • Maureen McGovern (20th Century, 1973)
"Top of the World" • Carpenters (A&M, 1973)
"The Way We Were" • Barbra Streisand (Columbia, 1973)
"My Melody of Love" • Bobby Vinton (ABC, 1974)
"Could It Be Magic" • Barry Manilow (Arista, 1975)
"Rhinestone Cowboy" • Glen Campbell (Capitol, 1975)

In August of 1975, the *Billboard* Hot 100 featured records by Paul Anka, the Carpenters, Barry Manilow, Helen Reddy, Olivia Newton-John, Glen Campbell, Captain & Tennille, Freddy Fender, Neil Sedaka, Morris Albert, and John Denver. Is it any wonder NASA chose that month to send *Viking 1* to Mars to look for signs of life?

Despite the emergence of funk, reggae, disco, and several other politically and sexually charged styles, the early seventies showed remarkable tolerance for MOR (Middle of the Road)—the only kind of pop music that requires no reinterpretation to become Muzak. Pre-rock crooners like Frank Sinatra, Perry Como, and Andy Williams were still pop stars. Roberta Flack, Neil Diamond, and Anne Murray were Grammy winners. Sammy Davis, Jr., Bobby Vinton, and Wayne Newton were gold-record holders. In those days, you played Vegas *before* your pop career was over.

Sometimes MOR came from Broadway. Show tunes were crossing over less frequently than they had in the days of *My Fair Lady,* but Judy Collins's "Send in the Clowns" (1975, from *A Little Night Music*) and "Day by Day" (1972, from *Godspell*) both went Top 20.

The movies, too, launched a few easy-listening hits. "Candy Man," the theme from *Willy Wonka and the Chocolate Factory,* was a dentally incorrect smash—the Anti-Crest—and, with the possible exception of "Barretta's Theme (Keep Your Eye on the Sparrow)," is the only reason anyone under thirty remembers Sammy Davis, Jr. "The Way We Were," the ageless title song from Sydney Pollack's 1973 film, transcended the genre and displayed Barbra Streisand's staggering emotional range without cloying, love-theme sentiment. Fresh from her first attempts at rock, the buttah-voiced diva of Brooklyn was resplendent and had not yet hit upon the sometimes not-so-great notion of recording duets with Neil Diamond, Donna Summer, and Barry Gibb.

Love-among-the-ruins specialist Maureen McGovern was the voice on "The Morning After" (from *The Poseidon Adventure*) and "We May Never Love Like This Again" (from *The Towering Inferno*), both Oscar winners for Best Song. Disaster movies, home of topsy-turvy ocean liners, flaming zeppelins, nose-diving 747s, and the indomitable Charlton Heston, were the early seventies' most notorious contribution to the cinema. Their paint-by-numbers approach to plot and character worked for songwriters, too—what are Mac Davis's four big hits "Baby Don't Get Hooked on Me," "One Hell of a Woman," "Stop and Smell the Roses," and "Rock N' Roll (I Gave You the Best Years of My Life)," after all, but the MOR equivalent of *Airport, Airport 1975, Airport '77,* and *Concorde—Airport '79*?

Unlike most of his country colleagues, Davis visited the pop charts regularly. Nashville headliners like George Jones, Tammy Wynette, Conway Twitty, Tanya Tucker, Loretta Lynn, and Willie Nelson couldn't often get past the lower reaches of the Hot 100 because regional airplay in the South didn't translate into the kind of national numbers that could make a C&W hit a mainstream success. When country songs did chart high enough to register in Yourtown, it was the MOR audience that made the difference. Hits by reformed rocker Charlie Rich ("The Most Beautiful Girl," "Behind Closed Doors"), Tex-Mex star Freddy Fender ("Before the Next Teardrop Falls," "Wasted Days and Wasted Nights") and ex-teacher Donna Fargo ("The Happiest Girl in the Whole U.S.A.," "Funny Face") succeeded because they registered high on the romance scale and low on the redneck scale.

Country-MOR encompassed not only pop ballads high in corn content (B. J. Thomas's "[Hey Won't You Play] Another Somebody Done Somebody Wrong Song," 1975) or country iconography (Glen Campbell's "Rhinestone Cowboy," 1975), but side trips by an angelic Australian (Olivia Newton-John) and a honey-voiced Canadian (Anne Murray). Newton-John is remembered variously as breathless balladeer, *Grease*-ette, and aerobics poster girl, but there was a down-home streak in her early work that extended from her twangy cover of Dylan's "If Not for You" (1971) to the lonesome-saloon saga "Please Mr. Please" (1975). Murray's acoustic hits ("Cotton Jenny," "Danny's Song," "Love Song") spoke to her small-town roots and generated a large country following for her in the United States that included, of all people, Burt Reynolds. Songs like the harmonically intriguing "Talk It Over in the Morning" suggested Murray had an urban side as well, but she continued (and continues) to represent the acoustic end of the MOR spectrum, far from Las Vegas fare like Wayne Newton's "Daddy Don't You Walk So Fast."

The center of the MOR universe was Vegas—a sucker's paradise that existed in a *Twilight Zone* where rock had never happened. In 1974, the year of Bobby Vinton's "My Melody of Love," the town without pity cleared a million dollars a day in gambling earnings for the first time, and the casinos' entertainment departments had attracted many of those tourist dollars with MOR headliners. Hapless Fred Flintstones ("Bet! Bet! Bet!") were more apt to play trust-fund roulette if they had been softened up by Ann-Margrock first.

For those disinclined to actually visit Nevada, there was always the TV variety show. Almost every MOR star had one. You probably remember *This Is Tom Jones, The Andy Williams Show, Donny and Marie, The Mac Davis Show,* and *The Glen Campbell Goodtime Hour.* You may have blocked out *The Engelbert Humperdinck Show, The Bobby Goldsboro Show, The Marilyn McCoo and Billy Davis, Jr., Show, Tony Orlando and Dawn,* and *The Bobby Vinton Show.* But admit it—those glitzy, virtual-Vegas hours were always a good test for that new color set.

The human embodiment of Vegas was, of course, Elvis Presley. Obese, rich beyond his wildest dreams, spiritually bankrupt, stripped of his rock-and-roll credibility, and divorced by Priscilla, Elvis maintained contact with his fans more through TV specials like *Elvis: Aloha from Hawaii* than through his recordings. He covered hits by MOR artists like Humperdinck, Sinatra, and Tony Bennett. Apart from the hunk-o' hunk-o' gold he collected for 1972's too-goofy-to-spoof single "Burning Love," he received scant notice for his later records. By 1977, the year of his death, he was as worn out physically as he was musically.

Though Neil Diamond's rock credentials were no match for Elvis's (whose were?), he was taken more seriously than any other MOR man. From his experience as a Brill Building songwriter to his appearance in the Band's *The Last Waltz* (1978), his résumé challenged easy-listening stereotypes. His records, however, didn't. While 1974's lush "Longfellow Serenade" is more effective than many Diamond dogs, it's just as affected as the rest of his lonely-guy seventies catalog ("Song Sung Blue," "I Am . . . I Said," etc.). But don't knock him too loudly—statistics say you are probably within 100 meters of a Neil Diamond fan right now.

Barry Manilow, a man with no apparent integrity, never had to face the accusations of "sellout" that nouveau-schmaltzers like Elvis endured. His pre-"Mandy" assignments had included writing and/or singing jingles for Pepsi, Dr. Pepper, and McDonald's ("You Deserve a Break Today"). There was nowhere to go but up. Before Eric Carmen adapted Rachmaninoff, before Billy Joel adapted Beethoven, Manilow adapted Chopin, turning the Polish master's "Prelude in C Minor" into "Could It Be Magic" in 1975. Maybe Manilow, the small-"r" romantic songwriter, secretly wanted to be a big-"R" Romantic composer. Maybe he was just showing off. Or maybe he knew he wouldn't have to pay royalties to a man who had been dead for 125 years.

There's no shame in doing covers, of course. It certainly worked for the Carpenters, the biggest MOR act of the seventies. Chalking up eleven Top 5 hits in six years, they drew on the talents of illustrious songwriters like Leon Russell ("Superstar"), Burt Bacharach ("Close to You"), Carole King ("It's Going to Take Some Time"), Neil Sedaka ("Solitaire"), and Paul Williams ("We've Only Just Begun," "Rainy Days and Mondays," "I Won't Last a Day Without You"). It didn't earn them any respect at the time, but if the participation of alternative rockers like Sonic Youth in the 1994 tribute album *If I Were a Carpenter* is any indication, Karen and Richard are getting cooler all the time.

That may mean the 5th Dimension is due for a comeback. Interpreters of material by Bacharach ("One Less Bell to Answer"), Sedaka ("Puppet Man"), and Laura Nyro ("Stoned Soul Picnic," "Sweet Blindness," "Wedding Bell Blues"), the quintet had by the early seventies become an R&B analog of the Carpenters, with Marilyn McCoo in the role of Karen. Rock, folk, and country already had black superstars (Sly Stone, Richie Havens, and Charley Pride), so why not MOR? As it happens, the 5th Dimension was more successful before its approach softened, but that may have more to do with Nyro's hiatus from songwriting than with the group.

Bell, the 5th Dimension's record label throughout the seventies, specialized in MOR. Its roster included Barry Manilow, the Partridge Family, Vicki Lawrence, Terry Jacks, and Tony Orlando & Dawn. Orlando's "Knock Three Times" and "Tie a Yellow Ribbon Round the Ole Oak Tree" were hard records to avoid, whatever you thought of them; they were both multiple-week Number 1s, and "Ribbon" was the top single of 1973. To this day, they are titles that can silence anyone defending the seventies.

Uh . . .

Dawn's hot streak was mercifully brief, ending around the time the group's cringe-making TV series debuted. But the musical damage was done. "Knock Three Times" was the first Number 1 single of the post-Beatles era, and "Tie a Yellow Ribbon" became a lounge standard and all-purpose homecoming anthem. And consistency? Starting in August 1974, Tony and female bookends Telma Hopkins and Joyce Vincent spent more than *thirteen consecutive months* on the U.S. charts.

Flight was futile; even if you found a country on which Orlando hadn't Dawned, some other MOR horror would find you. Telly Savalas had a hit with "If" in England. Holland's George Baker crooned "Una Paloma Blanca." Spain? Mocedades' "Eres Tu." And you could forget about fleeing to Canada—that is, unless you wanted to hear "Seasons in the Sun" a couple of hundred more times. No, you were trapped. Like *Viking 1,* the best you could hope for was life on Mars.

LOVE AMERICAN STYLE
Ballads

"Your Song" • Elton John (Uni, 1971)
"Colour My World" • Chicago (Columbia, 1971)
"Day Dreaming" • Aretha Franklin (Atlantic, 1972)
"The First Time Ever I Saw Your Face" • Roberta Flack (Atlantic, 1972)
"Time in a Bottle" • Jim Croce (ABC, 1973)
"My Love" • Wings (Apple, 1973)
"I Honestly Love You" • Olivia Newton-John (MCA, 1974)
"My Eyes Adored You" • Frankie Valli (Private Stock, 1974)
"Mandy" • Barry Manilow (Bell, 1974)
"You Are So Beautiful" • Joe Cocker (A&M, 1975)

The history of mainstream pop is the search for new ways to say "I love you." The new wrinkle in the seventies was explicitness; you no longer had to say "love" when you meant "sex," or "happiness" when you meant "ecstasy," or "face" when you meant "booty." That's not to say that all the barriers were down—Isaac Hayes was still shushed by his backup singers when he said "bad mutha . . ."—but the days of merely "Groovin' " on a Sunday afternoon were over.

Aretha Franklin's "Day Dreaming" (1972) typified the new breed of soul ballad. It contained traditional sentiments like " 'til death do you part," but its frank promises of pleasure were altogether new. Whether "day dreaming" was a euphemism for self-pleasure is another question, one only the track's insistent, slow-motion groove can answer. Franklin contemporaries Minnie Riperton ("Lovin' You"), Diana Ross ("Touch Me in the Morning"), Gladys Knight ("Help Me Make It Through the Night"), and Roberta Flack ("Feel Like Makin' Love") also got highly musical results from blurring the line between love and lust. On the men's side, check the O'Jays' "Let Me Make Love to You," Al Wilson's "Show and Tell," and Luther Ingram's "(If Loving You Is Wrong) I Don't Want to Be Right."

Of course, traditional pop balladry was still alive and well. Specialists like the Bee Gees ("My World"), the Carpenters ("Top of the World"), the Stylistics ("You Are Everything"), and Bread ("Everything I Own") were producing slow-dance fodder faster than AMC was producing Pacers. All the major pop artists had at least one big ballad in their catalogs: "Your Song" started Elton John's career; "Best of My Love" was the Eagles' first Number 1; "My Love" was Paul McCartney's first gold record with Wings; and "I'll Be There" has become the Jackson 5's most covered song. Stevie Wonder, known in the seventies for edgy singles like "Superstition," joined the soft parade with "All in Love Is Fair" (covered in 1974 by Barbra Streisand). Three Dog Night interrupted its string of up-tempo hits with "An Old Fashioned Love Song," one of the few Paul Williams songs not originated by the Carpenters.

Chicago cut ballads like "Just You 'N' Me" from the same cloth as their other brassy hits, enlisting the help of future tour-mates the Beach Boys for "Wishing You Were Here." "Colour My World," their most original love song, began as one part of *Chicago II*'s "Ballet for a Girl in Buchanan," made it to the B side of 1971's "Beginnings," took on a life of its own on radio, got youngsters everywhere practicing their piano arpeggios, and ultimately became the top "last dance" of the decade ("Stairway to Heaven" allowed more time for vertical expression of horizontal desire, but there was that fast part at the end).

For every positive statement like Joe Cocker's croakingly tender "You Are So Beautiful," there was a Bridget-loses-Bernie scenario lurking in the shadows. "Goodbye to Love." "This Masquerade." "Midnight Blue." The have-a-nice-day decade was capable of profound, romantically induced melancholy. Try playing Nilsson's "Without You," the Bee Gees' "How Can You Mend a Broken Heart," and the Spinners' "How Could I Let You Get Away" in one sitting. If you don't have a lump in your throat after that, get your estate in order—you may well be dead. If you have the lump, but haven't actually wept, go to the next level and listen to the Al Green version of "How Can You Mend a Broken Heart." It's unlike the Bee Gees'—dead slow and starkly arranged—but the vocal is the most heart-wrenching sound you'll ever hear. (This track is also a good place to start if you're not

sure why everyone makes such a fuss over Reverend Green.)

After September 20, 1973, every Jim Croce song had built-in potential for sadness. Croce and his band were killed in a plane crash that day, even as "Bad, Bad Leroy Brown" was logging its twenty-second week on the *Billboard* Hot 100. "Time in a Bottle," Croce's most popular ballad, went to Number 1 by year's end. Its "If"-style lyric and acoustic setting probably would have found a lovelorn audience even if the composer had still been alive, but there was new impact to its now-ironic line: "There never seems to be enough time."

Rockers knew how to write ballads too, as evinced by the Rolling Stones' "Angie" and "Wild Horses." The former, reportedly named for David Bowie's wife, is a gloomy little masterpiece that contains some of Jagger and Richards' best couplets ("With no loving in our souls / And no money in our coats . . ."). The latter was released in 1971, the same year Nevada enacted a law to control its burgeoning wild horse population. Fortunately, the power ballad hadn't been invented yet, so rock bands didn't feel obliged to write ballads unless they had a good idea for one ("Beth" notwithstanding).

10cc's "I'm Not in Love" was a brilliant stroke. It didn't take Woodward and Bernstein to figure out the character was lying about his feelings, but the song's tape-loop orchestration and immortal "big boys don't cry" interlude made it a haunting presence in the summer of '75. (The whole thing might have seemed less romantic if more fans had known the band was named for the average volume of semen a man ejaculates.) Other defining ballads of the era:

- The Dramatics' "In the Rain," thematically identical to the Temptations' "I Wish It Would Rain" and marred only slightly by the group's tendency to rush through the climatic "let me go" sections
- The Hollies' "The Air That I Breathe," a study in rock atmosphere and a candidate for pop-standard status (if someone would just cover it)
- Elton John's "Someone Saved My Life Tonight," the story of Elton's rescue from dire straits (marriage to a dour straight)
- Roberta Flack's ponderous "The First Time Ever I Saw Your Face," the top record of the early seventies, according to chart expert Joel Whitburn
- Olivia Newton-John's "I Honestly Love You," an intimate, whispered confessional—the white "Pillow Talk"
- Frankie Valli's "My Eyes Adored You," a one-man argument for unabashed sentimentality (persuasive, too)
- Carole King's "So Far Away," a pop master's lament for her increasingly transient society
- Barry Manilow's "Mandy," the love song most likely to elicit modern-day grins of smug superiority

It took more than two decades for Elvis Presley's 1956 hit "I Want You, I Need You, I Love You" to subdivide into Marvin Gaye's "I Want You," America's "I Need You," and Donna Summer's "I Love You." During that time, rock and roll grew up, left home, got an apartment, and lost its virginity. The sexual arena changed forever. War between the sexes was declared. Yet through it all, ballads continued to try to define the "L" word, using traditional phrases and concepts in new contexts.

That's not to say there was any kind of consensus. For a while it seemed Joy Division's "Love Will Tear Us Apart" (1980) had refuted Captain & Tennille's "Love Will Keep Us Together" (1975), but the eighties witnessed a return to Tin Pan Alley sentiments like "Love Will Save the Day," "Love Will Find a Way," and "Love Will Conquer All." Those who thought people had had enough of silly love songs looked around them and saw it wasn't so. Oh, no.

THE NAME GAME

"Mandy" was one of many seventies entries in the venerable girl's-name genre. Match the artist to his musical mate.

Level 1

1. Angie	a) Steely Dan
2. Annie	b) Grand Funk
3. Sally	c) B. W. Stevenson
4. Fanny	d) The Rolling Stones
5. Julie	e) Rod Stewart
6. Maggie May	f) John Denver
7. Rikki	g) Dawn
8. Daisy Jane	h) Bee Gees
9. Candida	i) Bobby Sherman
10. Maria	j) America

Level 2

1. Marianne	a) Bill Amesbury
2. Adrienne	b) Blood, Sweat & Tears
3. Virginia	c) Hamilton, Joe Frank & Reynolds
4. Daisy Mae	d) Stephen Stills
5. Rosanna	e) Cymarron
6. Emma	f) Classics IV
7. Lisa	g) Tommy James
8. Sandy	h) Focus
9. Sylvia	i) Hot Chocolate
10. Valerie	j) The Hollies

Level 3 (Southern Division)

1. Francene	a) Sam Neely
2. Jackie	b) Pure Prairie League
3. Melissa	c) Johnny Cash
4. Jessica	d) Wet Willie
5. Leona	e) ZZ Top
6. Kate	f) Boomer Castleman
7. Josie	g) Ozark Mountain Daredevils
8. Amie	h) Kris Kristofferson

9. Judy Mae   i) The Allman Brothers
10. Rosalie   j) The Allman Brothers

Answers: Level 1 1d, 2f, 3b, 4h, 5i, 6e, 7a, 8j, 9g, 10c *Level 2* 1d, 2g, 3a, 4c, 5f, 6i, 7b, 8j, 9h, 10e *Level 3 (Southern Division)* 1e, 2g, 3i, 4j, 5d, 6c, 7h, 8b, 9f, 10a

"HARRY, KEEP THE CHANGE"
Story Songs

"Gypsys, Tramps & Thieves" • Cher (Kapp, 1971)
"Brandy (You're a Fine Girl)" • Looking Glass (Epic, 1972)
"Taxi" • Harry Chapin (Elektra, 1972)
"Tie a Yellow Ribbon Round the Ole Oak Tree" • Tony Orlando & Dawn (Bell, 1973)
"Bad, Bad Leroy Brown" • Jim Croce (ABC, 1973)
"The Night the Lights Went Out in Georgia" • Vicki Lawrence (Bell, 1973)
"Billy, Don't Be a Hero" • Bo Donaldson & the Heywoods (ABC, 1974)
"Piano Man" • Billy Joel (Columbia, 1974)
"The Night Chicago Died" • Paper Lace (Mercury, 1974)
"Wildfire" • Michael Murphy (Epic, 1975)

In an era notorious for its narcissistic excesses, the most remarkable thing about songs like "Brandy (You're a Fine Girl)" (1972), "Bad, Bad Leroy Brown" (1973), and "The Night the Lights Went Out in Georgia" (1973) was that they were about *things that happened to somebody else*. While many of the early seventies' best-known musical tracts were rendered in excruciating first-person singular (see "All By Myself"), these story songs turned their narrative gaze outward, often describing actual human activity instead of self-inflicted mental anguish.

"Brandy," especially, was a breath of fresh air. If the whiskey-slinging barmaid whose true love loved only the sea was a tragic heroine of decidedly minor proportions, the song's unsinkable spirit, dynamics, and unforgettable chorus more than compensated. Looking Glass founder and lead singer Elliot Lurie rendered his own lyric, full of loyalty, passion, and pain, in a dispassionate drawl worthy of fellow New Yorker Donald Fagen (legend has it Lurie was briefly considered for membership in Steely Dan), bringing what could have been overwrought sentiment into respectable territory. Whether you heard "what a good wife you would be" or, as we initially did, "what

a good life human being," "Brandy" was hard to resist, a burst of pure pop in the maudlin summer of "Alone Again (Naturally)," "Goodbye to Love," and "Daddy, Don't You Walk So Fast."

Conversely, "The Night the Lights Went Out in Georgia" milked its story of a wrongly executed backwoods cuckold for every drop of cheap intrigue. A kind of Southern soap operetta, it was the lone pop hit for *Carol Burnett Show* regular Vicki Lawrence and a strong argument for handgun control (Guns don't kill people, people *with* guns kill people). Its value today is strictly as a campy artifact, but at the time it produced the same entertaining feeling of dread as Helen Reddy's "Angie Baby" and Cher's "Dark Lady."

Cher's mid-seventies output is central to the story song explosion. From the psychic friend in "Dark Lady" to the chip-on-her-shoulder tandem of "Half-Breed" and "Gypsys, Tramps & Thieves," the svelte bride of Bono spun pulpy yarns whose commercial appeal was undeniable; her three pop parables combined for five weeks at Number 1. Cher's real life was almost as interesting as her heroines'—she married Southern rocker Gregg Allman, wore TV's skimpiest costumes, and endured public criticism for naming her daughter Chastity (call it "Daughtergate")—but her tawdry tales of impend-

ing doom, racial prejudice, and small-town prostitution fascinated radio junkies everywhere.

Less gloomy but more violent was the work of former truck driver Jim Croce; though songs like "Bad, Bad Leroy Brown" and "You Don't Mess Around with Jim" had a personable, tall-tale atmosphere, the eponymous tough guys inevitably wound up beaten or stabbed. Like James Taylor, who could move from "Machine Gun Kelly" to "You've Got a Friend" in the course of one album, Croce divided his time between these bloody scenarios and his world-beating ballads ("Time in a Bottle," "I'll Have to Say I Love You in a Song").

Croce's finely crafted wordplay (see also 1972's "Rapid Roy [The Stock Car Boy]") was miles away from the bubblegum approach of plot-heavy hits like "Billy, Don't Be a Hero" and "The Night Chicago Died," both written by British producers Peter Callander and Mitch Murray, both tear-jerkers in the "Leader of the Pack" tradition. Or were they? While "Billy, Don't Be a Hero" registered first as just another dead-boyfriend ditty, it may in fact have been a veiled anti-Vietnam protest: Billy's death is clearly for naught, and the military pomp that convinced him to enlist seems hollow at song's end, as his "young and lovely fiancée" throws away the letter proclaiming him a war hero. "The Night Chicago Died" is an even less likely social commentary, but in the age of *The Godfather* and the Hoffa disappearance, anything dealing with organized crime (even long-dead gangsters like Al Capone) was topical. More to the point, both songs were state-of-the-art hook-fests that lodged themselves in the collective brainpan of Generation Brady. Undercover aliens who claim to have been in the western hemisphere during the seventies can be exposed using the final chorus of "The Night Chicago Died": if the subject fails to break into a rousing "Na na na na na na na na naa naa naa na naaa!" at the right point, he/she/it is most certainly not of this earth.

The same can be said of any subject who doesn't know there were *a hundred* yellow ribbons waiting for the ex-con in Tony Orlando & Dawn's "Tie a Yellow Ribbon Round the Ole Oak Tree" (the song never revealed the narrator's crime, but whatever it was, the penal system seemed to have turned him into a lovesick puppy). "Ribbon," Number 1 for a month in 1973, was something of a sequel: Dawn's first chart-topper, "Knock Three Times" (1970) had involved a different, though no less novel, nonverbal affirmation of love—banging on the ceiling. Those who found the ribbon thing a bit much the first time around had a chance to relive their discomfort when yellow ribbons became the visual tribute of choice Stateside during 1991's Gulf War. Disliking Dawn suddenly became an act of treason.

The stakes are lower when you're reinvestigating Harry Chapin's "Taxi" and Billy Joel's "Piano Man," on-the-job testimonials from a cabbie and a cocktail pianist. "Taxi" 's proto-slacker hero "Harry" (Chapin?), a workingman with many outside interests—getting high *and* getting stoned—picks up an old girlfriend one night, and all nostalgia breaks loose ("How are ya, Harry?"). The signature acoustic guitar figure evokes the slow crawl of San Francisco on a rainy night, and Chapin's ear for dialog was never sharper. "Piano Man" 's lounge lizard "Bill" (Joel?) tunefully describes the denizens of his workplace: people like John, the amiable bartender; Paul, the frustrated novelist; and Davey, who's in the navy because it rhymes. It's like *Cheers* minus the laughs, but it was the beginning of one of pop's great careers; though Joel had only one other early-seventies hit (1974's "The Entertainer"), he would explode in the second half of the decade with seven Top 30 hits.

Michael Murphy's "Wildfire" (1975), a folky ballad about a dead woman riding a dead horse ("Gee, your mare smells terrific!"), belonged to the popular story-songs-about-animals category, which also included Henry Gross's "Shannon," Lobo's "Me and You and a Dog Named Boo," and America's "A Horse with No Name." Its tragic tone was understandable, of course, but there were *human* bodies piling up as well. In David Geddes's "Run Joey Run" (1975) Joey's pregnant girlfriend takes one for the team when her gun-toting father flies off the handle (Papa, *please* preach); in Tommy Roe's "Stagger Lee" (1971) some dude named Billy gets shot in a gambling-related altercation (as per the 1959 Lloyd Price original); and in Hot Chocolate's "Emma" (1975) the title character commits suicide when her dreams of movie stardom fail to materialize (the song sounds like the blueprint for many a Prince classic, particularly "When Doves Cry").

Character studies like Elton John's "Levon" and "Daniel" were story songs, too, as were early-sixties reruns like Johnny T. Angel's "Tell Laura I Love Her" and Wednesday's "Last Kiss," but the heart of the genre was the high pop drama of "Brandy (You're a Fine Girl)," "Billy, Don't Be a Hero," and "The Night Chicago Died." Catchy, arranged to the hilt, and hopelessly earnest, these songs now amount to one of the best time capsules of the early seventies we have. If "Billy" 's fife-and-drum intro doesn't take you back to the days of lip gloss, Fresca, and stretchy jeans, maybe you weren't there. Maybe you should go back to your home planet.

SEVENTESE
Buzzwords

"Hot Pants (Part 1)" • James Brown (People, 1971)
"When You're Hot, You're Hot" • Jerry Reed (RCA, 1971)
"Rip Off" • Laura Lee (Hot Wax, 1972)
"Keep On Truckin' (Part 1)" • Eddie Kendricks (Tamla, 1973)
"Get Down" • Gilbert O'Sullivan (MAM, 1973)
"The Streak" • Ray Stevens (Barnaby, 1974)
"Dynomite—Part 1" • Bazuka (A&M, 1975)
"Convoy" • C. W. McCall (MGM, 1975)
"Hijack" • Herbie Mann (Atlantic, 1975)
"Have You Never Been Mellow" • Olivia Newton-John (MCA, 1975)

David Niven was preparing to introduce Elizabeth Taylor at the 1974 Academy Awards ceremony when he was streaked. A man named Robert Opal, who had escaped the notice of backstage security, ran across the stage au naturel, to the delight of the international TV audience. As Opal exited stage left, the unflappable Niven made a remark about the inadvisability of revealing one's "shortcomings," then went on with the show. Now, 1974 was a remarkable year—a U.S. president resigned in disgrace; runaway inflation threatened the world economy; Patty Hearst joined the Symbionese Liberation Army—but if you're looking for a defining personage, look no further than Opal, the Oscars' dangling participant.

Streaking was an oddly upscale phenomenon, having originated on college campuses like Yale (where four streakers were currently on probation). Closely related to the less courageous practice of mooning, it made exhibitionism fun again and, like all good trends, demanded a musical response. Predictably, spoofster Ray Stevens stepped up to the mic. "The Streak" was business as usual for Stevens (his "Ahab, the Arab" had rocked the novelty casbah in 1962), and its ascent to Number 1 was as unstoppable as the song's main character, a dowdy but hot-blooded voyeur named Ethel. Despite her husband's protests, Ethel simply refused to avert her eyes when streaked at the supermarket, the gas station, and the basketball game—she liked to watch.

Less a song than a wacky pseudo-documentary, "The Streak" might have been dismissed as just another white-trash-clashes-with-dashing-flasher story had it not been part of a movement—the buzzword movement. Whether they came from the worlds of rock (John Lennon's "Mind Games"), soul (Laura Lee's "Rip Off"), funk (Kool & the Gang's "Jungle Boogie"), or pop (Olivia Newton-John's "Have You Never Been Mellow"), buzzword hits had this in common: They were all based on modern idioms and slang expressions.

Sometimes the intent was pure gimmickry. "When You're Hot, You're Hot," Jerry Reed's shit-kicking tale of a craps game gone wrong, was just a good excuse to put a popular expression (which translates roughly as "I'm in the zone") to music. For the millions who had watched comedian Jimmy Walker deliver his overwrought signature line ("Dy-no-mite!") on TV's *Good Times,* the attraction to Bazuka's "Dynomite—Part I" was purely burlesque, although it wasn't a bad little Average White Band–style jam. Ian Lloyd & Stories, having pushed racial boundaries the previous year with "Brother Louie," furthered their own cause in 1974 with a song based on the hedonistic T-shirt slogan "If It Feels Good, Do It."

At other times, the genre transcended its limitations. By 1973 "Keep On Truckin' " was a worn-out hippie phrase associated with cartoonist R. Crumb, but it also helped establish ex-Temptation Eddie Kendricks as a solo artist. Kendricks chose a fresher expression, "Boogie Down," for his next effort. Thirteen years after "Short Shorts" had titillated teens, James Brown funkified the concept with "Hot Pants (Part 1)," a wicked three-minute come-on whose deep groove suggested that the recent departure of bassist Bootsy Collins for Parliament/Funkadelic wasn't going to be a problem for the JBs. (The roughly contemporary Brown-produced Bobby Byrd hit "Hot Pants—I'm Coming, I'm Coming, I'm Coming" gets our nod for title of the decade.) And Lennon's "Mind Games" turned a euphemism for passive-aggressive manipulations into a majestic, positive statement.

The newly emerging dance culture—and black culture in general—accounted for many buzzword hits, foreshadowing the prominence street slang would have in rap and hip-hop in the nineties. Not counting songs that had "disco" in their titles, which must have numbered in the thousands, words and phrases like "funky," "boogie," "get down," and "get it on" accounted for dozens of records between 1971 and 1975. The phrase "get it on" was so popular that British rockers T. Rex had to change the title of their so-named hit to "Bang a Gong" for its American release to avoid confusion with Chase's "Get It On." Ditto "get down," which attracted Gilbert O'Sullivan, Curtis Mayfield, and the Dramatics (whose variation was to get up and *then* get down). And "funky"—well, it got so you could put that word in front of just about anything and have yourself a hit record: "Funky Stuff," "Funky Nassau," "Funky Weekend," "Funky Worm" . . . Soul great Rufus Thomas's "Do the Funky Penguin" (a follow-up to "Do the Funky Chicken," which needed a sequel like Barry White needed a date) indicated things were going south at Soulsville, U.S.A., Memphis headquarters of Stax Records.

And speaking of sequels, remember "Old Home Filler-up an' Keep On A-Truckin' Cafe"? Of course you don't. But it was the 1974 C. W. McCall single that led to "Convoy," the novelty smash that put trucking and CB radios on the rock-and-roll map. How about "Dance the Kung Fu"? No? It was the sound of Carl Douglas trying to recapture the strange magic of "Kung Fu Fighting." "You Think You're Hot Stuff"? Jean Knight's "Mr. Big Stuff," Volume 2.

If songs about dancing, streaking, trucking, and martial arts represent the lifestyle portion of this discussion, records inspired by the 1973 Arab oil embargo, the environment, and terrorism represent the current-events portion. Dickie Goodman's "Energy Crisis '74," Charles Wright's "Solution for Pollution" and especially Herbie Mann's "Hijack" did respectable business—"Hijack" was one of the top disco hits of the seventies—but smacked of opportunistic topicality. Germany had paid $5 million to hijackers in 1972 in exchange for hostages, and records like "Hijack" and Johnny Taylor's "Hijackin' Love" seemed to make light of the life-and-death gravity of the international terrorism epidemic.

There was perhaps more honor in cutting lightweight records about intrinsically lightweight subjects, like heavyweight champions.

"Black Superman," Johnny Wakelin's 1975 tribute to Muhammad Ali—Ali had defeated Joe Frazier and George Foreman in 1974 to reclaim his title—was the musical equivalent of a Howard Cosell pro-Ali rant and one of many sports-pop crossovers in the seventies. Think of Joe Namath going west in *The Last Rebel* (1971), Jean-Claude Killy planning a heist in *Snow Job* (1972), or O. J. Simpson rescuing a cat in *The Towering Inferno* (1974). (Come to think of it, it's too bad Wakelin never recorded a tribute to Simpson, who set the NFL rushing record in 1973; it would have enjoyed some airplay a couple of decades later.)

The word "superstar" hit it big around 1971, when three records by that name made the charts. All of them—Murray Head's "Superstar," Carpenters' "Superstar," and the Temptations' "Superstar (Remember How You Got Where You Are)"—were about more or less the same thing: a famous dude who had forgotten his humble beginnings (a simple philosophy, a lover, the little people). In the age of the ego trip, such behavior was commonplace; mean, ego-driven types included Superman's arch-rival Lex Luthor, Stax control freak Isaac Hayes, and suave city cop Kojak. All bald, yes, but super bad. Lieutenant Kojak's catchphrase "Who loves ya, baby" may or may not have directly inspired the 4 Seasons' "Who Loves You"—Frankie Valli and the boys never sounded very macho and Telly Savalas was a guy who looked mean even with a lollipop in his mouth—but given pop culture's incestuous tendencies, it's a pretty good bet that it did.

The buzzword movement was exhaustive, going through popular phrases as quickly as Secretariat went through horseshoes. "Check It Out." "Hang Loose." "Do Your Thing." "What It Is." It spawned more than a few good records, mostly by artists who had long ago proven themselves (James Brown, John Lennon, Marvin Gaye), but it also provided the seventies with some of its worst squirmers. Listen, if you can, to the Jimmy Castor Bunch desperately quoting their two earlier hits, "Troglodyte" and "Hey, Leroy, Your Mama's Callin' You," as they vainly endeavor to be recognized amidst the hideous cacophony that is "The Bertha Butt Boogie." Falling as it does into two important buzzword categories ("Butt" and "Boogie"), it's a good example of just how far wrong this kind of thing could go. Choose your favorite trendy abomination from the buzzwords master list below.

BUZZWORD	SONG	ARTIST	YEAR
FUNKY	"Do the Funky Penguin"	Rufus Thomas	1972
FUNKY	"Funk Factory"	Wilson Pickett	1972
FUNKY	"The Funky Gibbon"	The Goodies	1975
FUNKY	"Funky Music Sho Nuff Turns Me On"	Edwin Starr	1971
FUNKY	"Funky Nassau"	The Beginning Of The End	1971
FUNKY	"Funky Party"	Clarence Reid	1974
FUNKY	"Funky Stuff"	Kool & The Gang	1973
FUNKY	"Funky Weekend"	The Stylistics	1975
FUNKY	"Funky Worm"	Ohio Players	1973
FUNKY	"I Don't Know What It Is, But It Sure Is Funky"	Ripple	1973
FUNKY	"Make It Funky"	James Brown	1971
BOOGIE	"The Bertha Butt Boogie (Part 1)"	The Jimmy Castor Bunch	1975
BOOGIE	"Boogie Bands and One Night Stands"	Kathy Dalton	1974
BOOGIE	"Boogie Down"	Eddie Kendricks	1974
BOOGIE	"Boogie On Reggae Woman"	Stevie Wonder	1974
BOOGIE	"Boogie Woogie Bugle Boy"	Bette Midler	1973
BOOGIE	"Boogie Woogie Man"	Paul Davis	1972
BOOGIE	"Jungle Boogie"	Kool & The Gang	1973
BOOGIE	"Steppin' Out (Gonna Boogie Tonight)"	Tony Orlando & Dawn	1974
GET DOWN	"Get Down"	Curtis Mayfield	1971
GET DOWN	"Get Down"	Gilbert O'Sullivan	1973
GET DOWN	"Get Down, Get Down (Get On the Floor)"	Joe Simon	1975
GET DOWN	"Get Down Tonight"	K.C. & the Sunshine Band	1975
GET DOWN	"Get Up and Get Down"	The Dramatics	1971
GET DOWN	"Time to Get Down"	The O'Jays	1973
GET IT ON	"Baby—Get It On"	Ike & Tina Turner	1975
GET IT ON	"Bang a Gong (Get It On)"	T. Rex	1972
GET IT ON	"Get It On"	Chase	1971
GET IT ON	"Let's Get It On"	Marvin Gaye	1973
GET IT ON	"We've Got to Get It On Again"	The Addrisi Brothers	1972
KUNG FU	"Chinese Kung Fu"	Banzaii	1975
KUNG FU	"Dance the Kung Fu"	Carl Douglas	1975
KUNG FU	"Kung Fu"	Curtis Mayfield	1974
KUNG FU	"Kung Fu Fighting"	Carl Douglas	1974

SUPERSTAR	"Medley from *Superstar*"	The Assembled Multitude	1971
SUPERSTAR	"Superstar"	Carpenters	1971
SUPERSTAR	"Superstar"	Murray Head & The Trinidad Singers	1971
SUPERSTAR	"Superstar (Remember How You Got Where You Are)"	The Temptations	1971
HOT PANTS	"Hot Pants"	Salvage	1971
HOT PANTS	"Hot Pants—I'm Coming, I'm Coming, I'm Coming"	Bobby Byrd	1971
HOT PANTS	"Hot Pants (Part 1)"	James Brown	1971
NATURAL	"Mr. Natural"	Bee Gees	1974
NATURAL	"Natural High"	Bloodstone	1973
NATURAL	"Natural Man"	Lou Rawls	1971
BELL BOTTOM	"Bell Bottom Blues"	Derek & The Dominos	1971
BELL BOTTOM	"Bell Bottom Blues"	Eric Clapton	1973
BOOTY	"Booty Butt"	The Ray Charles Orchestra	1971
BOOTY	"Loose Booty"	Sly & the Family Stone	1974
CHECK IT OUT	"Check It Out"	Tavares	1973
CHECK IT OUT	"Check It Out"	Bobby Womack	1975
FUTURE SHOCK	"Future Shock"	Curtis Mayfield	1973
FUTURE SHOCK	"Future Shock"	Hello People	1975
HIJACK	"Hijack"	Herbie Mann	1975
HIJACK	"Hijackin' Love"	Johnny Taylor	1971
MELLOW	"Ain't Understanding Mellow"	Jerry Butler & Brenda Lee Eager	1971
MELLOW	"Have You Never Been Mellow"	Olivia Newton-John	1975
STRUT	"Afro-Strut"	Nite Liters	1972
STRUT	"Struttin' "	Billy Preston	1974
MISC.	"Black Superman— 'Muhammad Ali' "	Johnny Wakelin	1975
MISC.	"Convoy"	C. W. McCall	1975
MISC.	"Crude Oil Blues"	Jerry Reed	1974
MISC.	"Crunchy Granola Suite"	Neil Diamond	1971
MISC.	"Do Your Thing"	Isaac Hayes	1972
MISC.	"Dynomite—Part 1"	Bazuka	1975
MISC.	"Energy Crisis '74"	Dickie Goodman	1974
MISC.	"Groove Me"	King Floyd	1971
MISC.	"Hang Loose"	Mandrill	1973
MISC.	"Hot Wire"	Al Green	1973
MISC.	"If It Feels Good, Do It"	Ian Lloyd & Stories	1974
MISC.	"Jive Turkey (Part 1)"	Ohio Players	1974
MISC.	"Keep on Truckin' (Part 1)"	Eddie Kendricks	1973

MISC.	"Love Means (You Never Have		
	to Say You're Sorry)"	Sounds of Sunshine	1971
MISC.	"Mercy Mercy Me		
	(The Ecology)"	Marvin Gaye	1971
MISC.	"Mind Games"	John Lennon	1973
MISC.	"Motorcycle Mama"	Sailcat	1972
MISC.	"Rip Off"	Laura Lee	1972
MISC.	"Sexy Mama"	The Moments	1974
MISC.	"Solution for Pollution"	Charles Wright	1971
MISC.	"The Streak"	Ray Stevens	1974
MISC.	"What It Is"	The Undisputed Truth	1972
MISC.	"When You're Hot, You're Hot"	Jerry Reed	1971
MISC.	"Who Loves You"	The 4 Seasons	1975

BOOGIE DOWN
The Dawn of Disco

"Rock Your Baby" • George McCrae (T.K., 1974)
"Rock the Boat" • The Hues Corporation (RCA, 1974)
"Dancing Machine" • The Jackson 5 (Motown, 1974)
"Never Can Say Goodbye" • Gloria Gaynor (MGM, 1974)
"Doctor's Orders" • Carol Douglas (Midland International, 1974)
"Get Dancin' " • Disco Tex and the Sex-O-Lettes (Chelsea, 1974)
"The Hustle" • Van McCoy and the Soul City Symphony (Avco, 1975)
"Get Down Tonight" • KC & the Sunshine Band (T.K., 1975)
"Fly, Robin, Fly" • Silver Convention (Midland International, 1975)
"7-6-5-4-3-2-1 (Blow Your Whistle)" • The Gary Toms Empire (PIP, 1975)

New York City almost went bankrupt in 1975. It had borrowed itself into near insolvency and could no longer handle its huge debt load. Only the establishment of a new financial body called the Municipal Assistance Corporation enabled the city to avoid disaster.

Of course, the whole crisis might have been averted sooner if Mayor Beame had simply imposed a disco tax. One dollar from every cover charge collected at a disco could have been siphoned directly into the city's coffers. If that seemed too direct, hidden taxes could have tapped disco's infrastructure: manufacturers of spandex garments, whistles, rhinestone jewelry, and coke spoons, for example, could have been hit at the wholesale level. Electricity for blow-dryers could have been routed through a separate utility, with exorbitant monthly billings. Perhaps a surcharge on Harvey Wallbangers. New York would have been debt-free before you could say, "Yowsah, yowsah, yowsah."

But it was not to be. Disco continued to operate without financial constraints, spreading across the five boroughs—and the five continents—like some *Andromeda Strain*–style virus. By 1975, the

scene was almost entirely above-ground; disco records were topping
the charts ("Rock Your Baby," "Lady Marmalade," "Get Down
Tonight"), selling in the millions ("Rock the Boat," "Love's Theme,"
"I Love Music"), and winning Grammy awards ("Fly, Robin, Fly,"
"The Hustle," "TSOP"). Conservative estimates had more than 20,000
discos operating in the United States. Having started in the so-called
Crisco discos (gay men's nightclubs) of New York in the early seventies, disco had become an international phenomenon that was
causing more arguments than capital punishment.

The music itself was relatively easy to figure out: a repetitive
vocal hook, usually an exhortation to dance, was accompanied by
lush orchestration, a forward-lurching bass line, Latin percussion,
and a kick drum on every beat, generally at the rate of about 120
thumps per minute. More horizontal than vertical—that is, more a
rhythmic continuum than a series of discrete musical events—a
disco song tended to exist in its entirety only on a twelve-inch single; the "hit" version, often subtitled "Part 1" or "Part 2," usually contained numerous tape edits. In the clubs, disco songs became raw
material to be divided into connected fragments by all-powerful dee-

jays. The deejay, in effect, was the artist. The whole night's music was the song.

Less obvious was disco's sociological significance. Though it begged not to be taken seriously—remember Disco Tex & the Sex-O-Lettes?—its sheer pervasiveness guaranteed a strong negative response. Was it:

a) the soundtrack for a permissive new singles scene in which Mr. and Ms. Goodbar cruised each other for joyless sex?

b) pure escapism, a natural response to the end of a period of economic prosperity?

c) a trance-inducing tonic for drunk, stoned urbanites who had abandoned all pretensions to social conscience?

d) a good excuse for reveling in everything that was cheap, trashy, and superficial in the seventies?

e) all of the above?

Whatever it was, it wasn't rock and roll. Just ask the thousands of Chicago White Sox fans who chanted, "Disco sucks!" as a crate of disco records was set ablaze in Comiskey Park on July 12, 1979. In retrospect, it's ironic that rockers took disco so personally; after all, rock continued unfettered throughout the disco boom, galvanized for once by the presence of a clear opposition (sort of like a musical cold war). Disco did much more serious damage to black music.

Most soul and funk acts recognized the commercial necessity of getting down. Joe Simon's "Get Down, Get Down (Get On the Floor)," James Brown's "Get Up Offa That Thing," the Undisputed Truth's "Let's Go Down to the Disco," Diana Ross's "Love Hangover," the Ohio Players' "Feel the Beat (Everybody Disco)," Johnnie Taylor's "Disco Lady," Earth, Wind & Fire's "Boogie Wonderland," and Joe Tex's "Ain't Gonna Bump No More (With No Big Fat Woman)" represent only a partial list of disco converts. Veterans who couldn't (or wouldn't) join the party faded commercially after 1975—the Stylistics, the Chi-Lites, Al Green, Aretha Franklin, and Sly & the Family Stone were among the casualties.

Disco shifted R&B's emphasis from personality to danceability.

The new genre's stars (KC & the Sunshine Band, Donna Summer, Gloria Gaynor) were not soul singers; they lacked the individuality and the passion of their predecessors. Though disco appeared to be delivering on soul's lustful protestations by describing ("Rockin' Chair"), selling ("Lady Marmalade"), and simulating ("Love to Love You Baby") sex, it frequently came off as cold, robotic, almost asexual. Soul was intimate; disco was standoffish. Soul was aggressive; disco was just loud.

Still, it's possible to distinguish between good disco and bad disco. Many of the best tracks are from 1974 and 1975, before the formula became oppressive. The Hues Corporation's "Rock the Boat" and George McCrae's "Rock Your Baby" entered the charts one week apart in the spring of '74, announcing the disco craze to the world at large, and both records went to Number 1 in July. McCrae recorded for T.K. Records, the label that would soon make Miami the most important disco center outside New York (other T.K. talent included Betty Wright, Timmy Thomas, KC & the Sunshine Band, the Beginning of the End, and McCrae's wife, Gwen). "Rock Your Baby," riding on an electronically generated bossa nova drum pattern, was spare, simple, and sweet, a strangely *emotional*-sounding disco record cowritten by none other than Harry Wayne Casey ("KC").

Casey's own KC & the Sunshine Band recordings were even more successful—"Get Down Tonight," "That's the Way (I Like It)," and "(Shake, Shake, Shake) Shake Your Booty" were consecutive Number 1s—but they were not as memorable. If you thought of them as disco, they were funkier than average; if you thought of them as funk, they were way too disco. Still, they helped establish the Miami sound, a brash mix of American and Caribbean dance music.

Producer Van McCoy popularized disco's first big dance step, the Hustle, in 1975. His single "The Hustle," a great groove record masquerading as a disco novelty, was used as ammunition on both sides of the Disco Does/Doesn't Suck debate and sparked spinoffs like the Salsoul Orchestra's "Salsoul Hustle" (the dance itself was descended from the Stroll). The Jackson 5's "Dancing Machine" was a perfect song for the Robot, that jerky mime thing everyone used to do on *Soul Train.* As for the Bump: The ol' purple-hip special felt best when the groove was mid-tempo and funky ("Shame, Shame,

Shame," "Boogie On Reggae Woman," "7-6-5-4-3-2-1 [Blow Your Whistle]"), not fast and skittering ("Doctor's Orders," "Everlasting Love," "It Only Takes a Minute").

Disco, contrary to popular belief, was not an entirely American phenomenon. The first disco hit, in fact, was African saxophonist Manu Dibango's "Soul Makossa," a loose, exotic-sounding jam that broke in New York's underground clubs before Atlantic licensed it for the United States in 1973. Jamaican Errol Brown's U.K.-based band Hot Chocolate contributed "Disco Queen" and "You Sexy Thing" to the scene. The "Eurodisco" sound began in Munich, Germany, home of Silver Convention ("Fly, Robin, Fly"), Giorgio Moroder ("Son Of My Father") and, at the time, Donna Summer. Moroder produced Summer's controversial "Love to Love You Baby" and much of her later catalog, and can take partial credit (blame?) for a great deal of current dance music. Today's Ecstasy-mad ravers doing their take on the seventies club scene should thank their lucky stars New York City was at least *morally* bankrupt back in '75—it made for some interesting nightlife.

CONCLUSION

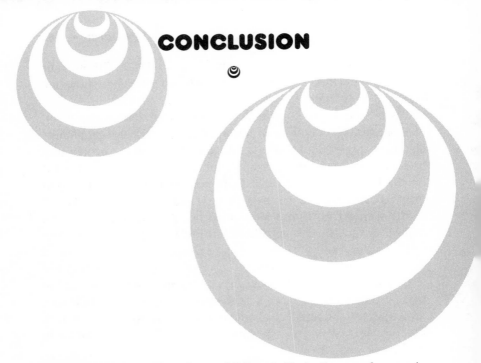

Soon after we found our childhood 45s in the crawl space in 1985, we had a "Seventies" party. Before oldies stations became as prominent as "contemporary" stations, before Burger King used "Mr. Big Stuff" and Mercedes-Benz used *Mannix, Kojak,* and *Baretta* to move product—and *way* before *The Brady Bunch Movie*—we invited some friends over to listen to some music from the early seventies.

The instructions were simple: Come dressed as someone or something specific to the first half of the decade. The concept of a party to celebrate the seventies was still a new one (cries of "Disco sucks!" were still echoing across the land and people were a bit tentative about such things), but the turnout was impressive.

For everyone there, this 1985 party became the first step in the long process of reclaiming the seventies. Although it had been universally mocked and denied, the decade at last got its due on that snowy evening in Kingston, Ontario. The costumes were not a disappointment. There was a wisecracking couple dressed as Sonny and Cher, a gun-toting Shaft, a bespectacled Elton John, an orange H. R. Pufnstuf, a chubby Jimmy Osmond. One person came as the entire

Jackson 5. Still another mysteriously arrived in business attire claiming to be Quinn Martin (the successful producer of television "crime dramas"). "Edith Bunker's cousin" (Maude) was there. Woodward and Bernstein were there. And—not seen in Canada since being banned in the latter half of the seventies—a lethal pair of clackers was there (two rubber balls on the end of two ropes tied to a ring balanced on the reveler's head).

The best costumes of all were conceptual. One woman, dressed in the charred remains of a lacy gown, claimed to be "Helen Reddy's bra." Another guest, perfectly symmetrical on four sides, came as the "secret square" from *Hollywood Squares*. Still another was unrecognizable as a huge, swollen prosthetic (Marcia Brady's broken nose). Finally, and most mystifying of all, there was the perfectly silent guest who dressed in white from head to toe and wore snippets of audiotape draped around his neck and hanging from his pockets (it wasn't until the end of the party that someone guessed right: that this guest had come as the "eighteen-and-a-half-minute gap in the White House tapes").

Here, then, in one room, was a representative sampling of early-seventies pop culture. And acting as the soundtrack for all that costumed eclecticism were our scratchy vinyl records (none of us had yet gone digital) of the best and worst music of the era. We were members of an unnamed generation, and we were owning up to—embracing—the crazed diversity of our Top 40 past.

The early seventies in general thrived on diversity. And it was in the *de*segregated, *un*formatted world of AM radio that this anything-goes philosophy was typified. Radio's "tribal magic" (McLuhan's phrase) was intact, and through it, a racially and generationally mixed AM audience—*listening to the same station*—was galvanized by its willingness to survey a bizarre variety of pop styles. "School's Out" and "Amazing Grace." "Billy, Don't Be a Hero" and "Lady Marmalade." "Smoke on the Water" and "The Entertainer." If there are lingering questions—like who is to be held accountable for the fact that "My Ding-A-Ling" will go down in history as Chuck Berry's only Number 1 record, and why, if Sade is pronounced "Shar-day," Slade was not pronounced "Shlar-day"—nothing can distract from the essential fact that the early seventies represent the last time that one mainstream radio station could accommodate that kind of variety.

The party raged on. Hit song after memorable hit song filled the room. Screams of recognition were heard. Earth shoes and clogs tripped the light fantastic as song lyrics emerged fully formed from long-locked memory files. The last person to arrive wore a hoop-zippered, stretchy orange "top," striped bell-bottoms, and gold North Star sneakers (two stripes). He had come as himself circa 1971. In many ways, that's what we have tried to do in this book, retracing our steps with the kind of gut-level responses that we shared when we first began listening to pop music twenty-five years ago.

They were precious years and they were few, but from 1971 to 1975, North America's cultural diversity found expression in the melting pot of AM radio. There was no dominant musical force to parrot, and artists were not yet confined to the stylistic cages that would come later, so the playing field was wide open; it was still possible to avoid formula and be rewarded with Top 40 airplay. And yet, in the pantheon of popular music, this five-year period—falling between the breakup of the Beatles and the onslaught of punk and disco—has been the victim of an almost conspiratorial code of silence. It has been pop music's eighteen-and-a-half-minute gap.

APPENDIX:
Grammy Nominees and Winners, 1971–75

List excludes awards that fall outside the scope of this book. Winners are in bold type.

14TH ANNUAL (1971) GRAMMY AWARDS
Announced March 14, 1972

Record of the Year
"It's Too Late"
Carole King (Ode)
Lou Adler, producer
"Joy to the World"
Three Dog Night (Dunhill)
Richard Polodor, producer
"My Sweet Lord"
George Harrison (Apple)
George Harrison and Phil Spector, producers
"Theme from *Shaft*"
Isaac Hayes (Enterprise)
Isaac Hayes, producer
"You've Got a Friend"
James Taylor (Warner Bros.)
Peter Asher, producer

Album of the Year
Tapestry
Carole King (Ode)
Lou Adler, producer
All Things Must Pass
George Harrison (Apple)
George Harrison & Phil Spector, producers
Carpenters
Carpenters (A&M)
Jack Daugherty, producer
Jesus Christ Superstar
London Production (Decca)
Tom Morgan, producer

Shaft
Isaac Hayes (Enterprise)
Isaac Hayes, producer

Song of the Year
"You've Got a Friend"
Carole King, writer
"Help Me Make It Through the Night"
Kris Kristofferson, writer
"It's Impossible"
Sid Wayne and Armando Manzanero, writers
"Me and Bobby McGee"
Kris Kristofferson and Fred Foster, writers
"Rose Garden"
Joe South, writer

Best New Artist of the Year
Carly Simon
Chase
Emerson, Lake & Palmer
Hamilton, Joe Frank & Reynolds
Bill Withers

Best Pop Vocal Performance, Female
Tapestry
Carole King (Ode)
"Gypsys, Tramps and Thieves"
Cher (Kapp)
"Me and Bobby McGee"
Janis Joplin (Columbia)
"The Night They Drove Old Dixie Down"
Joan Baez (Vanguard)

"That's the Way I've Always Heard It
Should Be"
Carly Simon (Elektra)

Best Pop Vocal Performance, Male
"You've Got a Friend"
James Taylor (Warner Bros.)
"Ain't No Sunshine"
Bill Withers (Sussex)
"I Am, I Said"
Neil Diamond (Uni)
"If You Could Read My Mind"
Gordon Lightfoot (Reprise)
It's Impossible
Perry Como (RCA)

Best Pop Vocal Performance, Group
Carpenters
Carpenters (A&M)
"All I Ever Need Is You"
Sonny & Cher (Kapp)
"How Can You Mend a Broken Heart"
Bee Gees (Columbia)
Jesus Christ Superstar
London Production (Decca)
"Joy to the World"
Three Dog Night (Dunhill)

Best Rhythm & Blues Song
"Ain't No Sunshine"
Bill Withers, writer
"If I Were Your Woman"
Clay McMurray, Laverne Ware, and
Pamela Sawyer, writers
"Mr. Big Stuff"
Joseph Broussard, Ralph Williams
and Carrol Washington, writers
"Never Can Say Goodbye"
Clifton Davis, writer
"Smiling Faces Sometimes"
Norman Whitfield and Barrett
Strong, writers

**Best Rhythm & Blues Vocal
Performance, Female**
"Bridge Over Troubled Water"
Aretha Franklin (Atlantic)
Contact
Freda Payne (Invictus)
"I Love You (Call Me)"
Diana Ross (Motown)
"Mr. Big Stuff"
Jean Knight (Stax)
Pearl
Janis Joplin (Columbia)

**Best Rhythm and Blues Vocal
Performance, Male**
"A Natural Man"
Lou Rawls (MGM)
"Ain't Nobody Home"
B. B. King (ABC)
"Inner City Blues (Make Me Wanna
Holler)"
Marvin Gaye (Tamla)
"Never Can Say Goodbye"
Isaac Hayes (Enterprise)
"We Can Work It Out"
Stevie Wonder (Tamla)

**Best Rhythm & Blues Performance,
Group**
"Proud Mary"
**Ike and Tina Turner (United
Artists)**
"If I Were Your Woman"
Gladys Knight & the Pips (Soul)
"Respect Yourself"
The Staple Singers (Stax)
"Theme from *Shaft*" (Instrumental)
Isaac Hayes (Enterprise)
"You've Got a Friend"
Roberta Flack and Donny
Hathaway (Atlantic)

15TH ANNUAL (1972) GRAMMY AWARDS

Announced March 3, 1973

Record of the Year
"The First Time Ever I Saw Your Face"
 Roberta Flack (Atlantic)
 Joel Dorn, producer
"Alone Again (Naturally)"
 Gilbert O'Sullivan (MAM)
 Gordon Mills, producer
"American Pie"
 Don McLean (United Artists)
 Ed Freeman, producer
"Song Sung Blue"
 Neil Diamond (Uni)
 Tom Catalano and Neil Diamond, producers
"Without You"
 Nilsson (RCA)
 Richard Perry, producer

Album of the Year
The Concert for Bangla Desh
 George Harrison and Friends (Apple)
 George Harrison and Phil Spector, producers
American Pie
 Don McLean (United Artists)
 Ed Freeman, producer
Jesus Christ Superstar
 London Production (Decca)
 Tom Morgan, producer
Moods
 Neil Diamond (Uni)
 Tom Catalano and Neil Diamond, producers
Nilsson Schmilsson
 Nilsson (RCA)
 Richard Perry, producer

Song of the Year
"The First Time Ever I Saw Your Face"
 Ewan MacColl, writer
"Alone Again (Naturally)"
 Gilbert O'Sullivan, writer
"American Pie"
 Don McLean, writer
"Song Sung Blue"
 Neil Diamond, writer
"The Summer Knows"
 Marilyn Bergman, Alan Bergman, and Michel Legrand, writers

Best New Artist of the Year
America
 Harry Chapin
 Eagles
 Loggins & Messina
 John Prine

Best Pop Vocal Performance, Female
"I Am Woman"
 Helen Reddy (Capitol)
Anticipation
 Carly Simon (Elektra)
"Day Dreaming"
 Aretha Franklin (Atlantic)
Quiet Fire
 Roberta Flack (Atlantic)
"Sweet Inspiration/Where You Lead"
 Barbra Streisand (Columbia)

Best Pop Vocal Performance, Male
"Without You"
 Nilsson (RCA)
"Alone Again (Naturally)"
 Gilbert O'Sullivan (MAM)
"American Pie"
 Don McLean (United Artists)
"Baby Don't Get Hooked On Me"

Mac Davis (Columbia)
"The Candy Man"
Sammy Davis, Jr. (MGM)

Best Pop Vocal Performance, Group
"Where Is the Love"
Roberta Flack and Donny
Hathaway (Atlantic)
Baby I'm-A Want You
Bread (Elektra)
"A Horse with No Name"
America (Warner Bros.)
"I'd Like to Teach the World to Sing
(In Perfect Harmony)"
The New Seekers (Elektra)
"Summer Breeze"
Seals & Crofts (Warner Bros.)

Best Rhythm & Blues Song
"Papa Was a Rolling Stone"
Norman Whitfield and Barrett
Strong, writers
"Back Stabbers"
Leon Huff, Gene McFadden, and
John Whitehead, writers
"Everybody Plays the Fool"
Rudy Clark, J. R. Bailey, and Kenny
Williams, writers
"Freddie's Dead"
Curtis Mayfield, writer
"Me and Mrs. Jones"
Ken Gamble, Leon Huff, and Cary
Gilbert, writers

Best Rhythm & Blues Vocal
Performance, Female
Young, Gifted and Black
Aretha Franklin (Atlantic)
"Clean Up Woman"
Betty Wright (Alston)
From a Whisper to a Scream
Esther Phillips (Kudu)

"In the Ghetto"
Candi Staton (Fame)
"Oh, No Not My Baby"
Merry Clayton (Ode)

Best Rhythm & Blues Vocal
Performance, Male
"Me and Mrs. Jones"
Billy Paul (Philadelphia
International)
"Drowning in the Sea of Love"
Joe Simon (Spring)
"Freddie's Dead"
Curtis Mayfield (Curtom)
"I Gotcha"
Joe Tex (Dial)
"What Have They Done to My Song
Ma"
Ray Charles (Tangerine)

Best Rhythm & Blues Vocal
Performance, Group
"Papa Was a Rolling Stone"
The Temptations (Gordy)
"Help Me Make It Through the Night"
Gladys Knight & the Pips (Soul)
"I'll Be Around"
The Spinners (Atlantic)
"I'll Take You There"
The Staple Singers (Stax)
"What Have They Done to My Song
Ma"
Ray Charles (Tangerine)

16TH ANNUAL (1973) GRAMMY
AWARDS
Announced March 2, 1974

Record of the Year
"Killing Me Softly with His Song"
Roberta Flack (Atlantic)
Joel Dorn, producer

"Bad, Bad Leroy Brown"
　Jim Croce (ABC)
　Terry Cashman and Tommy West,
　producers
"Behind Closed Doors"
　Charlie Rich (Epic)
　Billy Sherrill, producer
"You Are the Sunshine of My Life"
　Stevie Wonder (Tamla)
　Stevie Wonder, producer
"You're So Vain"
　Carly Simon (Elektra)
　Richard Perry, producer

Album of the Year
Innervisions
　Stevie Wonder (Tamla)
　Stevie Wonder, producer
Behind Closed Doors
　Charlie Rich (Epic)
　Billy Sherrill, producer
The Divine Miss M
　Bette Midler (Atlantic)
　Joel Dorn, Barry Manilow, Geoffrey
　Haslam, and Ahmet Ertegun,
　producers
Killing Me Softly
　Roberta Flack (Atlantic)
　Joel Dorn, producer
There Goes Rhymin' Simon
　Paul Simon (Columbia)
　Paul Simon, Phil Ramone, Paul
　Samwell-Smith, Roy Halee, and
　M.S.S. Rhythm Studio, producers

Song of the Year
"Killing Me Softly with His Song"
　Norman Gimbel and Charles
　Fox, writers
"Behind Closed Doors"
　Kenny O'Dell, writer

"Tie a Yellow Ribbon Round the Ole
　Oak Tree"
　Irwin Levine and L. Russell Brown,
　writers
"You Are the Sunshine of My Life"
　Stevie Wonder, writer
"You're So Vain"
　Carly Simon, writer

Best New Artist of the Year
Bette Midler
　Eumir Deodato
　Maureen McGovern
　Marie Osmond
　Barry White

Best Pop Vocal Performance, Female
"Killing Me Softly with His Song"
　Roberta Flack (Atlantic)
"Boogie Woogie Bugle Boy"
　Bette Midler (Atlantic)
"Danny's Song"
　Anne Murray (Capitol)
"Touch Me in the Morning"
　Diana Ross (Motown)
"You're So Vain"
　Carly Simon (Elektra)

Best Pop Vocal Performance, Male
"You Are the Sunshine of My Life"
　Stevie Wonder (Tamla)
"And I Love You So"
　Perry Como (RCA)
"Bad, Bad Leroy Brown"
　Jim Croce (ABC)
"Daniel"
　Elton John (MCA)
There Goes Rhymin' Simon
　Paul Simon (Columbia)

Best Pop Vocal Performance, Group
"Neither One of Us (Wants to Be
the First to Say Goodbye)"
   Gladys Knight & the Pips
   (Soul)
"Diamond Girl"
   Seals & Crofts (Warner Bros.)
"Live and Let Die"
   Paul McCartney & Wings (Apple)
"Sing"
   Carpenters (A&M)
"Tie a Yellow Ribbon Round the Ole
   Oak Tree"
   Dawn featuring Tony Orlando
   (Bell)

Best Rhythm & Blues Song
"Superstition"
   Stevie Wonder, writer
"The Cisco Kid"
   War, writer
"Family Affair"
   Sylvester Stewart, writer
"Love Train"
   Ken Gamble and Leon Huff,
   writers
"Midnight Train to Georgia"
   Jim Weatherly, writer

Best Rhythm & Blues Vocal
Performance, Female
"Master of Eyes"
   Aretha Franklin (Atlantic)
Alone Again (Naturally)
   Esther Phillips (Kudu)
Etta James
   Etta James (Chess)
"I Can't Stand the Rain"
   Ann Peebles (Hi)
"Pillow Talk"
   Sylvia (Vibration)

Best Rhythm & Blues Vocal
Performance, Male
"Superstition"
   Stevie Wonder (Tamla)
"Call Me (Come Back Home)"
   Al Green (Hi)
"I'm Gonna Love You Just a Little
   More Baby"
   Barry White (20th Century)
"Keep On Truckin' "
   Eddie Kendricks (Tamla)
Let's Get It On
   Marvin Gaye (Motown)

Best Rhythm & Blues Vocal
Performance, Group
"Midnight Train to Georgia"
   Gladys Knight & the Pips
   (Buddah)
"Be What You Are"
   The Staple Singers (Stax)
"The Cisco Kid"
   War (United Artists)
"Could It Be I'm Falling in Love"
   The Spinners (Atlantic)
"Love Train"
   The O'Jays (Philadelphia
   International)

17TH ANNUAL (1974) GRAMMY
AWARDS
Announced March 1, 1975

Record of the Year
"I Honestly Love You"
   Olivia Newton-John (MCA)
   John Farrar, producer
"Don't Let the Sun Go Down on Me"
   Elton John (MCA)
   Gus Dudgeon, producer
"Feel Like Makin' Love"
   Roberta Flack (Atlantic)
   Roberta Flack, producer

"Help Me"
Joni Mitchell (Asylum)
Joni Mitchell and Henry Lewy,
producers
"Midnight at the Oasis"
Maria Muldaur (Reprise)
Lenny Waronker and Joe Boyd,
producers

Album of the Year
Fulfillingness' First Finale
Stevie Wonder (Tamla)
Stevie Wonder, producer
Back Home Again
John Denver (RCA)
Milton Okun, producer
Band on the Run
Paul McCartney & Wings (Apple)
Paul McCartney, producer
Caribou
Elton John (MCA)
Gus Dudgeon, producer
Court and Spark
Joni Mitchell (Asylum)
Joni Mitchell and Henry Lewy,
producers

Song of the Year
"The Way We Were"
Marilyn Bergman, Alan
Bergman, and Marvin
Hamlisch, writers
"Feel Like Makin' Love"
Eugene McDaniels, writer
"I Honestly Love You"
Jeff Barry and Peter Allen, writers
"Midnight at the Oasis"
David Nichtern, writer
"You and Me Against the World"
Paul Williams and Ken Ascher,
writers

Producer of the Year
Thom Bell
(Spinners, Stylistics, Johnny
Mathis)
Rick Hall
(Paul Anka, Mac Davis, Candi
Staton)
Billy Sherrill
(Tammy Wynette, George Jones,
Charlie Rich, Tanya Tucker)
Lenny Waronker
(Gordon Lightfoot, Maria Muldaur,
Randy Newman)
Stevie Wonder
(Stevie Wonder, Syreeta Wright)

Best New Artist of the Year
Marvin Hamlisch
Bad Company
Johnny Bristol
David Essex
Graham Central Station
Phoebe Snow

Best Pop Vocal Performance,
Female
"I Honestly Love You"
Olivia Newton-John (MCA)
Cleo Laine Live at Carnegie Hall
Cleo Laine (RCA)
Court and Spark
Joni Mitchell (Asylum)
"Feel Like Makin' Love"
Roberta Flack (Atlantic)
"Jazzman"
Carole King (Ode)

Best Pop Vocal Performance, Male
Fulfillingness' First Finale
Stevie Wonder (Tamla)
"Cat's in the Cradle"
Harry Chapin (Elektra)

"Don't Let the Sun Go Down on Me"
Elton John (MCA)
"Nothing from Nothing"
Billy Preston (A&M)
"Please Come to Boston"
Dave Loggins (Epic)

Best Pop Vocal Performance, Group
"Band on the Run"
Paul McCartney & Wings
(Apple)
Body Heat
Quincy Jones (A&M)
"Rikki Don't Lose That Number"
Steely Dan (ABC)
"Then Came You"
Dionne Warwick & Spinners
(Atlantic)
"You Make Me Feel Brand New"
The Stylistics (Avco)

Best Rhythm & Blues Song
"Living for the City"
Stevie Wonder, writer
"Dancing Machine"
Harold Davis, Don Fletcher, and
Dean Parks, writers
"For the Love of Money"
Ken Gamble, Leon Huff, and
Anthony Jackson, writers
"Rock Your Baby"
H. W. Casey and Richard Finch,
writers
"Tell Me Something Good"
Stevie Wonder, writer

Best Rhythm & Blues Vocal
Performance, Female
"Ain't Nothing Like the Real
Thing"
Aretha Franklin (Atlantic)

"(If Loving You Is Wrong) I Don't
Want to Be Right"
Millie Jackson (Spring)
"St. Louis Blues"
Etta James (Chess)
Tina Turns the Country On!
Tina Turner (United Artists)
"Woman to Woman"
Shirley Brown (Truth)
"(You Keep Me) Hangin' On"
Ann Peebles (Hi)
"You've Been Doing Wrong for So
Long"
Thelma Houston (Motown)

Best Rhythm & Blues Vocal
Performance, Male
"Boogie On Reggae Woman"
Stevie Wonder (Tamla)
"Boogie Down"
Eddie Kendricks (Tamla)
"Hang On in There Baby"
Johnny Bristol (MGM)
Marvin Gaye—Live
Marvin Gaye (Tamla)
"Rock Your Baby"
George McCrae (T.K.)

Best Rhythm & Blues Vocal
Performance, Group
"Tell Me Something Good"
Rufus (ABC)
"Dancing Machine"
The Jackson 5 (Motown)
"For the Love of Money"
The O'Jays (Philadelphia
International)
"I Feel a Song (In My Heart)"
Gladys Knight & the Pips
(Buddah)
"Mighty Love"
The O'Jays (Philadelphia
International)

18TH ANNUAL (1975) GRAMMY AWARDS
Announced February 28, 1976

Record of the Year
"Love Will Keep Us Together"
  Captain & Tennille (A&M)
  Daryl Dragon, producer
"At Seventeen"
  Janis Ian (Columbia)
  Brooks Arthur, producer
"Lyin' Eyes"
  Eagles (Asylum)
  Bill Szymczyk, producer
"Mandy"
  Barry Manilow (Arista)
  Clive Davis, Barry Manilow, and
  Ron Dante, producers
"Rhinestone Cowboy"
  Glen Campbell (Capitol)
  Dennis Lambert and Brian Potter,
  producers

Album of the Year
Still Crazy After All These Years
  Paul Simon (Columbia)
  Paul Simon and Phil Ramone,
  producers
Between the Lines
  Janis Ian (Columbia)
  Brooks Arthur, producer
Captain Fantastic and the Brown Dirt Cowboy
  Elton John (MCA)
  Gus Dudgeon, producer
Heart Like A Wheel
  Linda Ronstadt (Capitol)
  Peter Asher, producer
One of these Nights
  Eagles (Asylum)
  Bill Szymczyk, producer

Song of the Year
"Send in the Clowns"
  Stephen Sondheim, writer

"At Seventeen"
  Janis Ian, writer
"Feelings"
  Morris Albert, writer
"Love Will Keep Us Together"
  Neil Sedaka and Howard
  Greenfield, writers
"Rhinestone Cowboy"
  Larry Weiss, writer

Producer of the Year
Arif Mardin
(Average White Band, Bee Gees,
Judy Collins, Mama's Pride,
Richard Harris)
Peter Asher
  (Linda Ronstadt)
Gus Dudgeon
  (Elton John, Kiki Dee)
Dennis Lambert and Brian Potter
  (Evie Sands, Tavares, Glen
  Campbell)
Bill Szymczyk
  (J. Geils Band, Eagles)

Best New Artist of the Year
Natalie Cole
  Morris Albert
  The Amazing Rhythm Aces
  The Brecker Brothers
  K.C. & the Sunshine Band

Best Pop Vocal Performance, Female
"At Seventeen"
  Janis Ian (Columbia)
"Ain't No Way to Treat A Lady"
  Helen Reddy (Capitol)
"Have You Never Been Mellow"
  Olivia Newton-John (MCA)
Heart Like a Wheel
  Linda Ronstadt (Capitol)

"Send in the Clowns"
   Judy Collins (Elektra)

Best Pop Vocal Performance, Male
Still Crazy After All These Years
   Paul Simon (Columbia)
"Bad Blood"
   Neil Sedaka (Rocket)
Captain Fantastic and the Brown Dirt Cowboy
   Elton John (MCA)
"Feelings"
   Morris Albert (RCA)
"Rhinestone Cowboy"
   Glen Campbell (Capitol)

Best Pop Vocal Performance, Group
"**Lyin' Eyes**"
   Eagles (Asylum)
A Capella 2
   The Singers Unlimited (MPS)
"Love Will Keep Us Together"
   Captain & Tennille
"My Little Town"
   Simon & Garfunkel (Columbia)
"The Way We Were/Try To Remember"
   Gladys Knight & the Pips (Buddah)

Best Rhythm & Blues Song
"**Where Is the Love**"
   H. W. Casey, Richard Finch, Willie Clark, and Betty Wright, writers
"Ease On Down the Road"
   Charlie Smalls, writer
"Get Down Tonight"
   H. W. Casey and Richard Finch, writers
"That's the Way (I Like It)"
   H. W. Casey and Richard Finch, writers

"Walking in Rhythm"
   Barney Perry, writer

Best Rhythm & Blues Vocal Performance, Female
"**This Will Be**"
   Natalie Cole (Capitol)
Never Can Say Goodbye
   Gloria Gaynor (MGM)
"Rockin' Chair"
   Gwen McCrae (Cat)
"Shame, Shame, Shame"
   Shirley & Company (Vibration)
"What a Diff'rence a Day Makes"
   Esther Phillips (Kudu)

Best Rhythm & Blues Vocal Performance, Male
"**Living for the City**"
   Ray Charles (Crossover)
Chocolate Chip
   Isaac Hayes (Hot Buttered Soul)
"L-O-V-E (Love)"
   Al Green (Hi)
"Love Won't Let Me Wait"
   Major Harris (Atlantic)
"Supernatural Thing—Part I"
   Ben E. King (Atlantic)

Best Rhythm & Blues Vocal Performance, Group
"**Shining Star**"
   Earth, Wind & Fire (Columbia)
Cut the Cake
   Average White Band (Atlantic)
Fire
   Ohio Players (Mercury)
"Get Down Tonight"
   K.C. & the Sunshine Band (T.K.)
"How Long (Betcha' Got a Chick on the Side)"
   The Pointer Sisters (Blue Thumb)

BIBLIOGRAPHY

Bangs, Lester. *Psychotic Reactions and Carburetor Dung*. New York: Vintage, 1988.

Bernstein, Carl, and Bob Woodward. *All the President's Men*. New York: Simon and Schuster, 1974.

Bronson, Fred. *The Billboard Book of Number One Hits*. New York: Billboard Publications, 1985.

Brown, Peter, and Steven Gaines. *The Love You Make: An Insider's Story of the Beatles*. New York: McGraw-Hill, 1983.

Christgau, Robert. *Rock Albums of the '70s: A Critical Guide*. New York: Da Capo Press, 1990.

Dannen, Fredric. *Hit Men: Power Brokers and Fast Money Inside the Music Business*. New York: Random House, 1990.

Davis, Clive, with James Willwerth. *Clive: Inside the Record Business*. New York: William Morrow & Co., 1975.

DeCurtis, Anthony, James Henke, and Holly George-Warren, eds. *The Rolling Stone Illustrated History of Rock & Roll*. New York: Random House, 1992.

George, Nelson. *The Death of Rhythm & Blues*. New York: Dutton, 1989.

———. *Where Did Our Love Go? The Rise and Fall of the Motown Sound*. New York: St. Martin's Press, 1985.

Giuliano, Geoffrey. *Blackbird: The Life and Times of Paul McCartney*. Toronto: McGraw-Hill Ryerson, 1991.

Goddard, Peter, and Philip Kamen, eds. *Shakin' All Over: The Rock 'n' Roll Years in Canada*. Toronto: McGraw-Hill Ryerson, 1989.

Guralnick, Peter. *Sweet Soul Music: Rhythm and Blues and the Southern Dream of Freedom*. New York: Harper & Row, 1986.

Hall, Ron. *The Chum Chart Book*. Toronto: Stardust, 1984.

Jackson, Rick. *Encyclopedia of Canadian Rock, Pop and Folk*. Kingston: Quarry Press, 1994.

Jancik, Wayne. *The Billboard Book of One-Hit Wonders.* New York: Billboard Publications, 1990.

Jasper, Tony. *Simply Pop.* London: Queen Tune Press, 1975.

Kael, Pauline. *For Keeps: 30 Years at the Movies.* New York: Dutton, 1994.

Kennedy, Pagan. *Platforms: A Microwaved Cultural Chronicle of the 1970s.* New York: St. Martin's Press, 1994.

Knobler, Peter, and Greg Mitchell, eds. *Very Seventies: A Cultural History of the 1970s from the Pages of Crawdaddy.* New York: Fireside, 1995.

Marsh, Dave. *The Heart of Rock & Soul: The 1001 Greatest Singles Ever Made.* New York: New American Library, 1989.

Nite, Norm N. *Rock On: The Illustrated Encyclopedia of Rock 'n' Roll.* New York: Harper & Row, 1984.

———. *Rock On Almanac: The First Four Decades of Rock 'n' Roll.* New York: Harper & Row, 1989.

Romanowski, Patricia, and Holly George-Warren, eds. *The New Rolling Stone Encyclopedia of Rock & Roll.* New York: Fireside, 1995.

Russell, Tom, and Sylvia Tyson, eds. *And Then I Wrote: The Songwriter Speaks.* Vancouver: Arsenal Pulp Press, 1995.

Schipper, Henry. *Broken Record: The Inside Story of the Grammy Awards.* New York: Birch Lane Press, 1992.

Smith, Joe. *Off the Record: An Oral History of Popular Music.* New York: Warner, 1988.

Stokes, Geoffrey. *The Beatles.* New York: Times Books, 1980.

Sweet, Brian. *Reelin' in the Years.* London: Omnibus Press, 1994.

Swenson, John. *Stevie Wonder.* London: Plexus, 1986.

Tobler, John. *This Day in Rock: Day by Day Record of Rock's Biggest News Stories.* London: Carlton, 1993.

Toffler, Alvin. *Future Shock.* New York: Random House, 1970.

Vonnegut, Jr., Kurt. *Wampeters, Foma & Granfalloons.* New York: Delacorte Press, 1974.

Waldron, Vince. *Classic Sitcoms: A Celebration of the Best of Prime-time Comedy.* New York: Macmillan, 1987.

Whitburn, Joel. *The Billboard Book of Top 40 Hits.* New York: Billboard Publications, 1989.

———. *Billboard Hot 100 Charts: The Seventies.* Menomonee Falls, WI: Record Research, 1990.

White, Adam. *The Billboard Book of Gold and Platinum Records.* New York: Billboard Publications, 1990.

Williams, Otis. *Temptations.* New York: Fireside, 1988.

Wilson, Mary. *Dreamgirl: My Life as a Supreme.* New York: St. Martin's Press, 1986.

Zappa, Frank, with Peter Occhiogrosso. *The Real Frank Zappa Book.* New York: Poseidon Press, 1989.

INDEX